UNDERSTANDING
ORGANIZATIONAL
EVOLUTION

UNDERSTANDING ORGANIZATIONAL EVOLUTION

Its Impact on Management and Performance

Douglas Scott Fletcher and Ian M. Taplin

QUORUM BOOKS
Westport, Connecticut • London

Library of Congress Cataloging-in-Publication Data

Fletcher, D. S. (Douglas S.)
    Understanding organizational evolution : its impact on management and performance /
    Douglas Scott Fletcher and Ian M. Taplin.
        p. cm.
    Includes bibliographical references and index.
    ISBN 1–56720–474–0 (alk. paper)
    1. Organizational change. 2. Performance—Management. I. Taplin, Ian M. II. Title.
    HD58.8.F553 2002
    658.4'06—dc21   2001019592

British Library Cataloguing in Publication Data is available.

Library of Congress Catalog Card Number: 2001019592
ISBN: 1–56720–474–0

First published in 2002

Quorum Books, 88 Post Road West, Westport, CT 06881
An imprint of Greenwood Publishing Group, Inc.
www.quorumbooks.com

Printed in the United States of America

The paper used in this book complies with the
Permanent Paper Standard issued by the National
Information Standards Organization (Z39.48–1984).

10 9 8 7 6 5 4 3 2 1

Copyright Acknowledgments

The authors and publisher gratefully acknowledge permission to reproduce the following material:

An early version of Chapter 4 appeared as "Organizational Evolution: The American Life Cycle" by Douglas S. Fletcher and Ian M. Taplin in *National Productivity Review,* Autumn 1999. Copyright © 1999, John Wiley & Sons, Inc.

An early version of Chapter 10 appeared as "Operating Reviews Meetings Enhance Teamwork" by Douglas S. Fletcher and Ian M. Taplin in *National Productivity Review,* Spring 1997. Copyright © 1997, John Wiley & Sons, Inc.

Contents

List of Figures

Preface

Businesses enter the twenty-first century with a mixture of optimism and anticipation regarding what the future will be for American firms. In an era of increased globalization, there has been a tendency to assume that the U.S. market system will become the operating norm for businesses worldwide. While there is evidence that global business practices are increasingly reflecting those that occur in the United States, it would be foolish to ignore the many variables that constrain firms in some countries from adopting the U.S. model in its entirety.

For example, the state remains a powerful influence in many societies, and the resulting different institutional frameworks set different agendas for businesses. In addition, legal frameworks differ markedly from society to society, giving a free hand to managers in some countries while severely curtailing those in others. The role of organized labor also varies; and in some societies, women play a more important role in the workplace than in others. These are just a few of the wide range of variations that limit and structure international models of business.

Any structure of business rarely remains static. To assume that the system that America now has will continue unchanged in the future is naïve. What worked ten years ago might be problematic today and conceivably will be completely inappropriate in ten years time. One certitude about capitalism is its dynamic nature. Systems evolve and organizations change, and they often do so in a paradigmatic way. Innovative organizations lead the market, but competitors are quick to follow, and new practices become the received wisdom for potential market entrants. In this fashion, America has moved from craft systems to mass production to mass customization.

In this book, we address these issues, paying particular attention to understanding how organizations (and to some extent societies and individuals) evolve over time. We clarify how the behavior of businesses reflects external influences as well as the internal needs of employees as they mature over time.

Key to our analysis is the interplay of the firm's *purpose*, business *processes* and *people* needs as they interact to shape the direction of organizational change. In charting the evolution of organizations we point to the ways organizations meet the challenges associated with each of these elements. In doing so we provide simultaneously an historical illustration, an analytic framework, and a model that can be of use to practicing managers.

The illustration is that of firms and how they evolve in an increasingly global system of capitalism. The analytic framework focuses on the resolution of tensions within organizations. Because firms must change, they must address what increasingly become organizational contradictions. Identifying such tensions, both generically across sectors as well as in firm-specific cases, and establishing how firms respond to them provide the substance for much of the book's discussion.

Finally, we offer a framework of action that enables managers to make their organizations successful. We do not pretend to provide a simple model for organizational success, since that would ignore the multitude of differences that occur among businesses. But we do offer a recipe that provides a systematic delineation of key operational issues. If nothing else, the following chapters should help the reader to recognize and identify problems in a pro-active way.

THE PARADOX OF CONTEMPORARY MANAGEMENT

As the size and complexity of an organization increases, firms go through predictable stages of organization evolution in which what worked in the past fails to work in the future. In these transitions, managers have to juggle the three variables of organization evolution—the *purpose* or direction of the firm, business *processes*, and *people* issues—and keep them in balance as they reinvent new ways of structuring the firm. In the firm's growth, tension develops as one variable is stressed at the expense of the others.

Over-controlling people, rather than effectively managing them, can cause a clash between autonomy and ego. If, on the other hand, firms are too people centered, cost can get out of line requiring tougher management processes to hold people accountable. Finally, sometimes firms stumble and lose their way because of a loss in focus of the firm's purpose and the ability to execute strategy. All of these are crucial management issues. Dealing with one or even two of them at the expense of the other(s) can be fatal for an organization.

In order to forestall these problems managers have a tendency to centralize decisionmaking in order to know what's going on and to reaffirm their control. This centralization is both natural and inevitable in the hierarchical organizations that predominate today. Furthermore, managers dislike change especially if it might threaten the status quo. In time, because they can't stay on top of all the details, the firm spins out of control. Consequently, firms go through cycles of centralization then decentralization as they try to find the right system and negotiate this "corridor of crisis." Managing in today's network organization requires a different kind of control. When managers stick to their traditional ways of insuring they are in control, they misuse teams, stifle creativity and innovation, and stumble in their strategic efforts.

The digital revolution and information technologies are helping shape a new economy, and they too are having a profound effect on organization structures. The ability to store, access, and analyze huge amounts of data and information is accelerating the shift towards the horizontal corporation and network structures. However, it is only recently that software tools have become available to ensure that the command and control model of management could give way to electronic methods of planning and reviewing results. In turn, this has released layers of middle managers once assigned the responsibility of coordinating disparate elements of vertically integrated businesses.

Often, it seems as though managers have trouble in knowing just what to do when confronted by changes such as the technological breakthroughs cited above. They typically rely on either/or thinking in which one management fad replaces another, neither of which has been proven effective by research data. Instead, what is required is the ability to delegate decision making without abdicating overall control of the organization. Firms have to find a balance of increasing but equal amounts of *management* toughness, attention to people and their needs, and *leadership* with a vision that promotes growth, direction, and a common goal for *people* to follow.

The model that is developed in this book derives from our understanding of how successful firms have managed these tensions, and what sorts of things need to be uppermost in the minds of those who acquire the mantle of leadership in the twenty-first century. While there are many books about teams, this book talks about teamwork in the context of wider performance and process issues. It is also not just another book about the personality traits of great leaders—ones that argue for a combination of toughness and insight, and the institutionalization of charisma. Instead, we discuss the tensions within authority structures as senior managers attempt to reconcile organizational logics (history and past practices that have sustained the firm) and their own definition of the problems that face the firm.

It is also not another book on creating tensions to confront change. Contradictions are inherent in any organization, and we argue that such contradictions follow a pattern. Either managers can ignore the underlying instability or confront it in ways that will ease the transition and sustain the organization's dynamic nature. Doing the latter might not guarantee success, but it will help them be better prepared to chart a future course.

This book has been several years in the making. It is a product of extensive consulting projects and academic research into organizations, in which the same sorts of problems were repeatedly identified. Time and again, we both, often in different contexts, recognized why firms were experiencing problems. We were struck by the fact that many senior managers seemed unable or unwilling to acknowledge the existence of a problem. When the inevitable crisis hit, they were forced into a reactive mode that was often too little, too late. We decided to explore these issues in more detail and to try and conceptualize the key factors that we encountered. This book is the product of these deliberations.

Along the way, discussions with many people have helped shape and form our final arguments. Doug Fletcher would like to acknowledge the many clients who have helped hone a pragmatic approach to the logic of management-leadership, Dwight Stewart Jr., John Petas, Roger Beach, Marty Miller, Michael Basta for his pragmatic insights, Jessica Haile for her critical thinking and editing skills, and Mary Fletcher who encouraged me to coauthor this book.

Ian Taplin acknowledges the insights provided in conversations with the following: Roger and Julia Cornish, Christopher Dandeker, Mike Lawlor, Jone Pearce, Brad Walker, Sharman Walker, Jonathan Winterton, John Wise, and Ned Williams. However, none of these people should be held accountable for any of the claims we make. Their contributions lie in stimulating our thought processes so that the eventual manuscript could come to fruition. He is also grateful for the tremendous support of Cindy Kelly throughout this project.

Finally, we would like to acknowledge the help of Debbie Singleton, who assisted with the final preparation of the manuscript, and our editor at Quorum Books, Hilary Claggett, who added the final clarity to some of our ideas.

PART I

EVOLUTION OF THE ORGANIZATION

Managers want to know what's going on in their organization. When they are accountable for results, they want to be—and should be—in control. The particular methods they use to maintain control naturally change over time. For managers to understand why the methods they use change and for them to keep control in the future, they need to understand the evolution of their organization and they must become familiar with the symptoms that indicate a need for change in their management practices.

The best management practices for controlling an organization depend on its size, complexity, and maturity. Management control also evolves in response to individual management styles, as well as to changes in competition, technology, and society. In Part I, we examine the early phases of organizational evolution, paying particular attention to the interaction between internal and external factors influencing any organization.

Just as with any human society, every business has its own life cycle. As it grows in size and complexity, an organization moves through distinct phases that can be likened to pre-adolescence, adolescence, and adulthood. To grow into the next phase, an organization must successfully negotiate a crisis that typically occurs in each phase if it wants to grow beyond it. These crises must be dealt with before they become critical, as any one could cause the organization's premature death.

Astute managers can forestall such a fatality. They can develop a perspective for managing change successfully by studying the phases and the control techniques applied during each phase. The key to gearing for change is knowing that organizational evolution *is* somewhat predictable.

Figure I.1
Organization Evolution

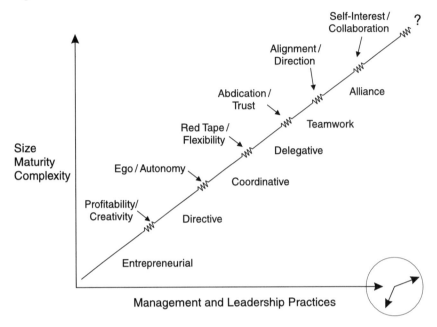

If managers can learn to recognize the particular phase their company is passing through, they can anticipate the problems of the next phase before they become painful. They can then plan for continued smooth growth.

The six phases identified in Figure I.1 typify the evolutionary stages that organizations go through as the size and complexity of the firm increases. We have built upon Larry E. Greiner's[1] pioneering work in this area, elaborating on some of the key problems that occur within the phases. These phases, characterized by the primary management or leadership practices dominant in each phase, are: entrepreneurial, directive, coordinative, delegative, teamwork, and alliances. The first three chapters discuss these phases in three groups. Chapter 1 addresses the evolution of an organization during the entrepreneurial and directive stages. When an organization enters the phases of coordination and delegation, it experiences perhaps the most difficult time of its development. Chapter 2 discusses organizational evolution during this "corridor of crisis." Chapter 3 covers the evolution during the last two phases, teamwork and alliances. During these mature phases, the organization's senior executives must become very specialized in management-leadership.

Each phase lasts anywhere from three to fifteen years and contains its own unique structure, systems, and management or leadership style. The horizontal axis in Figure I.1 indicates the growth of the typical organization over time. The vertical axis indicates the size, maturity, and complexity of the organization. The number of people in the organization measures "size." "Maturity" means the ability of the people in the organization to work together. Mature organizations typically have formal management processes to resolve strategic, capital allocation, and priorities between competing groups. Further, they have institutionalized ways of constructively dealing with and using conflict to achieve an integration of interests. For example, arguing among departments, fixing blame on others, and a noncooperative attitude between labor and management reflect a low level of maturity. "Complexity" refers to the diverse nature of the business, its different product lines, the dispersion of its facilities, the number of departments, and the like.

The management phases are listed under the diagonal trend line in Figure I.1 and the corresponding crisis points are above the line. The crisis points are actually tensions demanding resolution. Symptomatic of an organization that has outgrown its present management practices, the tensions around crisis points are learning opportunities. Tensions force managers to change their practices, which stimulates organizational growth.

Crisis points are sets of oppositions, which, like the management phases they correspond to, are predictable. Most crisis points can be characterized as: profitability/creativity, ego/autonomy, red tape/flexibility, abdication/trust, alignment/direction, and self-interest/collaboration. Note that the first variable in the set of opposites deals with organizational control; the second with what workers want. The management-leadership challenge is to constantly balance these as the organization evolves.

Without a plan, the negotiation of these crisis points does not occur naturally or smoothly, regardless of the strength of top management. Because of organizations' differences in foresight, strengths, and understanding of how to make the transition between phases, each organization experiences transitions differently. However, as Greiner has shown, the phases and the transitions between phases are commonly enough experienced for managers to use them in planning for an organization's future and in dealing with the crises between phases.[2]

Although senior managements' understanding of the evolution of the typical organization has a lot to do with how quickly an organization grows, the growth of industry will, of course, contribute significantly to the actual slope of the trend line. For high-tech businesses, the slope is steep. These companies typically go through each management phase rapidly because the life cycle of their product is short. In industries that are somewhat stable, such as food, oil, and heavy manufacturing, the slope is much flatter, with many years between phases.

If managers fail to understand their organization's evolution and the tensions surrounding the transition from one phase to another, they risk undermining the viability of their organization. Some organizations falter, plateau, fail, or are acquired. For example, GE before Jack Welch and IBM before Lou Gerstner both suffered badly in the coordination phase when sophisticated management systems evolved into rigid bureaucracies. The key to success in the coming decades will be to understand these phases of growth and to deftly balance the paradoxes or points of tension that run through the development, operation, and continual transformation of the organization.

Figure I.1 may seem confusing to those who are not familiar with the concept of organizational evolution that Greiner developed. The concept is clarified in Chapters 1 through 3 with an in-depth examination of each evolutionary phase and its corresponding crisis point.

NOTES

1. Larry E. Greiner, "Evolution and Revolution as Organizations Grow," *Harvard Business Review* (May–June 1998): 55–67.

2. Ibid.

1

The Early Phases

As any small and start-up business owner knows, the first few years are critical to the business' success. As we enter the twenty-first century, the explosion and demise of many Internet dot.coms is an ideal backdrop to understand this first stage of organization evolution. It is a testimony to how fast start-ups can burn through their initial capitalization. With so many going out of business or merging as the Internet economy unfolds, it is vital to understand the dynamics of this phase. Any start-up must set up all facets of the business. It must have the leadership and energy from the top to change quickly to match the demands of the market, to figure out how to become profitable quickly, and to turn over aspects of the business to professional managers as it grows beyond the entrepreneur's own capabilities. These early years see the organization evolve from having an entrepreneurial to a directive style of management.

THE ENTREPRENEURIAL PHASE

Nearly every organization begins with an entrepreneurial form of management. Typically, strong natural leaders have either founded or have been chosen to run a newly formed organization. Because they feel most comfortable doing almost everything themselves, they will centralize decision making so that they control almost everything that is important. Usually the entrepreneur is a technical expert. Generally speaking, the centralized decision making enables the organization to survive in its infancy. In the early phases, employees usually do not have a very clear

idea of where the company is going, and they look to the leader for vision.

By definition, leaders have followers. Leaders attract followers because
people have faith in what the leader stands for. Leaders use vision, charisma, and technical skills to persuade people to follow them. Often on the
world stage, the "pure" leader has no direct command authority over the
followers; they follow by choice. These followers may never have personal
contact with their leaders, and many never even see those who lead them.
This is particularly true of political leaders, such as Ghandi; religious leaders, such as Jesus and Pope John Paul II; and others who attract large
followings. It is the perceived authority, or what sociologist Max Weber
called "charismatic authority," of the leader that inspires followers.

In the business world the leadership skill is the same, but here the leader
knows the followers. These natural leaders tend to be risk takers; they
challenge the status quo, inspire, celebrate successes, and lead the way.
They display a self-confidence some may interpret as arrogance. They actively seek opportunities that test and develop their abilities to accomplish
results. They like difficult tasks, competitive situations, unique assignments,
and "important" positions. They undertake responsibilities with an air of
"I can do it!" and, when they have finished say, "I told you it could be
done."

The natural leader can usually maneuver the company successfully
through both the entrepreneurial and early directive phases of evolution.
Because leadership is so important to the young organization, we discuss
below the most typical business practices characteristic of the natural
leader, along with some of the pitfalls of natural leadership in a growing
organization. These practices are less dominant in the entrepreneurial phase
but build with time and become the signature of the directive phase. The
directive leadership style usually occurs when the entrepreneur gets in financial trouble and a strong personality or management expert is brought
in to turn the situation around.

Takes Intuitive Action

The natural leader tends to act first, think later. When problems arise,
the inclination is to assess the facts based on surface appearances and
plunge into corrective action immediately. As a group, natural leaders are
sharp, alert, and dynamic. They have to be to survive. For them, intuitive
action gives quick and effective results. When they stumble, they are thinking and moving fast enough to stay ahead of the minor setbacks. However,
intuitive action tends to be short-lived and does not anticipate long-term
consequences. Each decision builds a foundation for the organization that,
sooner or later, may be poorly constructed for a more mature organization
and must be torn down or rebuilt.

Centralizes Decision Making. The natural leader gets used to making all the decisions alone and resists attempts by subordinates to make their own decisions. Data is absorbed daily in tremendous amounts so the leader can analyze it for making decisions. Centralized decisionmaking is seen as expeditious and becomes habit-forming. For example, the oil industry is full of natural leaders who are technical experts in geology, petroleum engineering, drilling, and other fields. When they get to the top, it becomes hard for them to keep hands-on involvement in the daily results of the drilling program. Because of the stakes involved, this tendency is understandable. The same can be said for leaders of engineering companies, retail businesses, and other organizations where the stakes are high and technical expertise is critical. However, when the boss insists on making all the decisions, lower levels of management can become demoralized.

Reacts to Operating Problems. The natural leader tends to get satisfaction from achieving results that are immediate and visible, and for which there is personal credit. Natural leaders want to be involved in the day-to-day operation of the business. For example, a sales manager who is a natural leader may devote his time and effort to direct selling. An engineering manager may consider herself first a technical engineer and only secondly a supervisor or manager. She operates in this fashion because she *prefers* it this way. The preference to be involved in an area of previous experience, handling the familiar and feeling self-assured, is a natural one. Because natural leaders enjoy being involved in day-to-day operating problems, they handle emergencies very capably and enjoy doing so. Therefore, much time is spent in fire fighting. As the company grows, the natural leader hires assistants to collect data needed for decision making. This style leaves little time or energy to concentrate on the more difficult work of developing company infrastructure and people that will allow the business to grow.

Gives Task Assignments. Once decisions are made, tasks are assigned. This is not delegation! (Delegation is discussed in Chapter 10.) Leaders who assign tasks spell out duties for the individual or group, defining what to do, where to do it, when to do it, who is to do it, and how to do it. Subordinates often don't know the "why" behind task assignments because it remains locked in the head of leaders who feel that explaining it would take as long as doing it themselves.

Communicates from the Top Down. Natural leaders are concerned primarily with making others understand what they want. Leaders influence others by force of character and persistence. Communication in the organization is primarily in one direction: down. Although there may be a tremendous amount of data flowing upward, two-way dialogue channels have not yet been developed. Bosses' decisions are communicated as directives. As the number of employees grows, however, they can begin to feel that the leaders make little effort to listen to and understand the feelings or requirements of others.

Works Hard. Natural leaders are doers; they get the job done. They have a high energy level and judge others by their ability to accomplish tasks quickly. Often they end up doing the work of their subordinates in addition to their own work. They are always on the phone, take their briefcases home, and feel that, if it were not for them, the whole organization would stop.

Controls by Inspection. The natural leader conducts operating reviews and follow-ups in person, by phone, or in meetings as though he or she were always "inspecting" to see if they have been performed correctly. The standard, or "right way," is the way the leader wants it done. However, control by personal observation becomes both limited and limiting because the leader eventually cannot be in control of everything. In addition, the leader's personal oversight may minimize employees' opportunities to use their own initiative and creative thinking.

Organizes Work Around People. Work is assigned to those who can do it best, not necessarily by logical function. Subordinates are seen as an extension of the leader's ability to process data and dictate task assignments. The primary concern is whether the individual can do the work satisfactorily. This approach to organization tends to be successful over the short term. Sooner or later, however, the strong individuals accumulate diverse and unrelated responsibilities. Most likely, their successors will not have the unique combination of talents or the experience necessary to satisfactorily perform all the varied tasks. Consequently, each new individual entering the group tends to trigger reorganization and the redistribution of work.

Promotes Personal Interests. Often the natural leader is paternalistic in dealing with subordinates and wants to be seen as fair and understanding, even "one of the gang." In truth, the natural leader often needs acceptance, is interested in popularity, and is egocentric. Although the leader may be truly friendly and interested in employees, his or her underlying goal is to make the organization successful.

Uses Carrot-and-Stick Motivation. To get subordinates to follow their directions, natural leaders use pay, time off, lavish parties, and personal recognition as motivational "carrots." The drawback of this type of motivation is that it can create an inner circle of workers recognized by the leader and rewarded for their superior accomplishments. In addition, if used repeatedly, carrot-and-stick motivation can become based primarily on employees' fear and intimidation. Although there are potential drawbacks to these typical characteristics, imposing management discipline at the entrepreneurial stage of growth would hamper the organization's ability to survive. The entrepreneur's ability to quickly monitor results, collect data, analyze it, and make the appropriate decisions reduces the need to formalize.

Leadership Skills

With the current trend in the United States toward downsizing and the growth of entrepreneurial start-ups, natural leadership skills are essential. They are skills that have changed little over the last twenty years. John P. Kotter's 1971 Harvard study, "What Effective General Managers [natural leaders] Really Do," was revisited in 1999. Kotter concluded that, "They 'wasted' time walking down corridors, engaging in seemingly random chats with seemingly random people, all the while promoting their agendas and building their networks with far less effort than if they'd scheduled meetings along a formal chain of command."[1] What Kotter describes is pure leadership, not management. Part III points out there is a big difference between the two.

Each entrepreneur starts out with a vision for his or her organization and the technical skills to lead the company to that vision. When a business, division, department, group, or unit starts up, this natural leadership is crucial because *it gets the job done.* Employees have faith in the leader, and they follow the leader's direction. This combination of faith and readiness to follow is what makes the start-up grow. When the organization grows, the entrepreneur may lack the management skills and financial expertise necessary to continue building the business. A survey of more than 200 CEOs of small businesses indicates that the most important skill to survive this phase is financial acumen.[2] Ensuring profitability is the most common crisis a small organization first runs into.

This is the crisis of profitability versus creativity. The leader who, throughout the history of the organization, had been the creative director and promoter must suddenly become an expert financial manager as well, and must delegate some of the creative responsibility. He or she must pull away from the daily running of the organization and become a professional manager. When a business hits the crisis of profitability versus creativity, the leader may find his or her job in jeopardy. The leader must make the transition to professional management practices or face being replaced with someone who can get the organization under control and moving again.

The events that initially befell Apple Computer and its founder, marketing genius Steven Jobs, are classic examples of both an entrepreneurial business that has outgrown its administrative capability and one paralyzed by a crisis of ineffective management delegation. Apple's turbulent and troubling history is one that is familiar to much of the business community. Because of its rebirth in the late 1990s, we will use Apple as a case study in the application of leadership or management depending on the organization's evolutionary phase.

What Happened at Apple? Jobs and his college roommate, Steven Wozniak, the technical expert, literally created the personal computer industry when they built the world's first successful small computer in their improvised home workshop in 1976. Almost overnight, they parlayed the tiny company into a multibillion-dollar enterprise. However, in the early 1980s, Apple Computer's profits began a long, steady decline, and the value of its stocks plunged.

Industry analysts say that the company seemed gripped by a curious paralysis. As it got larger and more complex, structure and systems were added. Although this trend toward professionalization was resisted by Jobs (who referred to professional managers as "bozos"[3]), the new procedures were required for efficiency and control. However, many of these changes did not take root. Denial—and arrogance—undid Jobs. Consequently, Apple was unable to either produce new products or deliver promised improvements to dealers on time. For example, the Lisa computer was introduced without adequate software because the hardware and software groups refused to work together. Jobs and Wozniak became embroiled in internecine warfare over the control and direction of Apple. After continual battles, Wozniak quit the company. Soon after, Jobs himself was out of his job, and out of the company. Jobs' ouster occurred in a boardroom power play led by an executive Jobs had hired to restructure management and steady the floundering company.

A comprehensive history of Apple and the fate of its founders suggest that neither Wozniak nor Jobs had the management skills needed to lead Apple after it outgrew its entrepreneurial beginnings. They wanted to maintain the close control over the organization that they had in the early days, when they made the decisions and delegated little, if any, authority and decision making. What happened next at Apple is a saga of CEOs—one after the other—none of whom was able to get the organization under control. One of the expelled CEOs, Gil Amelio, indicated that a lack of management discipline had plagued Apple for years and caused his downfall, and that the same problem keeps Apple stuck.[4] The culture at Apple was formed by Jobs. He is known for throwing temper tantrums, referred to as "Steve-trums." His behavior created fiefdoms throughout the organization that cooperated infrequently, resisted direction, and acted just like the old Jobs even after his ouster.

Why didn't the company make progress after Jobs left? The reasons are complex and vary with each attempt to remedy the failing company, but each attempt failed mainly because those in charge were unable to tame the culture Jobs had created—a culture with a genetic predisposition to chaos. Jobs had instituted a culture that could be managed by one person alone, him; but no single individual could maintain control over such a large organization. One ex-employee clearly voiced the problem Apple faced: "When he [Jobs] left Apple [in 1985], his DNA stayed, and it's like people are willing to accept his leadership in a way that they wouldn't from anyone else."[5]

As employees now admit, Apple was in a death spiral back in the early

1990s. Sales and market shares were falling precipitously. Expenses were ballooning out of control. Departments battled one another and Apple became highly fragmented. For example, twenty-two marketing groups had sprung up around the company. Many top executives were in denial; many of the most talented were leaving.

When Jobs returned to Apple in late 1997, employees commented that he was able to enforce a coherence that was absent while he was gone. His leadership ignited the culture once again. Most top managers were replaced and he brought in a seasoned management team from Next. In an interview in *Fortune*, Brent Schlender had this to say about Jobs: "Friends, competitors, and even former foes agree that Jobs has wrung out much of whatever was dysfunctional in his mercurial style."[6] Couple this with the management infrastructure that was put into place by others over the years to control the business, and Jobs has the formula for organizational survival. Regardless of whether Jobs stays on as president, it is clear that leadership was required to inspire and provide a vision for Apple employees.

The Apple of the early 1980s is an example of an organization caught in a crisis of profitability versus creativity, impeded in its efforts to grow because of cultural legacies that emanated from a particular and inappropriate leadership style. It had too little management discipline and too much employee freedom, both of which indicate missing management strategies and processes. Despite its size, the organization was immature. What made this crisis particularly difficult for Apple was that Jobs, as the senior executive, debunked formal management techniques as the anathema that stifles freedom, flexibility, and innovation. As Shona L. Brown and Kathleen M. Eisenhart say, "Not surprising, these businesses [like the Apple example] have the reputation as fun places to work. But more often, these same businesses are less skilled at making their creative strategies actually happen. They are often described by analysts as 'inconsistent' and 'never fulfilling their promise.' And when they do have market successes, they may have difficulty following up with the next generation. Why? Because they are equally famous for poor or confused execution."[7]

Lessons. The telltale characteristics of an organization in the late stage of the entrepreneurial phase are:

1. **A loose structure.** Structures exist but are sometimes ignored. Responsibilities are unclear, tangible goals for profitability are weak, priorities conflict, deadlines come and go, and the chain of command is blurred.

2. **Random communication.** Communication is abundant, but usually no one knows what precisely is going on. Communication tends to be informal, random, and chaotic.

3. **Creativity versus profitability.** Creativity is what launched the firm. Profitability is what sustains its life. Balancing the two is often difficult for the technical

expert. The meltdown of Internet dot.com companies in the first year of the twenty-first century speaks to this reality.

At some point, start-ups must invest as much in improving internal operating processes as they do in generating new features, sales, and additions to the product line. That's the point when the entrepreneurial organization grows up—when it figures out whether it can maintain the can-do spirit that gave it birth while also instilling enough discipline to meet the expectations of the marketplace that ultimately controls its destiny.

THE DIRECTIVE PHASE

The directive phase is very similar to the entrepreneurial phase in its leadership characteristics. The major difference is the focus. Entrepreneurs concentrate on creative endeavors, whereas the directive phase requires operational leadership. If an organization (department, unit, group, or division) does a poor job of making the transition to managing the firm in a professional way and can't get operations under control, the ensuing crisis of profitability forces it into the directive phase.

Often at this stage, new management is brought in to centralize decision making and institute controls to get the business balanced. He or she must roll up his or her sleeves and get intimately involved with running the business. (In the case of Apple, new management was a seasoned John Scully with a background in running large consumer product companies.) They stay on top of things at every level, from day-to-day workings of employees to higher-level decisions. Rugged individualism is the most salient characteristic of the directive phase of leadership. The new leader may say, "I am the operational expert, look to me for direction," or "I will decide what you need to do," or "I'm the one who will save the sinking ship." When an organization enters the directive phase, it is no longer time for the type of creative individuality that plagued Apple. The leader has taken over a directive position, deciding what needs to be done and when. Often, such individualism is the only way to break the hold that the past has on the organization.

Management style in the directive phase, while tough minded, is usually paternalistic. The relationship that develops between leader and employee is often like a parent-child relationship, one where both are deemed part of a big family. A sense of teamwork is created by the paternalistic culture that encourages everyone to be loyal to the company. ("After all, we're all in this together, aren't we?") Management and subordinates attend company picnics together, and everyone works to build the business. The leader's operational expertise draws the workers together, creating a vision of the future that keeps the organization going.

Consider the fate that befell People Express in the mid-1980s. People

Express was a small but up-and-coming airline founded by the charismatic entrepreneur Don Burr, a graduate of Harvard Business School. By the time it was five years old, People Express had become a billion-dollar business and wanted to expand by taking over Frontier Airlines, a financially distressed small airline. Meanwhile, Burr and his wildly successful enterprise were praised by national publications, cited in textbooks, and held up to Harvard Business School students as a model of humanistic, participatory management.

The ink on some laudatory observations about Burr and People Express was hardly dry when the idealized public image collapsed. Burr moved suddenly to seize Frontier Airlines. When he did so, editors and business school professors—to their great surprise—learned that People Express was on the brink of bankruptcy. It was also in serious trouble with the IRS for nonpayment of back taxes. Within months, Texas Air (now Continental) swallowed both People Express and Frontier.

Burr blamed his troubles on rising costs, price wars, and stiff competition from bigger airlines. Some of his employees, however, further shocked and embarrassed editors and business school professors by denouncing the company's public image as "all a sham," its management style as "a one-man show." Burr, they said, was a "fantastic, charismatic person" but "an absolute dictator . . . you don't cross him" and a "master manipulator who did not treat them with dignity or respect."[8]

Like many organizations in the directive phase, People Express grew rapidly with its family approach. Employees recall that at first Burr was "like a father" who "ate pizza with them by day and drank beer with them by night." Every employee owned stock in the company, and Burr gave each of them fully paid medical, dental, and life insurance. "Everyone felt equal to everyone else," one employee recalls.[9] As Burr himself has said, he has "a hearty disrespect for bureaucracy and authoritarian styles" of management. Burr explained how he believed employees interpreted his philosophy: "If Don Burr says it, by God, that's what we want to do. Leadership is not pandering to what people say they need. It's *defining* what they need."[10] These remarks, contrary to what he believed, are the footprint of a leadership style taken too far.

Was Burr's paternalistic image really a sham, as some employees claimed? What really caused the death of People Express? Although it is difficult to be certain about the reasons behind the downfall of People Express, it seems obvious from Burr's words that he managed the fledgling company with a typical individualistic, even autocratic, style. This served People Express well during its early stage of growth, but it failed both Burr and his company in their efforts to cope with the inevitable tension between ego and autonomy that erupted when employees began to expect and demand the right to participate in decision making. Because of Burr's failure to make the changes crucial to propelling his company toward more professional management, he lost his once-thriving business by staying too long in the directive phase.

Another example of directive hubris occurred during the 1990s. The most common type of directive management during this period was labeled "slash and burn." It was identified with turnaround expert Al Dunlap, otherwise known as "Chainsaw Al."[11] Dunlap's brutal style involved lay-offs, plant closures, and crushing ingrown corporate cultures—all with the sole purpose of increasing corporate profits. His belief is that when the ship is sinking, people want the captain to tell them what to do—it is not the time to sit around and get a consensus on who should get in which life-boats.

Dunlap was good at cutting costs and increasing shareholder value to make a company attractive for sale, but his leadership style was not as good in promoting the long-term growth of the company. Although directive leaders like Dunlap maximize cost control, they tend to dampen the creativity and innovation that create the growth an organization needs to move on to the next phase in its evolution.

In the growing organization, a directive leader's ego, or ability to run the organization as an individual, comes into conflict with employees' desire to have some say in the decisions that affect them. Leadership by intimidation might get a company pointed in the right direction, but it cannot sustain that direction in the long run. Even the most loyal team workers may begin to chafe under the directive leader's management style. No longer satisfied with merely carrying out the leader's task assignments, subordinates naturally come to want the authority to make some decisions themselves. They also want the right to have more of a voice in decisions that affect them directly. They often believe, and rightly so, that they have more knowledge and expertise in their specialized field than the leader, who becomes more and more distant from the daily running of the organization.[12]

These developments may threaten the directive leader's ego. If so, the organization very likely will find itself in the grip of an ego-versus-autonomy crisis. Control is the central issue in the crisis ending the directive phase of an organization's evolution. If it is not resolved by effective management techniques—production control, inventory control, quality control, expense control—the crisis tends to pit the centralized control of a small number of senior executives against workers who want greater autonomy in their positions. Such a showdown can result in great casualties, including jobs, profits, and stock values. The company itself may suffer severe injury, even annihilation.

If an organization coming out of the directive phase is to effectively manage its size and complexity, it must build a solid infrastructure of management processes to run the business. Professional management is required with two fundamental characteristics:

1. **Direct authority downward**. Larger organizations are too complex for one individual to stay on top of all operating details. Therefore, managers must delegate their authority to individuals lower in the organization.

2. **Use of formal control systems**. Delegating authority creates the need for formal systems to plan and review results thus holding individuals or teams accountable for their commitments. These systems include a mechanism to set goals, monitor performance, and reward the desired performance.

SUMMARY

The entrepreneurial and directive phases of organizational evolution happen in the early years of launching a business. Both phases require strong direction from the top. The entrepreneurial leader is usually a technical expert in a specific area and success depends upon their creative ability to satisfy an evolving marketplace need. However, failure to ensure the profitability of the fledging firm often leads to terminal consequences.

What is required at this stage is an operational expert; a specialist who can restore profitability and continue to make the firm grow. Whether a turnaround expert or a seasoned executive, "directive leadership" best describes this leadership style. However, the Achilles heel of this often autocratic leadership is ego rather than reason. The developing tension between the leader's desire for control and employees' desire to have some say in decisions affecting them signals the need for change in how the business is managed. Since all of the operating levers cannot be manipulated from the top, middle-management coordination between functions is required. Success now depends on how well the firm builds its management infrastructure and controls its internal business processes with policies and procedures.

NOTES

1. John P. Kotter, "What Effective General Managers Really Do," *Harvard Business Review* (March–April 1999): 159.

2. N.C. Churchill and V.L. Lewis, "The Five Stages of Small Business Growth," *Harvard Business Review* (May–June 1983): 30.

3. Michael L. Tushman and Charles A. O'Reilly, "Ambidextrous Organizations: Managing Evolutionary and Revolutionary Change," *California Management Review* 38, no. 4 (Summer 1996): 13.

4. Peter Burrows, "From Apples to Sour Grapes," Rev. of *On the Firing Line: My 500 Days at Apple* by Gil Amelio and William L. Simon (New York: HarperBusiness, 1997), *Business Week*, 4 May 1998.

5. "An Ex-Insider's View of What Apple Needs," *Los Angeles Times*, 22 June 1998: Section D, p. 5.

6. Brent Schlender, "The Three Faces of Steve," *Fortune*, 9 November 1998, 96.

7. Shona L. Brown and Kathleen M. Eisenhart, *Competing on the Edge* (Boston: Harvard Business School Press, 1998), 34.

8. "Texas Air Gets Tentative Approval to Buy People Express and Frontier," *Orange County Register*, 15 October 1986, Section C, p. 3.

9. Ibid.

10. Ibid.

11. David Maharaj, "Sunbeam Gives the Ax to Chairman Chainsaw Al," *Los Angeles Times*, 15 June 1999, p. A1.

12. Michael Maccoby, "Narcissistic Leaders," *Harvard Business Review*, (January–Febuary 2000): 69–77.

2

The Corridor of Crisis

During the "corridor of crisis," which includes both the coordinative and delegative phases of an organization, managers must find a proper balance between centralizing control and decentralizing it. Figure 2.1 is a modification of Figure I.1 depicting organization evolution. It shows how the corridor of crisis is sandwiched in between the "entrepreneurial/directive" and "teamwork/alliance" styles of management.

The balance of control is very difficult during this transition partly because it constantly requires rethinking as customer demands, marketplace fluctuations, and the organization's complexity vary. Many companies end up going through a number of cycles of centralization and decentralization during this difficult period.

The mistake top executives often make, says Ralph H. Kilmann in his book *Managing Beyond the Quick Fix*, is relying on short-term solutions to organizational symptoms.[1] Most firms are too intent on making monthly revenue numbers, redrawing the organizational chart, distributing a revised mission statement, to focus on the real root cause issues; this explains why most change programs fail in this turbulent stage.

THE COORDINATIVE PHASE

As an organization begins to enter the coordination phase and the size and complexity of the firm increases, it adds professional managers to help with the work of the directive leader. Further, to cope with its growth, an organization may add corporate staff functions to help oversee its activities.

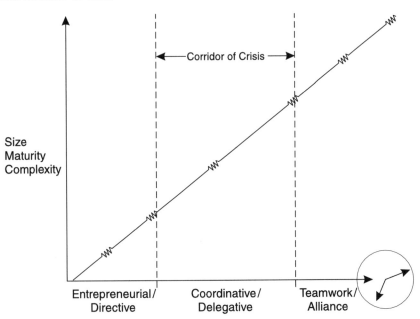

Figure 2.1
The Corridor of Crisis

To gain control of the confusion that may have developed in the directive phase, staff functions often create a series of policies and procedures to add to those the business already has. Upper management also uses its staff to collect and analyze data and to audit the line's results. Staffers often sit physically close to the boss and act as gofers; that is, they go for this and go for that. Senior executives often use them as personal assistants. After digesting operational data, senior executives, sometimes in discussion with corporate staff members, ask them to implement his or her decisions.

In this phase, top management maintains a certain amount of individual control, but they are no longer the sole enforcers of decisions and company policy. A cadre of corporate staff coordinates top management's directives, ensuring that the parts of the business work together to achieve defined company goals. As an organization in the coordination phase grows, so does the bureaucracy and red tape around its numerous policies and procedures.

Over time, as both the company and bureaucracy grow, using staff primarily to ensure that the goals of the top managers are met can cause friction between operating groups and the corporate staff. Red tape often gets tangled, and it becomes difficult to know who is really accountable for results. An organization facing such a crisis, the crisis of "red tape versus flexibility," tends to slip into "me-they" thinking. In such organizations, one group blames the other for problems and failures. Relationships become adversarial; one constantly hears the lament, "*They* don't trust me . . . *They* never follow through on their commitments." These complaints are partially valid; top managers *don't* entrust decision-making responsibility to lower levels. They don't want to give lower levels the flexibility they need to begin assuming accountability for the work they do.

Many of the so-called smokestack industries (notably U.S. Steel, for years known as "Big Steel" but officially renamed USX) found themselves smothered by this crisis during the 1970s and the 1980s. USX, which was particularly hard hit, finally emerged from the mire alive, but with its identity as a company changed forever.

USX's problems were typical of those of many smokestack industries. Their difficulties began when foreign competition, weak prices, and a glut of steel products on the world market plagued the steel industry for several decades. USX also suffered serious strife between labor and management, and many of its plants were crippled by labor disputes. In addition, the company also failed to make the necessary capital investments in new plants and machinery that could have augmented its future productivity, preferring instead to focus on short-term financial gains. Eventually, the forced closing of plants and the inevitable layoff of thousands of workers seriously weakened the company's infrastructure.

Like the typical company trapped in the coordination phase of evolution, USX fought the problem by adding more staff—that is assigning managers to manage managers, who managed other managers, who managed assistant managers, who managed supervisors, who managed assistants—until finally someone interfaced with the worker who actually did the work. Such a management strategy afflicts a company with bloated staffing, middle-management bulge, and a higher probability of worker mistakes, since such a strategy encourages lower-level people to follow direction rather than to think on their own.

To remedy the situation, companies like USX often renew their emphasis on regaining control by establishing more policies and procedures. Policy and procedures manuals grow in size and number. Separate departments write, edit, print, distribute, and keep track of all manuals in circulation. Bureaucracy grows and the red tape crisis begins to choke the organization. USX was caught in the classic tension between controlling operations from the top and giving employees more flexibility. Meanwhile, this same scenario was being played out in countless other firms during this period.

One reason that corporate raiders were so successful in the 1980s was that they came in and cleaned out the fat in the companies they were absorbing, like USX. Owners know that bloat, waste, and red tape are beyond managers' abilities to completely clean up; they have invested too heavily in the policies they helped create, and risk losing their jobs if they cut too much. But, if it wants to stay in business, the company must cut its own fat ruthlessly. It must trim the bulk and streamline unwieldy structures, drastically reducing organizational levels, eliminating staff authority duplication and position overlap, and imposing a decentralized system of management.

The raiding needed to cut the fat in companies such as USX can be seen as a temporarily directive style of management, like a brief return to the "slash-and-burn" strategy instigated by Al Dunlap. A single strong leader needs to come in, direct the cutting of corporate fat, reorganize the channels of responsibility and accountability down to the lower levels, and then get out to let the teamwork happen.

The downsizing efforts of the 1990s were primarily aimed at dealing with ineffective coordinative structures and reestablishing the productivity that U.S. companies had previously enjoyed. GM, Sears, IBM, and other well-known large companies have struggled with bloated corporate overhead, complacent overpaid middle management, and operational inefficiencies. Although Sears and IBM have successfully dealt with these issues, GM has not. It remains a messy, sluggish, inward-looking company that, so the joke goes, spends more time making organizational charts than cars. Because of its size and past market position, it felt immune to the competitive problems that beset other U.S. auto companies. It developed a culture of arrogance that belied the efficiency and foresight that its founder, Alfred Sloan, had created.

There will be no fixing the behemoth without first jolting management from its habitual lethargy. One of GM's chief problems is that management has failed to establish accountability at lower levels. Harvard industry analyst John P. Kotter says that at GM, "Employees guilty of mistakes—and there are plenty—are never identified, and trips to the woodshed are as rare as a snowless winter in Michigan."[2] GM's plight screams for a decisive manager who is not a product of the GM culture and who can cut the blinders off hide-bound management. Kotter says that at GM, "You've denial, complacency, depression—everything except urgency." GM's internal management troubles are coupled with labor disputes, such as the threatened strike at Saturn. But it would be wrong to place all the blame on labor. Management's behavior at GM demonstrates its dogged determination to dig in its heels to prove that it is right and that it still has the muscle over workers. This is precisely the sort of myopic behavior that will drive the firm further into red tape, chaos, and inefficiency.

Like GM, Boeing has become snarled in a transition period that has stalled many businesses. For Boeing, corporate culture is the problem. Like many other companies Boeing developed a paternal-like culture as it grew. As it entered the corridor of crisis, however, that culture became a drag on performance. In a family culture, bad performers are never thrown out; the culture is about seniority, not performance. The challenge Boeing faces in coming years is to stop the slide in market share being taken by Airbus. In a 1999 *Fortune* article, Kenneth Labich says the aircraft giant has decided to "become a tougher, leaner competitor. For that to happen, things have to get a lot less sleepy in Seattle."[3] Boeing is aiming for one of the greatest industrial transformations in U.S. history. They are deep into the corridor of crisis. If they don't change the way they do things, history indicates they will slowly fade away.

Even high-tech companies are not immune from the malaise of red tape. Two examples—one a hardware manufacturer, the other producing software—provide an insight into the bureaucracy that they face. Staffers at Microsoft with 30,000 employees, 183 different products, and at least five layers of management complain about red tape. A recent *Business Week* article sums up the Microsoft problems in a succinct fashion: "With decisions large and small being funneled to the top, the pair [Bill Gates and Steven A. Ballmer] became a bottle neck. Worse, they undermined the confidence of managers below. Ballmer and Gates were involved in every decision—from key features in the upcoming Windows 2000 to reviewing the response records for the company's customer support lines. Says Chris Williams, vice president of human resources, 'senior executives didn't feel like they were in control of their own destiny.' "[4]

Compaq promoted from within one of its own when it ousted CEO Eckhartd Pfeiffer after declining profits and a sinking stock price. An August 1999 article by *Fortune* quoted Compaq's Chairman Ben Rosen when he dug into the problems saying this about bureaucracy: "There was tremendous pressure for change, especially from four levels down in the organization. Decisions weren't getting made because of the structure."[5] The new top management group scrapped a cumbersome matrix organization that favored geography over functional accountability and set out clear profit-and-loss responsibility for each business unit.

If a company is to survive the red tape of the coordination phase and continue to grow, emphasis must be placed on self-control at the *point of control*. That is, the workers who do the work should be held accountable to exercise control over their delegated decision-making authority. The worker needs to become responsible for inspecting his or her work for quality and cost against predetermined and agreed-upon measures of performance. Data does not need to flow upward for top management inspection and staff control. Instead, it needs to flow horizontally to the workers who need it to do their jobs.

THE DELEGATIVE PHASE

The upper management of a company facing a crisis of red tape in the coordination phase usually realizes that decision making must be decentralized. The managers attempt to cope with the crisis by giving lower-level employees some authority to make decisions. Managers must often redefine expectations for middle managers, who may become threatened as the decision making they once enforced is moved to lower levels. Control is generally decentralized, with top management moving to a role of overseer rather than originator of decisions.

The danger with the delegative phase is that top management often fails to balance delegated control—trusting front-line workers—with appropriate and effective systems for monitoring what happens at the lower levels of decision making. It is easy to go too far in cutting middle management, which causes the bloat and sluggishness of the company in the coordination phase. When a company cuts too much, lower-level workers who are now making decisions once made by superiors tend not to get sufficient and timely feedback. Further, top management does not assume responsibility for conducting performance planning sessions, communicating goals, and reviewing results with lower-level decision makers, but it has not yet replaced its direction with local equivalents. While management refrains from "telling employees what to do," it abdicates its responsibility to plan and review the results. Inevitably, what top management fears most happens: poor decisions are made and these mistakes are not identified and addressed. Therefore, they cannot be corrected in time to prevent recurrences. As the company continues to grow, the results of bad decisions and unrectified mistakes can escalate into the crisis of "abdication versus trust."

The natural response to such a loss of control is to reinstitute the type of centralized control managers exercised in the coordination phase. The coordinative and delegative phases are termed the "corridor of crisis" in an organization's evolution precisely because of the difficulty of finding an appropriate balance between centralized and decentralized control. Companies that become stuck between these two phases find themselves cycling through systems of tight and loose control, without seeming to be able to find a proper balance.

One example of such a company is BankAmerica. During much of the 1980s, it found itself caught in this kind of trap. Once the largest bank in the world (with 80,000 employees) and a model of growth and profitability, BankAmerica enjoyed international clout; yet it approached the end of the decade as the nation's chief problem bank, on the brink of disaster. BankAmerica would recover, making an unusual comeback. It is ironic that Chief Executive A.W. (Tom) Clausen is both the culprit blamed for the near-fatal decline and the savior who snatched BankAmerica back from the edge of the precipice.

During its early years, BankAmerica flourished under the paternalistic hand of A.P. Giannini, its founder. Clausen, one of Giannini's successors, later encountered growing pains throughout the company and recognized them for what they were: a corporate struggle to come of age. BankAmerica had thousands of employees stationed in outposts all over the world. Clausen moved to decentralize control, sharing decision-making authority with managers at lower levels and allowing all employees more autonomy. He then moved on to head the World Bank, and installed new management at BankAmerica.

However, the new management failed to require that lower-level decision makers be held accountable for results. Management abdicated its responsibility to install a formalized short-term planning and review system. As a result, BankAmerica found itself with too many unwise loan decisions made by inexperienced employees. Worse, the corporation lacked adequate means of monitoring what was happening in far-flung offices, since its communications (computer) system was outmoded, slow, and ineffective. When profits disappeared, stocks fell, and debts increased, BankAmerica's board forced Samuel H. Armacost, Clausen's successor, to resign.

Armacost was unable to break through the bureaucracy and build a solid infrastructure of management processes to move the bank toward decentralization. BankAmerica had a portfolio of billions of dollars in loans gone bad, morale was low, staff ranks were bloated and inefficient, and key people were leaving. There was a mortgage scandal, the company's stock sagged, and a bank half the size of BankAmerica posed a takeover threat.

Armacost resigned under fire, and Clausen came back—like Steve Jobs at Apple—to save the ailing corporation, which was in shambles. Reapplying a directive leadership style (temporarily), Clausen managed to turn the corporation around. In BankAmerica's 1989 Annual Report, Clausen asserted that "the turnaround has been accomplished. The recovery is a fact. My job is done."[6] Since then, following its merger with NationsBank, BankAmerica has slowly built itself again into one of the biggest banks in the United States.

Jumping the Curve

Breaking through a crisis of abdication versus trust—trusting both subordinates and a decentralized management control system—such as that which beset BankAmerica is one of the most difficult transitions a company can make. To get out of the corridor of crisis, companies need a strategically formulated plan to jump the curve to a team-based structure made up of external alliances and internal business processes that are controlled horizontally by the people doing the work.

Jumping the curve means making the transition from one phase to another. Although any transition is hard, hanging on during the roller coaster ride through the corridor of crisis is especially difficult. Figure 2.2 shows the S-curve, a familiar concept seen in most things biological as well as manufactured products and organizations. Applied to all three the pattern is virtually the same: slow growth at the beginning, then rapid acceleration with a final slowdown. To survive and grow, it is critical to invest in the next product life cycle, or organizational phase, *before* such a move is

Figure 2.2
Jumping the Curve to New Heights

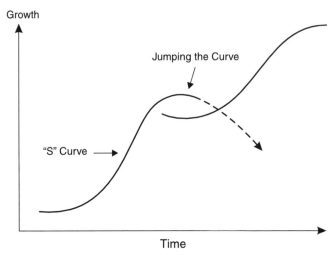

apparently necessary: when things look good and profits are at an all-time high. This is what jumping the curve means—looking forward to the next stage of evolution and planning for it in order to get there.

Dr. Jonas Salk, a major figure in the fight against polio, has described the biological underpinning of this phenomenon. The S-curve is a way to "reflect a law of nature that governs growth in living systems. [It] reflects the transformational character of change in our times."[7] Salk found that species threatened with extinction must adapt; successful organizations must do the same. A central part of the adaptation process is *creative destruction*. Jumping the curve requires leaving the past behind—which necessitates some destruction—and learning a new way to relate to the environment—which means being creative.

Toyota Takes the Long View. Figure 2.3 graphically illustrates the S-curve concept using research gathered at Toyota. Over many 55-year cycles, technology has migrated from canals to telecommunications. Using this data, Toyota made a strategic decision to invest in the next evolving technology. Toyota takes "a very long view" in its planning.[8] Not wanting to be known as a "buggy whip" manufacturer, Toyota is anticipating the future—which is already here—and preparing to jump the curve to the next new technology which is telecommunications and the Internet.

Toyota is not leaving the car business, but sees telecommunications and the Internet as the next growth opportunity. It is basing its decision on information it has gathered on the life cycles of industrial technologies. Figure 2.3 depicts some of this information. It suggests that the highway

Figure 2.3
Toyota Takes a Very Long View of the Future

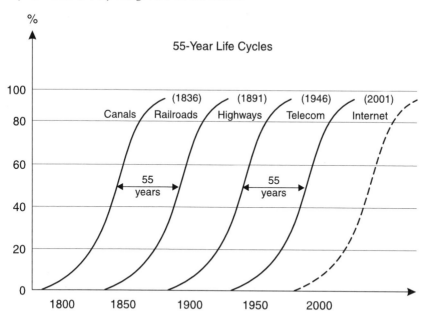

as a dominant infrastructure today has reached its zenith after a 55-year run. It is being eclipsed by the digital revolution.

The Dow Jones Industrial Average Puts on a New Face. Evidence of this shift is a change in the Dow Jones industrial average. At the end of the twentieth century, several tech companies replaced "smokestack" stocks—Chevron, Texaco, Goodyear Tire & Rubber, and Bethlehem Steel were out and Microsoft, Intel, and phone giant SBC Communications were in. As we enter the twenty-first century, nineteen of the thirty Dow components—or 63 percent—will represent service industries, including financial services, technology, and consumer products. To understand the updates in the 103-year-old Dow is to keep in touch with the massive shift in the U.S. economy away from heavy manufacturing and towards technology and services.

Figure 2.3 shows how telecommunications started in the early 1950s with the introduction of television. The Internet took off just before the year 2000. If it is truly a new technology and telecommunications is peaking, then society can look forward to a robust economy made up of information and knowledge industries built on the backbone of telecommunications, but with a digital twist.

The lesson here is that Toyota's managers see themselves as stewards of a long-standing enterprise. Their priorities match their commitment to the organization's long-term survival in an unpredictable world. Like careful bonsai gardeners, they prune yet encourage growth and renewal without endangering the plant they are tending.

Symptoms of a Need for Organizational Change. To successfully make the transition out of the corridor of crisis and grow free of the cycles of centralization and decentralization that make such a transition so difficult, managers and leaders need to recognize the symptoms that indicate a need for change. If managers watch for these symptoms they can plan ways to overcome a present problem and to avoid related ones in the future. Below are some of the most salient symptoms of a need for organizational change.

Going back to the past. When things don't work, managers resist change and begin to rely too heavily on what worked in the past, turning their backs on the new. When things still don't go well, they work even harder, doing what made them successful in the first place. Often they become overworked and irrational as more and more critical decisions drop between the cracks and are not resolved.

Adding assistants. In an attempt to preserve their status, handle the tremendous decision-making load, and relieve themselves of day-to-day administrative details and people problems, managers hire more assistants. However, this only adds to the long-term problems of bureaucracy and bloat that eventually develop.

Tightening the reins. Managers like the power that decision making gives them, partly because it preserves their status. They resist letting subordinates make decisions, fearing that by delegating authority they lose control. When things go wrong, centralized control becomes tighter. But the very thing that managers fear most actually happens. By trying to keep control, they actually find themselves increasingly losing control.

Extending the hand of the boss. Senior managers use staff as an extension of their own office. Staff personnel spend time collecting and analyzing information, then channeling it to the boss. The boss then gives staff task assignments and directives to "fix" the problem. It's not uncommon for a president to tell the comptroller, "See to it that costs are cut in XYZ Department." Quality control departments are instructed to "control" quality, and production control groups are ordered to "control" production, without any discussion about *how* that control should happen with the people doing the work.

Throwing in more money and people. When problems develop, the solution often is to throw more people and money at them. Further, when the natural leader insists on centralizing decision making, a paradox is created: he or she needs more people to carry out top-management dictates. Positions proliferate and middle managers become mere relay points for information being funneled up from the bowels of the organization or for dictates fired downward by the boss.

Bloating at the waistline. Minimum control spans—two or three direct reports—and many levels of management produce a middle-management bloat. It is common for managers to have only two direct reports, with hundreds under each one of them or, even worse, a one-on-one reporting relationship where an assistant separates the managers from lower-level subordinates. Because managers haven't learned to manage effectively and supervise using a broad span of control, the organization begins to add subordinate levels. This adds more and more to middle management, but growth is only vertical.

Working with the "walking dead." Policies and procedures, reports, and second-guessing stifle individual initiative. The message workers hear is: "Don't think, follow standard operating procedure." Those who remain become the walking dead, not the creative workers an organization needs.

Growing upward. Promotion is the only way to give managers a raise, so levels and new job titles are added to middle-management ranks, furthering the problem of management bloating. This expands the bureaucratization of management and adds to the dysfunctionality of the firm.

Reorganizing responsibilities. Work is often assigned to individuals randomly instead of by function. Many diverse and unrelated duties end up being assigned to a position. Often the successors don't have the unique talents of the incumbent, and this triggers a reorganization to fit the new person. When the work is assigned based on one's talents, fields overlap and duties duplicate, blurring line and staff authority.

Doing it "my way." Since a formal management system is lacking, each division head, manager, or supervisor manages based on what comes naturally or intuitively. When one manager leaves and a new one comes in, it's "throw out the old and do it my way." Subordinates become confused and frustrated as they try to learn a new set of rules and attempt to figure out where the new boss is coming from.

New Symptoms. As the firm moves towards increased decentralization, there is an emphasis to change management programs, talk of cross-functional teamwork, matrix structures, and a plethora of special task forces. While the residues of earlier symptoms remain, they do not go away, and a new set of symptoms exacerbates the frustrations of employees caught in the corridor of crisis as outlined below.

The maddening matrix. A formal mechanism to resolve the diverse and conflicting need of functional, product, and geographic management groups often leads to matrix management. However, a matrix is all but unmanageable—dual reporting relationships lead to conflict and confusion: the proliferation of channels created by informational logjams create a proliferation of committees and reports; and overlapping responsibilities produce turf battles and a loss of accountability.

Creating more committees and task forces. Managers set these up to look into problem areas and make recommendations. Top management uses the data they gather to make decisions. Used too often, these data-gathering techniques serve to encourage the centralization of control. For example, in a vain effort to rescue BankAmerica from crisis, President Armacost set up many new task forces and required a flurry of written reports from subordinates. In his own reports, he continued to reassure bank directors and stockholders that "the strategic plan is working." It was revealed later, of course, that Armacost's plan wasn't successful.

Distorting databases. Why was Armacost's plan a failure? Layers in the organization filter out what's really going on at lower levels. The result is that data is distorted as it goes up the chain of command and is changed to fit the expectations of what upper management wants to hear. Upper managers make decisions on the information they get. Distorted information at any level is detrimental to a company, and can even have disastrous consequences. For example, White House and Congressional investigators made the shocking discovery that middle managers of NASA's launch team at Houston Space Center did not inform top management that engineers wanted to scrub the launch of the *Challenger* spacecraft in January 1986. Their reason: the "O" rings on the vehicle's rocket boosters were unsafe in the freezing temperatures that blanketed the Florida launch pad on the morning of the flight. As the world knows, an "O" ring failure on the right rocket booster caused the *Challenger* to explode a few seconds after liftoff, killing all on board.

Ignoring suggestions. Top managers sometimes confront a problem by asking for suggestions, but instead of considering them, they often say, "When I was in the field we tried that (a subordinate's suggestion), but it didn't work." The only problem is that the world has changed dramatically over the last twenty years, and perhaps the suggested idea has become viable. Managers' decisions end up being made on experience that is often out of date, and decisions become more conservative and cease to reflect the realities of day-to-day operations.

Tolerating a loss of communication. As middle management grows, worker-supervisor communication begins to disappear. If the resulting problem isn't too serious, the "fix" is deemed a course in communications, a supervisory program, or something else to placate the workers and top management. However, this remedy treats the symptoms, not the underlying causes.

Taking "vacations." What's discussed in training sessions is often ignored and rarely implemented back on the job. The old-timers tell the "charm school" graduates, "Your vacation is over; now let's get back to work."

Attending more meetings. Middle-management officers typically spend 40 to 60 percent of their time in meetings, coordinating across departments, and solving interface problems. These meetings can last for hours, with nothing resolved except a decision to meet again. Since accountabilities are not clear, there is much needless finger pointing.

Persisting with outdated approval levels. In many organizations, expenditure requests may have to go all the way up to the executive committee for approval. Top management gets bogged down with such minor things as the selection of furnishings for lower-level management offices, review of expense accounts, and the approval of even the most minor expenses—all of which causes delays in decisions vital to the day-to-day operation of the business.

Blaming between departments. As an organization begins to polarize, teamwork breaks down and a "me-they" attitude develops. Loyalty to the company is replaced by loyalty to one's own group or department. One department starts blaming another. While certainly this is immature behavior, it is often the only way for employees to vent their frustration and anger at what they perceive to be a dysfunctional set of management practices. Departments become protective of their own areas, turf battles emerge, and groups maximize their own needs and results at the expense of others. Everyone plays politics to further his or her own best interests.

Losing the Exceptional Employee. Good people are hired, but they leave. The crisis of ego versus autonomy is widespread. Bright subordinates realize that their boss and the system he or she is part of are inflexible and egocentric; therefore, they leave. The organization is left with "yes men," and the leader complains that there is no one to replace *him/her*. This becomes a self-fulfilling prophecy.

Increasing grievances. When boredom sets in and the red-tape routine kills the fun, workers may use their initiative in undermining management and expressing their discontent. At the work level, grievances grow. Workers are "grieving" for recognition, attention, and the opportunities for individual initiative. They end up walking the line with management just like kids do with their parents to make work more interesting.

Managing by fire hose. There is never enough time for planned action, so managers usually have a fire hose in their hands. Their day is spent putting out one flare-up after the other.

Playing musical chairs and downsizing. The solution to increasing difficulties is often to cut the copier bill, not the fat. Get rid of people, not the system. The fat is an employee population out of control; the fault is not theirs, however. The management system is the culprit. W. Edward Deming, the quality guru of the 1980s, was fond of saying, "Eighty percent of the problems companies face are system problems, not the people." Unfortunately, most of the downsizing efforts have had only minimal success. It takes people to run the system. If the people are not involved in the redesign, they will not own the solution; they will, instead, resist, furthering the game of musical chairs.

OUT OF A CORRIDOR OF CRISIS

An effective management system is what Deming advocates. It's the way out of a corridor of crisis. Eric G. Framholtz and Yvonne Randle say in *Changing the Game* that transitioning to professional management depends, largely "on the design and implementation of effective performance management systems." They go on to suggest that "as a firm's management begins to plan for its transformation, they need to ensure that they have effectively designed every element in the firm's performance management system, along with each department's and each individual's clear account-ability."[9] In a performance management system accountabilities are linked to align the goals within an organization. If management abdicates its re-sponsibility to ensure that this vital work is done, it faces the crisis of "abdication/trust."

An in-depth discussion of the tools and techniques managers use to make the transition in an organization to a team-driven environment is covered in Part III, Chapter 10.

SUMMARY

Each one of these symptoms should tell the wise leader or manager that he or she needs to begin planning rational and effective ways to manage change. Only by doing so will the organization successfully jump the curve and grow out of the evolutionary corridor of crisis. Moving on to an or-ganizational system of teamwork means eliminating the symptoms created by red tape and a lack of trust in subordinate decision making.

Essentially, managers must figure out how to decentralize decision-making authority without exercising direct control. They must create an infrastructure that supports delegation, encourages teams, and sustains an information system that provides data on results to those being asked to do the work. They must create a culture of individual commitment that nonetheless recognizes that "we are all in this together."

NOTES

1. Ralph H. Kilmann, *Managing Beyond the Quick Fix* (San Francisco: Jossey-Bass, 1989).

2. Alex Taylor III, "Is Jack Smith the Man to Fix GM?" *Fortune*, 3 August 1998, 90.

3. Kenneth Labich, "Boeing Finally Hatches a Plan," *Fortune*, 1 March 1999, 101.

4. "Remaking Microsoft," Cover Story, *Business Week*, 17 May 1999, 108.

5. Alex Taylor, "Compaq Looks Inside for Salvation," *Fortune*, 16 August 1999, 126.

6. BankAmerica Corporation, 1989 Annual Report, p. 2.

7. Jonas Salk and Jonathan Salk, *World Population and Human Values: A New Reality* (New York: HarperCollins, 1981), 3.

8. David Holley, "Toyota Heads Down a New Road," *Los Angeles Times: OC Edition*, 16 March 1997, p. 1. D1.

9. Eric G. Flamholtz and Yvonne Randle, *Changing the Game* (New York: Ox-ford University Press, 1998), 243.

3

The Transition to Teams and Alliances

As an organization leaves the corridor of crisis and makes the transition from centralized control to the cross-functional management of business processes, it enters the teamwork phase. The ultimate management system that emerges from the transition is one that captures the energy and initiative of rugged individualism, yet combines those qualities with teamwork. The collaboration generated through teamwork is what helps synergize the system. People work together to create a system that none of the participants could produce alone.

The alliance phase is an external version of the teamwork required inside the firm. With proper management-leadership, the teamwork from inside the firm is turned outward to form alliances. The organizational skill is leadership. The integration of horizontal alliances and supply-chain partnerships into core business processes requires a top-level skill set focused on influence skills, personal relationships, and continuous improvement of business processes.

THE TEAMWORK PHASE

How does a system encourage people's individual expression while maintaining control? Is there a way to find that balance? Yes, there *is* a way. It is to truly value people as an asset and a resource rather than as an expense of production.

According to Robert B. Reich, a former U.S. Secretary of Labor, and now a professor at Brandeis University, "Companies are experimenting with a new operating system for the employer-employee relationship—one to replace the old set of practices that put employers and employees on opposite sides of the table. The model for the organization of the future aims to create tangible and intangible value that both sides can enjoy. It accepts as a core reality—rather than as a pleasant fantasy—the old saw that a company's people are its most important asset. And it builds on that reality to create a way of working that is profoundly human and fundamentally humane.

"It is a revolutionary notion: collaboration and mutual advantage are the essence of the organization. They can create flexibility, resiliency, speed, and creativity—the fundamental qualities of the company of the twenty-first century."[1] In this statement, Reich sets the tone for managing in the future, beginning with today.

GE Lights the Way in a Changing World

Jack Welch of GE is a master at building teamwork and balancing the tension paradoxes of running a big and complex business where people count. Focusing too much on either the *people* or the *process* side of a business traps most firms. Rare is the firm that balances *both* as its size and complexity increase. John Byrne of *Business Week* in an interview with Welch indicates that there is debate on this subject. "They [GE managers] grouse that despite the rhetoric about managing for the long term at GE, they are under too much pressure to produce short-term results. They say that for all that Welch talks about 'sharing best practices' and 'boundary-less behavior' they are still missing many opportunities. . . . Some worry that the company's gargantuan Six Sigma program . . . is allowing bureaucracy to creep back into GE." Welch's reply to them is what creates the tension, and the paradox. His retort: "You can't grow long-term if you can't eat short-term. Anybody can manage short. Anyone can manage long. Balancing those two things is what management is."[2]

Simultaneously managing opposites is the trick, whether the opposites are long- and short-term goals or the people and processes of the business. GE's massive Six-Sigma program focuses on pure *process management*. Yet, Welch spends more than 50 percent of his time on *people issues* and considers his greatest achievement the care and feeding of talent.

When John Naisbitt coined the phrase "high tech–high touch" a decade ago, he was referring to the need for more people interaction as technology accelerates. Jack Welch's focus on people and building teamwork, in addition to his being a tough manager intent on results, makes him a skilled management-leader in the twenty-first century. Managers must grow their companies while caring for and coaching people. This human side of enterprise coupled with rigorous process management creates the tension for

Figure 3.1
The Three-legged Stool Concept of an Operating System

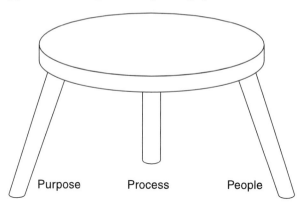

Purpose   Process   People

creativity and innovation. For most managers these two approaches are strange bedfellows, but as Welch says, that "is what management is."

In addition to pushing the people side of the system, Welch has pushed for a state of constant change. Change reflects the reality of what a company must do to survive in today's environment. GE's demanding regimen of constant change is one that other companies find difficult to adopt. Why? Because most people resist change. Even when the mind says change is normal, people find ways to resist. And yet, for leaders today, there is no other choice but to change. By adopting change as a strategy, the venerable GE has survived and thrived while erstwhile competitors such as Westinghouse have disappeared.[3]

Welch seems to be one of those rare individuals who might be called a management-leader. Management skills have to do with goal setting, operational processes, measuring results, and making the numbers. Leadership skills, on the other hand, deal with vision, people needs, building teamwork, and setting the company's direction. When a strategy of constant change is added to management and leadership, an organization's operating system becomes a three-legged stool—Leg 1: dealing with *purpose*; Leg 2: *process* controls; and Leg 3: the *people* of the firm, which is the future growth of the organization (See Figure 3.1).

It has been said that companies survive because they change, adapt, and reinvent themselves, not because they pursue a cautious, secure, stable path. Conservative behavior is the riskiest strategy, not the most prudent one. GE certainly exemplifies the ideal company and Welch, the management-leader. Judging by results—a 23-fold rise in its stock price since 1981—his strategy seems to be working.

HP Nurtures Culture

Another very well run team-based company is Hewlett-Packard. Most employees are known for doing things the "HP way," which includes a heavy dose of team consensus decision making and respect for coworkers. But there is a down side when overcommitting to any one technique, as HP risks doing. "True innovation requires radical ideas, and radical ideas can grow only in a climate of constructive dispute [that is, tension]."[4] For HP's traditional markets, its strong company culture may have nurtured fine organizational values. But as the author of a *Business Week* letter to the editor noted, "With the brutal commodization of technology in the Internet era . . . [the company's culture] has become a competitive disadvantage."[5]

Group-think, a lack of innovative products, poor measures of team performance, team versus individual compensation, and effective strategies to manage teams are just a few of the issues on the management radar screen at the teamwork-driven phase. Sensing this malaise, HP's Board took action in the middle of 1999. It was a surprise, however, when the Board selected not an engineer, but an outside marketing person to be the new CEO. The first woman to head a Dow-30 company was picked to jump-start HP's innovative machine. They recognized that in recent years the culture has turned into a bureaucratic, consensus-style culture that has a sharp disadvantage in the Internet-speed era.

After a little more than a year in the job she is collapsing eighty-three profit centers into twelve and centralizing decision making. This is part of the vicious cycle of decentralization and centralization of corporations caught in the corridor of crisis—when they don't get it right the first time. Her conclusion was that past management had crippled the business. Here is what she had to say about taking decentralization too far. "A company is a system. To change the company, you have to operate on the whole system—the strategy, the structure, the rewards, the culture. You have to have the courage and the capability to tackle everything at once."[6]

Her insight is astute. The concept that an organization is a system—that you can't change one part without simultaneously modifying all other subsystems—is our conclusion and recommendation that is found in Chapter 16.

Motorola's Strategic Shift Produces a Bumpy Ride

Motorola of Schaumburg, Illinois, is one American company that successfully operates in a changed management environment that maximizes human resourcefulness. Motorola's most significant characteristic is the shift to a team- and people-centered management style; it was one of the first organizations to recognize the human side of enterprise. People began to be treated more seriously and seen as an asset, leading to the emergence of a new corporate culture. Motorola's management preaches openness to new ideas, involvement, questioning of assumptions, and encouragement of bold proposals for change.

Under the guidance of its longtime CEO, Robert Galvin, Motorola adopted management techniques to get it ready for the brutal competition of the 1990s. Galvin's expectation was that people at any level must challenge any idea. Management encouraged questioning by involving people at all levels in its corporate planning process. The objective was not just to have a document called a plan, but also to get people *involved* in bringing it to life. He believed that people needed to think about where Motorola was going and how to get there. Plans looked ten years ahead, anticipating the unfolding of the information age.

Besides being involved in planning, Motorola's people have a real stake in the firm. Twenty percent of pretax profits go into an employee "bonus pool." To make this even more meaningful, the 95,000 worldwide employees of the firm are divided into decentralized "profit centers," then further divided into teams numbering between 50 and 250 each. Each of these teams has a bonus pool. Every employee is keenly aware of his or her contribution to personal bonuses, which are based on productivity, quality, housekeeping, and safety.

Motorola maintains high levels of communication, both vertically and horizontally. The CEO sets the pace by frequently eating in the employee cafeteria. Communication is more formally enhanced by a series of employee steering committees, consisting of only four levels from shop floor to top management. At Motorola, employee self-control is the key. Steering committees first negotiate output standards and other performance measures for the work groups that they represent. These set up clear expectations, frequent performance reviews, employee self-reviews with corrective action, and bonus awards for both individual and team success. Performance records are posted weekly.

Over the years, this approach to management has served Motorola well. However, in 1998, ten years after winning the Baldrige Award, Motorola received a scathing review in a *Business Week* article, "How Motorola Lost Its Way," which described the inside saga of warring factions and strategic blunders at the company. The article came at a critical time for Chris Galvin, grandson of the founder, who was made president at the age of forty-seven. The picture of what he inherited is consistent with what is found in most large organizations that can't control the size and complexity of their growing businesses and that are unable to create teamwork across divisions.

In Motorola's case, the young Galvin has "railed against a culture that he thinks, at times, has been too smug, too engineering driven, and too focused on internal rivalries. To foster cooperation [and teamwork] among divisions, he's starting to pay top executives based on company wide per-formance—not just their own division's results."[7] This is an example of the crisis of "alignment versus direction." Because of poor alignment around common corporate goals, each group maximizes its own interests at the expense of the corporation. Divisions, subordinates, and functional groups want direction, but when management does not provide enough leadership, employees, and therefore the corporation, can loose their way.

This type of crisis is characteristic of a large organization in the team-work phase. The crisis pits the integration of internal teams all pulling together toward a strategic company vision against enhancing the image and personality of select people. The crisis develops when there is too little teamwork at the top and autonomous divisions don't have a common stra-tegic vision and a set of company goals to which they are committed.

Motorola's tale is a cautionary one. It is a lesson in how an organization reaches a very successful industry position only to become blinded by suc-cess and a hubris that keeps executives from working in alignment as a top-level team. Without a solid performance management system with appropriate metrics to track performance and with management-leaders to provide direction, a crisis of "alignment versus direction" dogs the firm as it tries to manage in the network phase. This crisis is not often felt at the top—Motorola being an obvious exception—but at lower-management levels where frustration builds and lack of clear direction takes its toll.

THE ALLIANCE-ORIENTED PHASE

Figure 3.2 could very well be a picture of Motorola's growth. It is also a generalized picture of the typical progress of organizational evolution. As Figure 3.2 depicts, the evolution of a firm from the entrepreneurial to the alliance phase is not linear as represented in Figure I.1 in Part I. Usually the ride is a bumpy one, as firms negotiate the messy transitions from one stage to the other. Some firms are able to jump the curve at each crisis point; others falter, declining stock price often signaling when they are in trouble; others fail; and the weaker merge to survive.

Motorola as an Example

Motorola stands apart as an example for others to follow, even as it experiences a downturn in business. Motorola has a history of reinventing itself. Since its inception in 1928, past Galvin family members forced the company to go through the regular trauma of jumping the curve that then defined the company's product priorities. Accordingly, Motorola jumped from car radios, to walkie-talkies, to solid-state TV, to integrated circuits, to microchips, to wireless communications and, most recently, to the Irid-

Figure 3.2
The Roller Coaster Ride to Alliances

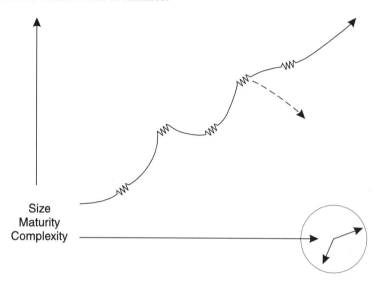

Size
Maturity
Complexity

ium satellite network—a risky and farsighted investment if there ever was one.

However, Motorola needs to reassess how it does business. Granted, many of its decisions depend on the developing high-tech industry, and the evolving more powerful technologies are creating a global paradox. These technologies enable large organizations to get smaller—as they outsource, form alliances, and forge partnerships—while smaller firms are becoming more important and powerful. Galvin has ventured into these strategic areas to discuss alliances with networking powerhouses, Cisco Systems and 3com.[8]

Motorola's example gives clear evidence of the need for organizations to find ways to build internal teamwork between powerful divisions and to jump the curve to the next organizational form, alliances, if they are to stay lean and flexible. This means developing outside relationships with vendors, suppliers, and even the competition—those who can supply non-core competencies—so the firm can concentrate on growing its unique business niche.

In this age of high-tech globalization and e-commerce, stronger firms today are becoming proactive by reaching out to build alliances to ensure their viability. While the joint venture/strategic alliance relationship is increasingly part of the business landscape, it has proven to be an operational challenge. Although the synergies between two parties may be apparent in concept, putting them into day-to-day practice is not easy. The ability to define shared goals and to foster their mutual achievement is a leadership skill. The operative skill is *collaboration*.

Collaboration, so important in the teamwork phase, is equally important in the alliance phase. In genuinely collaborative teamwork-driven firms, people learn how to focus on who has the relevant knowledge and expertise, not on who has the title or position. As more and more companies form alliances, these same collaborative skills are essential. These companies need to forge close, long-term relationships. They need to work hand in hand to refine products and components, respond to shifts in demand, and unclog bottlenecks—sharing at the same time sensitive information. Such high-trust relationships were once thought possible (in the vertically integrated firm) only with internal suppliers. But alliances do work if both sides use a mature collaborative approach.

Without collaboration, alliances are fraught with the same kinds of problems internal teamwork efforts face. As organizations move toward more alliances, alliance partners still must maintain their respective control. The tension created between the self-interests of the partners and the common goal that partners are trying to achieve can create frustration and disappointment. Yet, during the initial honeymoon period, alliances usually start well. Then, slowly, expectations not documented in the initial negotiations begin to surface, creating eventual resentment. Expectations, while subtly discussed initially, can never be put into a formal document. As in failed marriages, getting these expectations out on the table is very hard for executives not accustomed to this sort of intimacy.

Company culture plays a big part in how smoothly the alliance functions. Since it is almost impossible to define codes of culture that would ease the transition, and all too often a good dose of executive ego is thrown in, the honeymoon period can quickly dissipate.

Chrysler and Daimler-Benz

Mergers, which are formal alliances, provide a glimpse at how difficult it is to blend different cultures and top-level egos. Consider the merger of Chrysler and Daimler-Benz. Behind all the hoopla lies the enormous task of melding two huge institutions with proud heritages and vastly different cultures. It has not been easy. DaimlerChrysler officials admit that "70 percent of major mergers fail because of cultural conflicts; the inability to make timely, professional decisions; or a reluctance to address controversy."[9] Currently the merger is experiencing the same kinds of conflicts and tensions.

Citicorp and Travelers

Another huge merger is Citicorp and Travelers Insurance Group. The *Business Week* cover story "Citigroup: Can This Marriage Work?" concludes, "The Citigroup merger is going reasonably well. But there are signs of tension between Sanford Weill and John Reed."[10] At Citigroup, Reed is the *manager*, Weill the *leader*, and they are appointed CO-CEOs. Theirs is a marriage of opposites, yet is paradoxically beneficial. They have the opportunity to get synergism not from one, but from two very different work styles. The marriage metaphor is a good one. In many marriages, different personalities between husband and wife initially attract but often cause long-term friction. When each partner learns to value the skill, talent, and point of view of the other, and more importantly learns to manage the tension of the marriage, it works.

In the corporate world, where survival is often equated with individualism, the challenge is how to maximize human talent. Today's corporate reality is one of networks and team effort. With evolving supply-chain partnerships and strategic alliances, management-leadership is the solution. Both strong management and strong leadership are needed to assure the organization can perform as a fluid whole.

KLM and Northwest Airlines: A Turbulent Trip

This may be the case at KLM and Northwest Airlines. From afar, it looks like the perfect transatlantic marriage. To celebrate their oneness in the public eye, KLM Royal Dutch Airlines and Northwest have merged their logos into a single red-and-blue seal emblazoned on their 747s. However, as reported in a 1994 *Fortune* article, "Behind this scene lurks a marriage from hell, an eye-gouging, rabbit-punching slugfest, with accusations flying like dinner plates, and one combatant, KLM, running to court hurling charges of spousal abuse."[11]

Both sides think they know how best to run an airline. The Dutch want to blend both companies into a single, binational organization along the lines of Unilever and Shell. That suggestion horrifies the Americans, who are certain KLM would end up running the show. Their fear is that the real Dutch agenda is to control Northwest. So bitter is the clash for control that the Dutch and the Americans threaten to wreck an alliance yielding $200 million a year in operating profits.

In part, the fight is a classic clash in cultures, a collision of two different ways of doing business: the European way versus the American way. The marriage of these two airlines mints money, but towering egos and a bitter battle for power have begun to spoil it. KLM and Northwest display, in stark relief, the crisis point of "collaboration/self-interest"—the need to collaborate, yet at the same time yielding yet maintaining control over individual business interests.

The KLM–Northwest Airlines example is not stopping other U.S. airlines, such as United (its "Star Alliance" with 16 other carriers), Delta, and Continental, from rushing to form alliances. American carriers are rushing to go global, but not by buying new jets and adding routes. Instead, they are teaming up with foreign carriers to create huge worldwide alliances that generate healthy profits at little cost. The jury is out, but the ability to gain genuine collaboration between varied corporate cultures will be difficult—as in the KLM example. As more and more companies go global and attempt to leverage their corporate assets, the management challenge will be to overcome the crisis of self-interest versus collaboration.

Wintel Synergism

A more positive alliance, but one not without its ups and downs, is Wintel. For at least two decades, the relationship between Microsoft and Intel has been so symbiotic that the two have become known as Wintel—a contraction of Windows and Intel. Although the alliance between Microsoft and Intel is well known, it is bemoaned by many, especially the competition. A *Fortune* article sidebar entitled "Scenes From a Marriage" had this to say about their alliance: "The [Bill] Gates and [Andy] Grove alliance was not without friction. Both are high-decibel table pounders who wield sarcasm like a samurai sword. Their companies mirror their aggressive and sometimes intransigent personalities. Gates and Grove say occasional blow-ups are just part of the chemistry that makes the relationship work. Call it creative tension or perhaps a form of therapy. Whatever it is, it hasn't slowed the companies down much."[12]

Wintel is an alliance based on mutual respect, a long-term relationship, a strong common goal, and the ability to use *tension* to find a solution, preserve the alliance, and make the marriage work. Although the corporate cultures of the two partners are different, both Grove—who has since left Intel—and Gates worked through the pitfalls of an alliance where two strong egos learned to work together. Fortunately the partners, as in a good marriage, learned to communicate. They learned to say, "we enlarge our respective viewpoint to include the other person's viewpoint," and they learned effective ways to express their respective frustration.

Managing tensions emanating from different corporate cultures and sometimes battling egos in an alliance is surely a skill for the twenty-first century. Grove sums up the challenge this way: "I have to admit that a lot of our people at Intel are like what's found at Microsoft. So when you take their defensiveness and our obnoxious arrogance and mix them all up, it can be a pretty potent mixture."[13]

One of the three elements affecting the evolution of any firm is *maturity*, which was described in Part I. It is an institutionalized way of dealing with and using conflict to achieve understanding and avoid separation. Leaders achieve collaboration either by chance or by design. In the case of Wintel, neither Grove nor Gates lets self-interest get in the way of what was best for the alliance. This is not the case in most situations. The industrial revolution has left a legacy of command-and-control within the business community. Firms tend to fall back on standardized cookie-cutter thinking and organizational charts when approaching alliances. They rely on positional power. This is not the way to build alliances, but neither is the opposite: a reliance on a few in-house experts who serve as gunslingers of alliance knowledge.

Instead, as the authors of "Institutionalizing Alliance Skills: Secrets of Repeatable Success" suggest, alliances need to be individually tailored to the needs of each company. The process boils down to learning about a partner's unique business processes, how to take advantage of each other's strengths, determining conflicting management practices, and identifying sources of competitive advantage. Absorbing this embedded knowledge offers alliance partners a way to cut costs through economies of scale, or to access proprietary technology. The dynamic nature of this knowledge creates a *new corporation* that encompasses not only a specific firm, but also the web of relationships that surround and enmesh it. Relationships between companies grow or fail much like relationships between people. By paying attention to the human aspects of alliances, managers can leverage the maximum value from them. Collaboration is the glue that holds it all together.

SUMMARY

Although it is impossible to predict the future, there are current trends in industrial society that portend the direction in which organizations are moving. Companies worldwide are building neural networks to each other. The resulting web of inclusion may not always work, but they may well represent the new shape of global business. Clearly the former structure of the past—GM being the classic example—is no longer viable in an age of teams functioning as mini-organizations, alliance partnerships, horizontal communication across oceans, integrated process flows, and outsourcing of all but a firm's critical-core competencies. This implies that corporate levels of control are shifting from predominantly top-down to a blend of horizontal and vertical structures.

In terms of life cycle, corporations pass through preadolescence and adolescence before entering adulthood. At this later stage the parental "father knows best" is replaced with employee maturity, and differing points of view are resolved in mature ways. At this stage, interpersonal skills become as important as management controls.

Rosabeth Moss Kanter sums up best the interpersonal trend in her article, "Collaborative Advantage: The Art of Alliances." She concluded that alliances often tend to emphasize the legal or financial aspects of the deal. But smart managers know that alliances involve much more. Like all human relationships, business partners are living systems that have endless possibilities. And companies that know how to tap those possibilities and manage alliances effectively have a key corporate asset—call it a collaborative advantage. After completing a study of more than thirty-seven companies from eleven parts of the world, Kanter suggests that relationships between companies grow or fail much like relationships between people. By paying attention to the human aspects of alliances, management-leaders can leverage the maximum value from them.[14]

NOTES

1. Robert B. Reich, "The Company of the Future," *Fast Company* (November 1998): 150.

2. John A. Byrne, "How Jack Welch Runs GE," *Business Week*, Cover Story, 8 June 1998, 92.

3. James Flanigan, "With Asia and CNET, GE Again Embraces Change," *Los Angles Times, OC Edition*, 14 June 1998, p. D3.

4. Mark W. Fleischmann, "Hewlett-Packard Can No Longer Afford Consensus," *Business Week*, 3 August 1998, 10.

5. Ibid.

6. Patricia Sellers, "The 50 Most Powerful Women in Business," *Fortune* 16 October 2000, 132.

7. "How Motorola Lost Its Way," *Business Week*, 4 May 1998: p. 142.

8. Roger O. Crockett, "Motorola: Slow and Steady Isn't Winning Any Races," *Business Week*, 10 August 1998, 62.

9. Donald W. Nauss, "Auto Merger Celebrated Worlds Apart," *Los Angles Times*, 18 November 1998, p. C3.

10. Gary Silverman and Leah Nathans Spiro, "Citigroup: Can This Marriage Work?" *Business Week*, 7 June 1999, 126.

11. "Northwest and KLM: The Alliance from Hell," *Fortune*, 24 June 1998, 64.

12. "A Conversation with the Lords of Wintel," *Fortune*, 8 July 1996, 52.

13. Ibid.

14. Rosabeth Moss Kanter, "Collaborative Advantage: The Art of Alliances," *Harvard Business Review* (1 July 1994).

4

Maturing Societies and Nations

Chapters 1 to 3 explained how organizations in transition from one evolutionary phase to another exhibit symptoms that suggest change is necessary for continuing growth. Managers must recognize these signs and interpret them correctly to move smoothly from one phase to the next. They must also understand the changing culture within which they operate and how dynamic external forces shape the organization. Within this context, it is especially important for managers to recognize the emerging impact of information technology on organizational structures, external relationships, and how work gets done.

This chapter explores the external forces that shape an organization. It begins with an overview of the six phases of cultural evolution in most societies, using the United States both as an analogy and a backdrop. Not surprisingly, the typical evolution of an organization parallels the evolution of a culture. The chapter concludes with a look at how several other nations are dealing with their own evolutionary changes.

THE SIX PHASES OF EVOLUTION

All societies, cultures, and organizations inevitably experience change. Organizational and cultural evolution can be simply classified into six phases that range from the egocentric "I" to the interpersonal and somewhat remote "Us." How these phases parallel the organizational phases discussed in previous chapters can be seen in Figure 4.1, which is a modification of Figures 1.1 and 3.2. This new model realistically portrays the

Figure 4.1
The Six Phases of Cultural Evolution

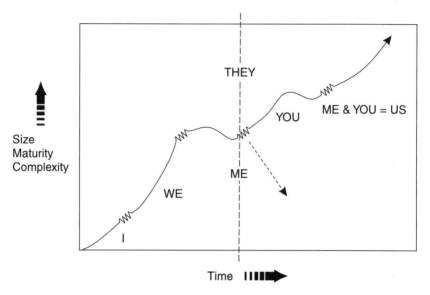

road as being bumpy rather than straight. It combines organizational evolution with societal evolution and depicts the life cycle of any organizational form, be it business, the family unit, or society itself.

On the vertical axis are size, maturity, and complexity; time is plotted on the horizontal axis. The crisis points of profitability/creativity, ego/autonomy, red tape/flexibility, abdication/trust, alignment/direction, and self-interest/collaboration are indicated—as sawtooth icons—on a larger life cycle representing the typical Western society. Instead of identifying the unique structure, systems, and management style assigned to each phase of organizational evolution, however, Figure 4.1 designates each cultural phase according to its type of energy and personality characteristic: "I," "we," "me" "me-they," "you," and "me + you = us."

The "I" Phase

"I" is the energy by which the American West was won. Rugged individualism was the reigning ethic, as it still is to a great extent in the American business world. Broadly interpreted, rugged individualism encompasses strong qualities of self-reliance, independence, individuality, and originality. People with a strong individual ethic, such as pioneers and, in the business world, entrepreneurs, have the philosophy that "I can do things other people can't. . . . I don't rely on anyone else. . . . I'm independent. . . . I can do it alone." Most businesses are founded and initially nourished on this ethic.

"We" Are in This Together

As America grew, the number and variety of people greatly expanded. It became known as the melting pot of the world. The country became more strongly unified and became aware of that unification during the two world wars, which helped forge the nation into a powerful economic force, smack in the middle of the industrial age. People were glad to have jobs, and those who did have a job worked under an ethic of hard work, saving money, and being loyal to the company and boss. As documented in the 1956 classic *The Organization Man*, the right answer for the middle manager in his gray flannel suit was, "Yes, Boss."[1] Americans from all walks of life worked hard to experience the "good life," and they worked together. Government became more *directive*—like the paternalistic head of the household—and most were proud to be American.

What about "Me?"

Then along came the 1960s, and people began to ask, "What about *me?*" The Baby Boomers, the generation born between 1946 and 1966, grew up in the grip of the most peculiar paradox. On the one hand, they were children of the boom years of the 1950s and 1960s. It was a period of optimism. People felt the economic prosperity would continue forever. On the other hand, they were children of the Cold War. They grew up with the idea of World War III as a kind of "future historical" reality. This created a most peculiar tension: the tension between the belief in a rosy, easy future and no future at all. The tension produced the Me Generation— a generation whose cry became, "Do your own thing."

The very thing that forged the melting pot in the United States—the diversity and togetherness of a variety of people—began to splinter. The *me* philosophy emerged from within the context of *we*-oriented groups. There were black, Native American, and gay movements. Women and minorities sought equal pay and equal access to promotions and to the management ladder. All employees wanted a greater say in decision making. People began saying, "I'm entitled to my individuality."

Entitlement programs proliferated from government-*coordinating* bodies. Lawyers fueled the trend by taking the individual's side and suggesting fault lay not with the individual but with the system in which the individual existed. Personal responsibility for one's actions was weakened. The nuclear family began to break down, and gangs grew—often to provide lost identity. Those entering the workforce were harder to manage. As the demands for rights and entitlements increased, there was a corresponding decline in responsibility and commitment. The glue of the community—whether in the neighborhood or at work—was no longer holding people together.

Peter F. Drucker correctly predicted and described America's transition in his book, *The Age of Discontinuity*, published in 1968. As a country, he said, America is no longer going to continue to grow using only the techniques of the past. The emerging force, he correctly predicted, is the knowledge worker. With the coming of the digital age, the foundations of the U.S. economic model have been undermined. People are struggling with why the old rules don't seem to work any more.[2] True to Drucker's predictions, many new values emerged from the turbulent years of the 1960s; the priorities of young people changed accordingly, and as they assumed positions of authority in business, the American work ethic was no longer the same.[3] For an in-depth discussion of these changes see Chapter 6, "The Changing Perception of Work."

"Me-They" Conflicts

"Me-they" conflicts in the 1960s began to develop as management tried to cope with the new aggressiveness in the workforce. Major conflicts occurred between labor and management and between government and industry. The crisis of red tape/flexibility burst on the scene as people began to question centralized control. People's own local issues came to be seen as more important than directives from above. At issue were discrimination, occupational safety, pollution, and unfair labor practices. Government's reaction was typically defensive. To the American people, "they" became almost anyone—government agencies, foreign competitors, management and even other groups of people. Whoever "they" were deemed to be, "they" were unfair.

Foreign competitors caused especially contentious conflicts among American workers as they, and especially Japan, began to beat the United States at its own game with better and cheaper cars, cameras, and television sets. Union workers vented their frustration by taking sledgehammers to Japanese cars and by blaming a resistant management for productivity declines. Better educated employees and those who spoke out became the targets of management wrath because managers saw them as being disloyal to the company. Management complained that leisure comes first, work second for these new and vocal workers, and that workers were more interested in self-expression and lifestyle than in doing the hard work their elders had done.

As workers and the American public asked, "Why should we do it your way?" management also began asking itself serious questions. The paternalistic approach minted in rugged individualism wasn't working anymore. What's more, it generated other problems that management wasn't ready to solve. Government faced similar difficulties. To support its entitlement programs, subsidies, foreign aid, military budgets, and other spending, government increased taxes. Capital investment declined and the budget deficit skyrocketed.

"You" Really Are Important

Pressured by the national moods and forces in the population, government and business conceded that "you" are important. The well-worn cliché "people are our most important asset" started to take on new meaning around 1980. Diversity in the workplace, especially in Silicon Valley, really did generate new and fresh ideas. There intelligent workers from around the world—especially Russians, Indians, and Israelis—began challenging basic technical assumptions, which stimulated innovation.

A similar sentiment was echoed in the corridors of Congress. Partly driven by growing budget deficits, the Federal Government transferred more and more activities to the state and local levels in the 1980s to avoid fiscal crises. This was a first step at trying to decentralize government. The operative words were "down with big government"—a rhetoric that translated into massive downsizing. Big government, like big business in its own sphere, was seen as being part of the problem. Though the reality of excessive military expenditures coupled with tax cutting was transparently problematic to some, the ideology of devolution was, nonetheless, embraced by many as a panacea. The reigning philosophy was: "Let people at the local level be responsible for solving their own problems. Remove the intrusiveness of centralized bureaucracies and empower local citizens. *Your* ideas and solutions are important; government cannot do it all." These admirable sentiments, although limited in practice, illustrated the new mood of "involvement."

Business and industry began to say to workers, "*You* on the assembly lines know better how to put cars together. We need your input. We should work together as a team." Greenfield assembly plants began to spring up, Saturn cars began rolling off the assembly line, and teams began tackling a whole host of corporate problems.

Business began thinking more about customers and customer satisfaction. To customers they began saying, "*You* really are important to us and we need to start listening more to you." In the other direction, business stopped looking at suppliers as adversaries and began working with them as vital extensions of their chain of value-added production. Partnerships, alliances, and outsourcing emerged as the vertical integration strategy that had worked during the directive systems of the industrial revolution began to wane.

In earlier phases, the industrial sector used manual labor, capital, and natural resources to create wealth. With the development of the "you" philosophy, workers became more important and more informed and knowledgeable. The developing information age used brains, not brawn, to create economic wealth. The Internet, Microsoft, Intel, GE, Sun Microsystems, Dell Computer, Motorola, and others have as their underpinning high "knowledge content," with manufactured components taking a back seat. As John Naisbitt observed in his provocative 1982 book, *Megatrends*, "We now mass produce information the way we used to mass produce cars. . . . This knowledge is the driving force of the economy."[4]

The impact of innovative computer software and information technology combined with corporate and government downsizing significantly improved profitability, reduced product cycle times, and enhanced customer satisfaction. Together these innovations created network infrastructures leveraging the information age that burst upon the scene with the Internet. Corporate intranets proliferated, improving communication, video conferencing, and e-mail. By the late 1990s, the United States was again leading the world in productivity gains.

Although the new emphasis on information and worker knowledge helped the U.S. economy grow in the late 1980s and 1990s, a host of other factors also converged to jump-start the American economy during this period. The Cold War ended in 1989, the economy of the Asian Tigers stumbled badly in one of their own corridors of crisis, and Europe's unification efforts created the possibility of renewal in the European life cycle.

Me + You = Us

These combined trends all helped focus attention on how interconnected society has become and on the need to work together. When "you" becomes indispensable to "we," the philosophy becomes "you" plus "me," or let "us" work together. This philosophy, however, requires leadership, a common cause, and *teamwork*. The concept of "us" is a lot like "we" without the paternalism. It requires a high degree of individual maturity and the willingness of players to subordinate their interests to a cause or goal greater than their own. In a 1980 book, *Managing in Turbulent Times*, Drucker predicted that American society would enter a corridor of crisis.[5] Looking back, this surely was the case. Drucker went on to suggest that if America was to survive, then most of its institutions, including its principal components—government, industry, and labor—must begin to work together toward a common goal. This is the "us" imperative.

Getting to such a teamwork-driven phase from an earlier phase is by no means easy. Much of the world today remains mired in "me-they" conflicts. Superpowers that don't always see eye-to-eye create economic or cold wars in a disguised attempt to prove their power. Nations that are still in a "me-they" phase tend to be most concerned about their own survival, which leaves little time or energy for team building.

Developments in technology and industry have made the transition to the "us" phase both more urgent and more difficult. From the telephone to railroads to semiconductors, each leap in technology has kicked up growth and living standards. The shift to a digital world promises to be just as, if not more, spectacular, speeding the need to build network structures. Some people tend to see technology as inherently paradoxical, with every positive quality countered by an opposite negative quality. As a *Harvard Business Review* editorial quotes a researcher, "Technology does not place us into an idyllic garden of paradise but, rather, into an unsettling garden of paradox."[6]

The developments in microprocessor technology accelerate the shift to a digital world. Don Tapscott, author of *The Digital Economy*, summarizes the massive events taking place in American culture this way: "Today we are witnessing the early, turbulent days of a revolution as significant as any other in human history. A new medium of human communications is emerging, one that may prove to surpass all previous revolutions—the printing press, the telephone, the television, the computer—in its impact on our economic and social life. The Internet is enabling a new economy based on the networking of human intelligence. In this digital economy, individuals and enterprises create wealth by applying knowledge, networked human intelligence, and effort to manufacturing, agriculture, and services. In the digital frontier of this economy, the players, dynamics, rules, and requirements for survival and success are all changing."[7]

The twentieth century has brought an incredible amount of technologic innovation and progress. People with extraordinary ideas have brought about more change during these last 100 years than in any other century. In *Business @ the Speed of Thought*, Bill Gates even suggests that businesses will change more in the next ten years than they have in the past fifty.[8] Driven by the Internet, personal computers, innovative software, and new generations of digital devices, rapid technological change will continue into the twenty-first century.

Much like the transition to alliances in the business world, the transition to the "us" phase is being made with the assistance of information technology making communications a top priority. Communications links are integrating organizations, global strategies are being merged with local priorities, diverse worldwide organizations are beginning to function and react as one, and suppliers and strategic partnerships are wired into supply-chain management and e-commerce software so the unit can perform as a fluid whole.

The above is a macro view of the American life cycle, from its entrepreneurial, individualistic beginnings to its evolving "us" philosophy. The twenty-first century will see not only the progression of digital technologies, but also a continuation of the trend toward the knowledge worker. American workers will continue to be better educated, more discriminating, more aware of themselves and their individual rights, more vocal, and more interested in personal advancement and in achieving their full potential as individuals. If a society is to flourish in the next century it must have a core workforce of analytic workers. These are the knowledge workers who will increasingly replace the production workers—the old footsoldiers of capitalism. These will be problem solvers: workers prepared to apply analytical skills to complex issues.

Emerging is a more human side of enterprise. It is built around people talking sideways to people, and it requires increased interpersonal skills. Contacts are between cross-functional peers and partners, and require management-leaders who supplement traditional management in running businesses. Management-leadership skills create the conditions for a tight-loose system: a management system based on performance and process controls, yet also free within those limits to create and innovate. In the modern world of business, the color of the suit is no longer gray. Not everyone dresses alike; clothing mirrors the diversity, creativity, and innovation of the times.

GROWTH WORLDWIDE

The changes that have been seen in the United States, especially over the last four decades, have happened in similar ways in other nations. Here are a few examples of the ways in which other nations have gone through and dealt with various phases of their evolution and the associated crises.

Dad Retires in Indonesia

Suharto had it all: limitless wealth, international respect, and unquestioned power. But what he didn't have was the ability to see that he was creating the conditions for his own downfall. His case shows the classic directive style in bold relief. Suharto was running the country, but running it into the ground. Within corporations, such people are known as autocrats. Within a country, they are dictators. Suharto joins a long list of deposed dictators who mistook public obedience for adulation.

In power for more than thirty-five years, Suharto never appreciated that the world and Indonesia had changed. Paradigm paralysis, hubris, and a phalanx of sycophants cut off the real world from Suharto and trapped him, like they had trapped so many others before him. A parent/child relationship develops under these conditions with a prevailing philosophy that "father knows best." It produces rebellious teenagers. Late in 1999, East Timor, a province of Indonesia, wanted to exercise its independence but Dad said "no." Thus began the struggle between parental control and the desire for independence. Fearing a loss of control, a bill with an anonymous vote was rushed through parliament enabling the armed forces to quell dissent activity. Thousands of Indonesian students took to the streets in protest because it gave the military the right to limit civil liberties.

Directive corporate cultures face the same dilemma as dictators. They unknowingly create "organizational children" with their parent/child leadership style. Over time, rebellious teenagers (employees) strike, call in sick, or engage in white-collar thefts. No matter whether it's a country, province, or a company, when the directive style endures for too long, the oppressed will rebel. As we outlined in Chapter 1, when the size and complexity of an organization increases, the maturity of those involved (workers and supervision) leads them to seek decision-making parity or a crisis, fueled by the clash of ego/autonomy, will result.

Russia Caught in Red Tape

General H. Norman Schwarzkopf gave the world a lesson in management when he dismembered the USSR's old command-and-control model used by the Iraqis in the Gulf War. Schwarzkopf's strategy against the Iraqis was to cut their lines of communication, for he knew that without direction from above, the troops in the field couldn't act on their own. He was proven to be correct.

Vladimir Putin is continuing Boris Yeltsin's process of dismantling Russia's dependence on centralized planning, including decrees and directives from a few people at the top. Not surprisingly, their decentralization efforts have run up against some of the classic problems organizations face as they fluctuate between centralization and decentralization. The battle Putin faces is against central planning, bureaucracy, staff groups, and the frustration of lower-level workers who are managed from the top.

The parallel between the old Soviet Union and many worldwide corporations that are monopolistic, bureaucratic, and insulated from real competition is striking. In the USSR, there were scores of vertically integrated ministries (functional departments in corporations) for almost every facet of business, transportation, government, and education. Breaking up these ministries is taking time; first Yeltsin, now Putin, are pushing hard for more privatization and anti-monopolistic structures, but culture is a resistant foe.

Many of Russia's problems come from the systems of government and the culture of governing that it inherited on the breakup of the USSR. The USSR had been described as a fear-driven, dehumanizing system that didn't support a core of humanistic values and economic incentives, which are precisely what has been required for Russia to shift quickly to a market economy. Russia's problem is systemic. People aren't lazy or unwilling to cooperate. The system creates indifference and resistant behavior. The cry to work harder for Mother Russia no longer motivates. The government created the system, and it is the system that is problematic, not the people.

The USSR wasn't always ineffective, however. Stalin used an idealistic and directive style of management to build upon Lenin's earlier transformations. At the time, it was a prudent strategy, for Lenin, a consummate pragmatist, had previously established the framework for hyper-industrialization that dragged the country out of its semifeudal past and into the industrial twentieth century. Stalin's leadership primed the pump and rebuilt the economy, but the country didn't shift gears into the next logical step, a decentralized government.

Instead, the USSR built a complex system of vertically integrated ministries, which were then overlaid with the web of the Communist Party. Russia has, therefore, inherited the world's most complicated and nonproductive structure. The ties between government and party remain, inhibiting progress. This is especially true, for example, in food production, which is still in the clumsy hands of Communist ideologues, and which, therefore, loses more ground each year to higher quality imports. But the deeper problem is institutional. The rush to create a market economy has floundered because the institutions that sustain market practices are either absent or immature. For decades, the prevailing institutional logic was based on centralized directives. The visible fist was the Soviet answer to Adam Smith's invisible hand.[9]

Now that such control ideologies and practices have been dismantled, a vacuum exists. Incipient market forces and the urge to consume are not sufficient to drive organizational efficiency. And without the institutions of capitalism or a strong centralized state authority, the immature marketplace is an inadequate mechanism to handle the exchange of goods. The result is not just capitalism without capital, but markets without equilibrating market forces. Even foreign investors have found this out, often to their cost.

The Soviet management system remains the biggest impediment to successful joint ventures between the United States and Russia says Charalambos Vlachoutsicos and Paul R. Lawrence in a 1990 *Harvard Business Review* article. "The core of Soviet hierarchy—the structural task unit (STU)—explains the interaction between Soviet management, workers, and outsiders. The largest STU is the enterprise itself; the smallest is the work brigade. This system produces excellent vertical integration, but inner solidarity tends to inhibit horizontal communication."[10] The dilemma in a society with centralized control is creating a structure within which people have the freedom to be creative, to choose, and to be innovative without the central command losing control.

This dilemma is no different from what is found in bureaucratic companies. For example, the walls between manufacturing and sales, quality control and manufacturing, and corporate and line functions create the same conditions. Two management principles emerge from Russia's example. First, small is better than large, for it is easier to manage smaller units than larger ones. Second, free-market coordination is superior to heavy corporate oversight. Changing Russia to follow these two principles requires a critical look at the existing control system. Russia needs a free market, it needs to coordinate interactions between interested parties, and it needs to push its admittedly broken system harder. To accomplish these things, it needs to create institutions that will simultaneously erode the red tape of bureaucratic control and provide workers and managers alike with a belief in the legitimacy of the marketplace.

Shifting Gears in Taiwan

Paternalistic China faces the same fate Russia is currently struggling with. At the moment China has created a schizophrenic political economy that is part market economy and part centralized state control—a form of market Leninism. It continues to try to do both, but with growing problems since reconciling the two systems is all but impossible.

While Russia and China continue to struggle with the crisis of red tape/flexibility, Taiwan is preparing to shift gears. In the late 1990s, Taiwan accounted for nearly one-half of the world's production of PC hardware. It has made manufacturing and electronic technology its specialty. In fact, the rise of Asian economies in the last fifty years has been based on their skill in manufacturing goods. Despite their importance, however, the region is in trouble. The Asian crisis, affecting all Asian Tigers, is signaling change. The main symptom of change is that the region is awash in overcapacity; however, this is only a symptom. What is really happening in Asia is that it is beginning to move from one industrial era to another. Consequently, Asian countries are being forced to rethink their theory of business.

An example of an Asian company caught in this transition is the Acer Group headquartered in Taiwan. Stan Smith, chairman of Acer, recognizes the crisis signals. His view is that the region's reliance on high-volume manufacturing is ending. He sees that mass production too soon becomes surplus production when Third World countries all try to compete for the same slice of the pie. He believes that "labor-intensive manufacturing of hardware is not sustainable long term for any country in Asia," and that every Asian country must preserve its manufacturing skills but must also build the skills that create value in managing supply-chain networks.[11]

Implementing the changes that Smith suggests will result in radical decentralization. Acer plans to spin off twenty-one units in the next four years. These will be stand-alone companies owned by shareholders in their respective countries.[12] Acer's strategy is proactive. It suggests that Acer will jump the curve. To Acer, small is better than large, decentralized better than centralized, and making units autonomous, yet tied to the parent, creates stability and the engine for creativity, local innovation, and satisfying local needs.

The evolving multinational model being adopted by Acer, which features local autonomy with close ties to a central core, reflects a tight-loose philosophy. It creates a tension paradox. It generates a healthy debate over what needs to be done and where. If other Asian companies follow suit and decentralize, they will be able to participate in the newly emerging global economic networks and structures.

Japan Stuck in Crisis

The picture for former Asian front-runner and model performer Japan is less rosy. During the last twenty years, when the United States was struggling with its own productivity crisis, Japan was being held up as the model approach to teamwork, efficiency, and organizational structure. However, since the late 1990s, Japan has been stuck in a crisis. The once strong and thriving economy is floundering. What happened?

The first problem facing Japan is its international perception. The West has believed Japan to be more advanced, according to Western standards, than it really is. What on the surface looks like participative management is not. Most of its corporations are top-down, directive, autocratic, and chauvinistic entities built on a clearly defined hierarchy.[13] Line managers know their success depends on giving bosses want they want and deliver recommendations designed to please them. The nation's labor markets are segmented. A core group of perhaps one-third of Japanese workers enjoys numerous benefits, such as guaranteed lifetime employment. The remaining two-thirds of the workforce enjoy no such privileges.[14] Often working long hours, in sometimes unsafe conditions, such workers are required to commit to trustful submissiveness.

Additionally, in many Japanese firms trust is limited to small groups of insiders. Close, trusting relationships are forged early in the typical Japanese company, usually in the employee's first year. Working most nights past midnight, commiserating over drinks, and rotating through similar overseas assignments produce strong bonds among coworkers. Finally, fear and the embarrassment of being left behind has sometimes driven the bold ventures that are often mistaken in the West for strategic planning.

The second problem in Japan is that it is struggling to relate its ancient and rich cultural tradition to the increasingly Westernized culture of international business. For example, the consensus and teamwork seen in Japan are culturally derived; they are not, for the most part, the products of management savvy. The consequence of such a strong teamwork philosophy can be bureaucratic paralysis. Third, the government is morbidly afraid of rising unemployment. This fear may explain the political paralysis over decisive bank restructuring, which would force a multitude of bankruptcies from bad business loans. Fourth, the Japanese are very conservative and committed to their values, even in crisis.

Finally, and most important, Japan's government lacks any center of accountability. As Robert Neff notes in a *Business Week* article, "Conflicting bureaucracies contend for power. Meanwhile, politicians remain toothless. This means that in a Confucian tradition where bureaucrats count the most, politicians suffer an information deficit."[15] Neither is held accountable. Politicians have no real power, and bureaucrats, cut off from economic reality, make decisions to protect the status quo of the very institutions they are responsible for overseeing. For example, bureaucrats are charged with reforming the banking industry with its mounds of low-interest debt—which is like asking the mouse to watch the cheese.

Japan's crisis of red tape versus flexibility is particularly difficult because of its cultural values and stubbornness of set organizational systems. As Drucker points out: "It is not even that the wrong things are being done. Indeed, in most cases, the *right* things are being done—but fruitlessly. What accounts for this apparent paradox? The assumptions on which the organization [society] has been built and is being run no longer fit reality."[16]

Perhaps most disturbing in the case of Japan is the rapid downturn after such prominent success. Such steep descents have plagued many countries—and organizations. Drucker explains: "The story is a familiar one: a company that was a superstar only yesterday finds itself stagnating and frustrated, in trouble and, often, in a seemingly unmanageable crisis. This phenomenon is by no means confined to the United States. It has become common in Japan and Germany, the Netherlands and France, Italy and Sweden."[17]

The British Sunset

Once a formidable military power as well as an economic one, the British Empire (on which proud Britons claimed "the sun never set") has been reduced to little more than a shadow of her former presence. Its problem is one of institutional impasse. The engine of early industrial growth is no longer appropriate or adequate. Unable to restructure its organizations and institutions to match the demands of twentieth century capitalism, Britain was doomed to decline before two world wars exposed its weaknesses for all to see. Its industrial culture was obsolete by the end of the nineteenth century. It remained a rigid class society in which indifference to professional management by its elite was surpassed only by the entrenched power of craft workers and their unions. The latter resisted changes that would increase productivity; the former preferred to muddle through. As a result, R&D expenditures were typically inadequate and new inventions failed to receive the funding that would make them commercially viable.

The inadequate Victorian craft-based system of manufacturing was no match for the emerging mass production of the United States, or even the technical specialization of incipient German industrialization. British institutions suited an entrepreneurial and industrializing economy, but not a progressive one. Organizationally, Britain couldn't embrace innovation because machinery was often viewed by the workforce as the enemy, since it undermined traditional status and independence. Unable to solve the tensions, the elite relied on past glories. It canonized the amateur and decried the educated specialist. All these contradictions were finally exposed during World War II.

In World War II, efficient German production, even in the midst of an embargo that severely curtailed imports of crucial raw materials, outstripped that of Britain. With massive infusions of American capital and resources, Britain struggled through the war. In victory, its leaders attempted to build a New Jerusalem, but the foundations were old and decaying. Britain's leaders and its ruling class proved incapable of recognizing that the old ways were no longer appropriate. This form of denial is not unique among societies and organizations that have seen better days. In Britain's case, as in many firms, that denial has led to uncertainty and decline. As its dreams and illusions faded one by one, all that remained, according to Correlli Barnett, was "a dank reality of a segregated, subliterate, unskilled, unhealthy, and institutionalized proletariat hanging on the nipple of state materialism."[18]

SUMMARY

In their *Lessons of History*, Will and Ariel Durant say, "Civilizations begin, flourish, decline, and disappear or linger on as stagnant pools left by once life-giving streams."[19] The same can be said of any society that loses a common purpose or direction and does not find a way to reinvent itself.

There is one caveat. An organization, society, or individual can jump the curve but cannot skip over development stages. Just as people have to pass through their teenage years to become adults, an organization or society has to be prepared to go through all the stages of development. It can't, for example, go to a free-market economy or decentralize decision making without assuring itself that it has a mature population to make sound decisions, a control system to ensure and monitor results, and an information system that provides timely red flags if results are off-track. While the speed of transition might vary from case to case, the sequence remains immutable.

In the last decade Americans have witnessed a few red flags. It is clear for example, that due to the Internet many of the old rules in both the United States and the world no longer work, and that new ones have not yet been devised, are not yet clearly understood, or are just now forming. To be effective in the twenty-first century, the United States and other nations will want to jump the technology curve. To do this they will have to assess the maturity of the people and rely on different strategies than in the past.

The next chapter reviews management control techniques in organization evolution and how they either help or hinder organizational growth.

NOTES

1. William H. Whyte, Jr., *The Organization Man* (New York: Simon and Schuster, 1956).

2. Peter F. Drucker, *The Age of Discontinuity: Guidelines to Our Changing Society* (New York: Harper & Row, 1968), 40.

3. "A Work Revolution in U.S. Industry," *Business Week*, 16 May 1983, 100–110.

4. John Naisbitt, *Megatrends: Ten Directions Transforming Our Lives* (New York: Warner Books, 1982), 16.

5. Peter F. Drucker, *Managing in Turbulent Times* (New York: Harper & Row, 1980).

6. David Champion, "Technology's Garden of Paradox," *Harvard Business Review* (July–August 1998): 12.

7. Don Tapscott, *The Digital Economy* (New York: McGraw-Hill, 1996), xiii.

8. Bill Gates, *Business @ The Speed of Thought* (New York: Warner Books, 1999).

9. The term "invisible hand," which Adam Smith coined in his book *Wealth of Nations*, 5th ed. (New York: Random House, 1994, 1st ed., 1776), refers to the coordinating mechanisms that are constantly at work in the marketplace, which are far better at allocating goods and services than any centralized planning staff, no matter how large.

10. Charalambos Vlachoutsicos and Paul R. Lawrence, "What We Don't Know About Soviet Management," *Harvard Business Review* (November–December 1990): 50–58.

11. James Flanigan, "Acer's Information Age Lessons," *Los Angeles Times: Orange County Edition*, 7 June 1998, D 10.

12. "Acer: A Global Powerhouse," *Business Week*, 1 July 1998, 95.

13. Linda Grant, "The Japanese Fight a Lot," *Fortune*, 22 June 1997: 164.

14. Satoshi Kamata, *Japan in the Passing Lane* (New York: Pantheon Books, 1982).

15. Robert Neff, "Why Japan Won't Act to Save Itself," *Business Week*, 18 May 1998, 144.

16. Peter F. Drucker, "The Theory of the Business," *Harvard Business Review*, (September–October 1994): 95.

17. Ibid.

18. Correlli Barnett, *The Audit of War* (London: MacMillan, 1986), 304.

19. Will and Ariel Durant, *The Lessons of History* (New York: Simon & Schuster, 1968), 90.

5

An Issue of Control

The previous chapter addressed the evolutionary process as it occurs in societies and cultures. This final chapter in Part I on the evolution of an organization builds on the previous four. Here the focus is on how societies and corporations maintain control in response to *external* forces, such as the available labor force, competition, government regulations, and capital markets. These external forces then shape the structure and *internal* control mechanisms that an organization develops to maximize results.

One external force particularly important for controlling businesses in the twenty-first century is the availability of information-based technologies. A great deal of managerial control lies in the information-based procedures that companies use to ensure results. As a general trend, face-to-face communication is initially the norm in controlling simple organizations. Later, as firms migrate to more complicated structures, information technology takes over to track and control results.

Figure 5.1 depicts the changing structural forms and their respective icons that emerge as the pace of change and information requirements increase. When knowledge and information are simple and the pace of change is stable, then a flat organization structure emerges with its characteristic entrepreneurial/directive leadership style. In a stable environment, these firms grow and become bureaucratic with layers of management whose tasks are coordinating the business activity. As size, complexity, and pace of change quickens with knowledge and information becoming a strategic advantage, then partnerships, alliances, and networks form.

Figure 5.1
Drivers of Structural Change

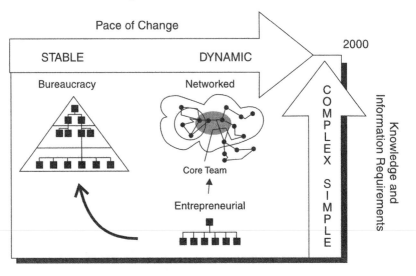

CONTROL STRATEGIES

Building on the developing nations' examples from the last chapter, we will show how early organization forms usually follow a directive approach. The available labor force is a determining factor in how the business is controlled. In developing nations workers have little education or education that is specific to a certain skill, and they tend to come into urban areas from the surrounding rural areas where alternative employment opportunities are rare. Because they are in low-skill jobs, such workers need a great deal of direction and are valued more for their hands than for their heads. They become extensions, or "cogs," of the organizational "machine." Control is maintained through strong directive channels, and is enforced through the threat of dismissal. Such organizations are run with order, predictability, linear thinking, and scientific management. The Asian Tigers and other societies in the throes of rapid industrialization tend to manage their workers in this way.

The United States went through such a phase during its industrial revolution, when Taylorism[1] reduced work to a set of prescribed tasks that took individual decision making out of the work process. However, the worldwide development of network structures has brought about a revolution in control strategies for large multinationals. Volatility, uncertainty, diversity in the workplace, the demand for knowledge workers, and the increased flow of information are a far cry from the environment of developing countries. Newer management control strategies to accommodate today's marketplace are evolving, but are not yet fully developed. In fact, organizations are still struggling with how best to use the most recent strategies—controlling through teams and alliances—in the global market.

Those experimenting with control strategies to function in today's business environment must find means of controlling networks within different cultures, societies, business climates, and traditions. One of the most difficult aspects of developing control strategies lies in managing the smooth transition from one stage of organizational development to another. For an organization working towards a networked structure, skipping organizational stages is often appealing, but is dangerous. The control practices for each stage must be undertaken sequentially. For example, the transition from a paternalistic, directive structure to a delegative structure takes time, employee education, and the building of a networked infrastructure that encourages teamwork and personal accountability. One of the mistakes that many U.S. multinational corporations have made is to try to move too quickly from one organizational stage to another.

Leapfrogging over management stages is especially appealing to firms that want to transport professional management practices to a subsidiary in a developing country. These subsidiaries often fail because the parent organization makes the mistake of not adequately assessing the labor force, culture, and society of the subsidiary country. This has been the case in Russia since the end of the cold war. U.S. firms have moved in too quickly and consequently, there are many failed attempts to establish business there. As Peter F. Drucker says, "To run an automobile factory in Malaysia is no different than to run one in Nagoya, Japan, or in Detroit. But relationships *are very different* between worker and supervisor and superintendent, and between the factory even though the management tasks are exactly the same."[2] Firms must recognize the institutional constraints and learn to work *with* these differences, which means considering how to manage *to* them during each phase of organizational evolution.

A similar discussion of the limits of control is at the heart of *The End of Corporate Imperialism*, by C.K. Prahalad and Ken Lieberthal.[3] When Western multinationals think about competing in big emerging markets like China and India, they have a tendency to think that they can customize existing products and services to meet the needs of the local marketplace without changing their business model. Not so. Reaching new customers in these emerging markets requires mirroring the societies' organization evolution. Prahalad and Lieberthal argue that not until multinationals let go of their imperial mind-set will these markets become profitable. It is common practice to talk about how corporations will change emerging markets. It is only recently that firms are reversing the question to ask how the emerging markets will change the way multinationals do business.

Failing to consider the local culture and the workforce means potential failure for any company moving into globalization strategies with a provincial view anchored in their home market. The same consideration applies when designing a control system for the firm. Understanding where the firm is in its evolution is vital.

INTERNAL AND EXTERNAL FACTORS

Clearly, as discussed in previous chapters, there are both internal and external influences on any organization. The ways in which an organization maintains and manages control is, therefore, influenced by such internal and external factors. The internal variables influencing control strategies, as in the three-legged stool illustrated in Chapter 3, are the *purpose, processes*, and *people* of the organization. These three factors determine the operating philosophy and drive internal control mechanisms, but are themselves influenced by external factors.

A curious feature of an organization's development is that the relative influence of internal and external factors on the organization's control strategies tends to vacillate. *External* factors such as those mentioned above (the labor force, competition, society, technology, etc.) tend to alternate with *internal* procedures and processes as the driver of the corporation's control strategy. For example, the external factor of the market is virtually the sole driver of the control strategies in an entrepreneurial organization. However, when that organization experiences the crisis of profitability/creativity, it has to become directive. Instead of the market dictating how things should be done, strong leadership from above takes over.

The shift between external and internal influences in an organization's control strategies tends to come at the crisis points for each phase, discussed in earlier chapters. As a reminder, these crisis points, or sets of tension paradoxes, are: profitability/creativity, ego/autonomy, red tape/flexibility, abdication/trust, alignment/direction, and self-interest/collaboration. Note that the first variable in each set deals with managerial *control*, while the second variable deals with freedom from control, or what *people* want.

Figure 5.2 again shows each of these crisis points. The horizontal axis gives the organizational phases previously discussed. For simplicity, they have been grouped into three. The vertical axis identifies the management concepts and techniques used to control a company at each stage of organizational evolution.

Another observable trend shown in Figure 5.2 is a gradual shift from natural leadership to management-leadership as can be seen on the vertical axis. As organizations evolve, they tend to go through roughly three different control strategies. First, they control people with task assignments; second, they install bureaucratic operating and process controls that monitor financial results; and third, they strike a management-leadership balance between leading (not controlling) people and managing processes.

To understand the nuances that take place in an organization's control

Figure 5.2
Control Strategies in Phases

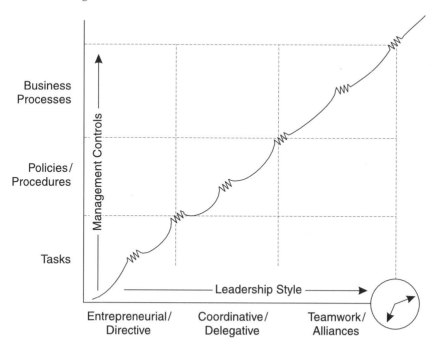

strategies during each phase of its evolution, we revisit each of the phases previously discussed in Chapters 1 through 3. Our focus is on both the oscillation between management and leadership as firms evolve and the oscillation between external and internal influences on control strategies.

The Entrepreneurial Phase

In the entrepreneurial phase, an adequate supply of capital and the *external* market control the destiny of the new company. The questions concern how well the company is meeting the needs of the marketplace with new innovative product and whether it has the necessary resources for success. In the case of a new group functioning like a mini-organization within a mature company, control rests with the department's internal customers— that is, with the other departments that need its services. In most instances, survival depends on customers wanting to buy, which means the organization or group must respond quickly and creatively to what customers want. In both cases, the controlling element is *external* to those providing the product or service.

In the start-up phase of a new business, constant face-to-face commu-

Figure 5.3
Task Assignments

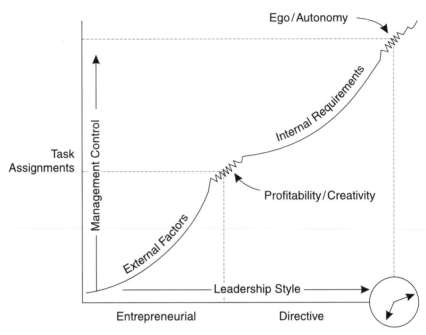

nication allows for the control of key aspects of the business without formal reporting structures. Technical leadership influences people to follow, task assignments are frequent, and informal communication and teamwork are actually getting the job done (see Figure 5.3).

If the start-up is not carefully planned in response to market demands, however, excessive creativity can outweigh practicality and profitability suffers. If the organizational unit gets in trouble, creditors or top management may bring in a turnaround specialist to get things moving again, or the firm may just go out of business.

The Directive Phase

The crisis of profitability/creativity, flowing out of the entrepreneurial stage, forces the organization to adopt a strong directive leadership style to bring the situation under control. The focus becomes primarily *internal*. Centralized decision making becomes the dominant control mechanism, with a simple chain of command and functional structure.

There are two variations of the control strategies of the directive style. The first relies on the power of position much like what is found in the military. It works well in a crisis and when a group is relatively isolated from external factors. The second variation is a one-person, one-way-to-do-things approach. It is like what brilliant people do who call all the shots and build industrial empires. These are the charismatic technical experts in engineering, marketing, and other disciplines. These experts use their own personal charm and intelligence to control events. Louis A. Allen, in the *Professional Manager's Guide*, describes the strong control characteristics of the directive leader.[4] The guide suggests that a directive leader holds as the standard his or her way, and sets levels of performance that others are expected to meet. Since the natural leader is usually an expert in the work of the people he or she supervises, standards tend to be high and demanding, and prompt good work is expected as the norm. The directive leader spends a great deal of time giving task assignments (not a form of delegation), personally inspecting results, and observing all aspects of business. Performance correction largely centers on the manager trying to get people to approximate the way he or she prefers work to be done.

In times of crisis, organizations generally tend to become directive, which is an appropriate response. "Chainsaw Al" is the classic example from the downsizing of the 1990s. The captain of a sinking ship does not seek a consensus on who will get into which lifeboats. He gives orders. The danger of a directive system of control, of course, is the limitation of formal management process controls and top management's paradigm paralysis brought on by ego and hubris.

The Coordinative Phase

To overcome the weaknesses of egocentric leadership in the directive phase and attempt to bring structure to an organization in the crisis of ego/autonomy, firms in the coordinative phase focus on getting their many disparate and growing parts to work together using middle managers as coordinators. These firms make it through the directive phase because they are financially healthy and are positioned in a growing market segment. The challenge they face is to maintain and grow market share. The controlling pressure therefore shifts to become *external*. Competition heats up, knock-off products emerge, and the need for low-cost volume production becomes paramount.

In response, a hierarchical organizational structure develops, there is a drive towards standardization, and the firm begins to function in a machine-like way. For centuries, organizations have been constructed in Newtonian terms as clock-like mechanisms composed of separate parts. This machine metaphor has dominated thinking, declaring that life and everything in it—physical, biological, or social—could be understood and controlled as machinery. In coordinative control strategy various line functions—marketing, R&D, manufacturing, and others—are given individual autonomy and are required to work together under the watchful eyes of staff control groups. These groups oversee quality control, production control, inventory control, expense control, and the proliferation of policies and procedures each generates. These are the mechanisms to safeguard assets and insure the system runs smoothly.

In responding to external competition, a bureaucratic organization tries to become more responsive and encourages people to work together in a matrix structure. Figure 5.1 depicts the conditions under which a matrix emerges. As an organization's bureaucracy grows, its focus of control must inevitably begin to turn inward. As the pace of change quickens, and as volatility increases, the stability of bureaucracy becomes a liability. In time the crisis of red tape/flexibility catches up with the organization. As Erica Schoenberger points out in *The Cultural Crisis of the Firm*, "Bureaucracies are very efficient in handling routine tasks in a stable environment. Routine and stability are the necessary underpinnings for a well-defined and enduring division of labor that, in turn, allows the bureaucratic machine to operate more or less automatically, according to known rules."[5] When those rules change—with changing market conditions, rising cost, and growing competition—the organization is forced to reassess its control system.

The Delegative Phase

The only way out of the crisis of red tape/flexibility created in the coordinative stage is to take a tight-loose approach to control.

"Tight" means that delegation of authority to lower levels is joined with a control system that predetermines—around key performance measures—the desired end results or the "what" of the business, and then reviews these results. This is a diagnostic control system. The focus of control in the delegation phase is *internal*—the requirement for stability and predictability (see Figure 5.4). This control strategy leverages the talent of workers where self-control at the point of control is needed. (Part III covers this subject more thoroughly.)

On the other hand, "loose" refers to the development of a corporate operating philosophy in which workers at all levels are encouraged to make decisions that benefit the corporation as a whole. This approach assumes workers will do the "right" thing if they know what "right" is, and so companies educate and articulate a vision and direction to enable them to make the best decisions. John P. Kotter's study of management-leadership concludes that control techniques do not always have to be quantitative; qualitative techniques are also effective. Kotter concludes that developing workers who are able to make decisions in a "loose" system requires: (1) articulating a company purpose that addresses what people want out of their job; (2) painting a picture that shows how their job can contribute to the company vision; (3) demonstrating enthusiastic support for effort; and (4) encouraging public recognition and reward for all successes.[6]

Figure 5.4
Navigating the Corridor of Crisis

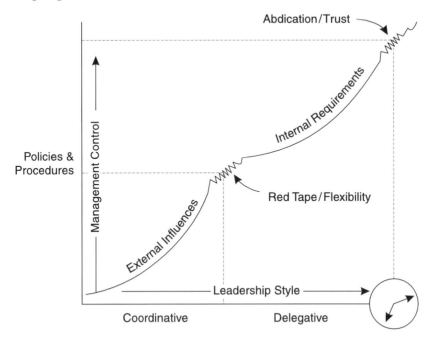

If a tight-loose control system is not well planned and implemented, de-centralizing decision making and empowering employees to make decisions can result in crisis. Remember the example of BankAmerica in Chapter 2. Its failure to implement a uniform quantitative control system when decision making was decentralized caused a near-fatal disaster. Control of reports was so poorly planned that feedback did not make it to either lower-level decision makers or to top management. One former executive described the control system thus: "When you sent a report to San Francisco, it was like throwing a piece of paper into the Grand Canyon."[7] The bank's outmoded computer technology—which was entirely inadequate for tracking such a sprawling system—exacerbated the control problem.

The BankAmerica example points to the importance of a well thought out and implemented decentralized control system. At BankAmerica, not enough management effort was focused internally to build a tight-loose control system and too much trust was granted prematurely and indiscriminately, resulting in the decentralization/centralization yo-yo effect evident in the corridor of crisis.

Delegation of authority with management processes to ensure operating goals are in place and reviewed on a frequent basis is the control strategy in the delegative phase. However, another failure in the crisis of abdication/

trust is not fully considering what constraints are needed when delegating. The freedom that teams are given in making decisions must be spelled out and boundaries must be clearly defined. For example, exploration teams in an oil company were told they were a profit-and-loss center and to act accordingly to maximize return on assets. The teams took their mission to heart. When internal drilling rigs were unavailable, they began going outside the company and subcontracting rigs to get their projects moving. When top management found out, it came down hard on the teams and said "no." The teams were left without a clear sense of their authority and with a battered trust in management.

The biggest single mistake corporate managers make when pushing decision making to lower levels is not considering the implications on existing policies and procedures. It is not enough to empower teams. One of the reasons they don't is that at this stage of organizational evolution, firms have a tendency to promote people into CEO positions with financial or legal backgrounds. These are not operating executives. In fact, their focus on increasing shareholder value and legal issues ties up much of their time. Little attention is paid to the implications of delegating decision-making authority, and this abdication of their management responsibilities causes countless problems.

The Teamwork-Driven Phase

To overcome the crisis of abdication/trust, an organization needs a good vertical infrastructure of tight control. With adequate vertical controls, horizontal restructuring of the organization becomes possible with teams made up of employees from different disciplines within the company. These teamwork structures emerge out of the matrix form—project teams—prominent in the coordinative and delegative phases. The interdependence that is key to successful teamwork began in these matrix structures.

In the teamwork-driven phase, however, coordination falls on the shoulders of the team. Through reengineering, layers of middle managers are gone. Lean manufacturing and cross-functional coordination require that groups no longer operate in isolation from one another. They need to understand that they respond to and are influenced by *external* upstream and downstream process teams within the organization, external suppliers, and the emergence of alliance partners. Managing these external influences is part of their job and it has a profound impact on their ability to produce results.

Control in the teamwork-driven phase is more complicated than ever before in the history of the organization. It lies not only with management-leaders, but also with the teams themselves. Management-leaders must provide adequate controls for the massive explosion of communication necessary to keep the teamwork-driven phase going. They must also balance internal controls with the increasingly important external sources to carry out its business. Chapter 12, entitled "Interactive Leadership," discusses further how top executives' roles evolve as the organization evolves. The teams themselves must consider many of the same control issues as the management-leader. They are, after all, like mini-organizations of their own within the larger organization. The larger organization functions for the team like an external influence.

Because teams must balance *internal* and *external* influences on their control strategies, the mechanisms teams use to manage themselves are very similar to that used by top management—an emphasis on obtaining commitments and follow-up. Quality time must be invested in preplanning and reviewing operating results. To do this, teams monitor their ongoing key operating indicators and members agree on projects needed to improve the ongoing work of the team.

In the teamwork-driven phase, not having balanced corporate control mechanisms can cause groups to go off in different directions. The firm then faces the crisis of alignment/direction, which hampers its ability to evolve into a horizontal corporation.

The Alliance-Oriented Phase

As core business teams extend their reach to an expanding external web of alliance partners, the ability of the host company to control results in this expanded network is reduced. Propelled by the explosive increase in information-sharing technology, the migration to network structures forces teams to change the way they control themselves. Team members doing the work control day-to-day details through electronic communication. Management-leaders find they must alter control strategies to accommodate the growing importance of outside allies. Enterprise resource planning software, e-commerce, supply-chain management, and on line data analysis tools are just a few of the many techniques networked firms use to manage in this phase. Chapter 9, "When Span of Control Becomes Span of Communication," discusses in more detail the impact of information technology on organizations in this teamwork-driven phase.

For most companies, information technology holds the promise of providing top management with a method of quickly and efficiently overseeing and analyzing data from cross-functional teams, both within and outside their corporate walls. Because of the already heavy use of networked technology systems in many high-tech start-ups, these companies offer an interesting variation from the pattern of evolution evinced by most companies. The networking fundamentally underpinning these companies allows them to pass much more quickly through the corridor of crisis than other types of firms, and provide a model of how to manage a network organization.

Figure 5.5
A Balance of Management-Leadership Control

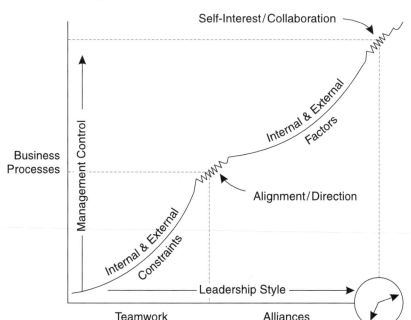

Alan Greenspan, Federal Reserve Board chairman, stressed the importance of the information technology trend in a 1998 University of California, Berkeley, speech. He said, "Important technological changes have been emerging in recent years that are altering, in ways with few precedents, the manner in which we organize production, trade across countries and deliver value to consumers."[8] The strength of many U.S. corporations today lies in the investments they made in computer technology and software during the 1990s. Societies and industries in all parts of the world are using technological innovations, in Greenspan's words, to "organize production differently and better."

However, to organize production differently and better, firms must first put in place a performance-management system to control results and processes at the lowest possible level. This means an alliance-oriented organization must ensure that a formalized lateral control system exists to align and integrate team efforts across many boundaries. In today's network organizations, commitments and cooperation must be obtained horizontally all along the end-to-end business processes by a combination of managerial controls and leadership influence (see Figure 5.5).

Without this glue, there is a high probability of slipping into the crisis of self-interest/collaboration. For example, recall from Chapter 3 how the self-interest of one partner hampered collaboration between KLM and Northwest Airlines, causing "an alliance from hell."

In the teamwork-driven and alliance-oriented phases, both external and internal forces influence the approach to organizational control. The ideal control strategies strike a balance of *internal* management controls and *external* leadership to ensure that the organization is glued together. This convergence of external and internal control requirements is why senior executives cannot be one dimensional in their skills. This is new to many old-line managers accustomed to having their own way, and it is one of the reasons why more and more emphasis today in large multinational corporations is being placed on leadership development. It is a skill too few managers possess and one that is hard to identify and develop.

Robert Simons, a professor of management at Harvard, sums up the challenge of control in *Levers of Control*. He says that today, "A new theory of control that recognizes the need to balance competing demands is required. Inherent tensions must be controlled, tensions between freedom and constraints, between empowerment and accountability, between top-down direction and bottom-up creativity, between experimentation and efficiency. These tensions are not managed by choosing, for example, empowerment over accountability—increasingly, managers [firms] must have both in their organizations."[9]

SUMMARY

Guiding the growth of a business first requires that senior executives understand where the firm is in its evolution. Business success depends upon knowing which external or internal set of forces materially shape the business and then structuring the appropriate response. Second, what controls a firm changes in each evolutionary growth phase. Control pressures oscillate back and forth between external forces that influence a firm's growth and internal requirements to remain profitable.

External factors such as financing and the marketplace initially control the destiny of a small newly formed entity. Control gradually drifts upward, away from where creativity and innovation reside, to the top. This upward drift is to obtain standardization and ensure profitability, but eventually it can precipitate the corridor of crisis. If not properly dealt with, the crisis causes a lack of marketplace responsiveness, a constant reshuffling of those at the top, or endless cycles of centralization and decentralization. Finally, migration to a team-driven and alliance-oriented phase requires a delicate balance of management (to control *internal* operations) and leadership (to influence people and *external* situations over which the leader has no command authority).

Six red flags to help senior management identify control issues are the crisis points defined as profitability/creativity, ego/autonomy, red tape/flexibility, abdication/trust, alignment/direction, and self-interest/collaboration. These early warning signals highlight the control strategy employed by top management and suggest that what people require to be effective may not be in alignment.

NOTES

1. Taylorism refers to the process pioneered by Frederic Taylor. It was of breaking jobs down into their component parts to minimize wasted motion in the early 20th century.

2. Patricia A. Galagan, "Peter Drucker," *Training and Development* (September 1998): 27.

3. C.K. Prahalad and Ken Lieberthal, "The End of Corporate Imperialism," *Harvard Business Review* (July–August 1998): 69.

4. Louis A. Allen, *Professional Manager's Guide* (Palo Alto: Louis A. Allen, 1969), 205.

5. Erica Schoenberger, *The Cultural Crisis of the Firm* (Cambridge, MA: Blackwell, 1997), 84.

6. John P. Kotter, *A Force for Change* (New York: The Free Press, 1990), 63.

7. "Back Again: Clausen Returns to Clean House," *Time*, 27 October 1986, 74.

8. James Flanigan, "On the Bright Side: U.S. Firms Taking Lead in Preparing for 21st Century," *Los Angles Times*, 13 September 1998, Section D1.

9. Robert Simons, *Levers of Control* (Boston: HBS Press, 1994), 4.

PART II

HISTORICAL PERSPECTIVES AND TRENDS

Part I explained how organizations evolve from entrepreneurial and centralized management through a decentralized network model of management to a greater reliance on teamwork and alliances, which will be especially important in the coming decades. In this section we shift gears somewhat and examine the historical perspectives and trends behind the evolution, focusing on the principal resource of most organizations—their employees.

Despite the fact that management gurus have been talking about the need to more meaningfully incorporate employees in the work process for decades, many firms remain blind to this sentiment. During the twentieth century, the paradigm of mass production predisposed managers to treat workers as a variable cost—just one of the many inputs to be controlled. Mass customization, a growing service sector, tight labor markets, and the emergence of the knowledge worker is forcing management to rethink its assumptions about work and what workers want out of jobs.

In Chapter 6 we examine the origins of the mass production paradigm and show how its legacy has proved resilient as managers cling to an ideology of hierarchical control. In the face of compelling reasons to change, many managers have proven themselves reluctant to abandon a system that has conferred status and wealth upon them. We look at what might be forcing change to occur but also recognize that inertia is a powerful force impeding change.

We then consider the shift to teamwork that has occurred in the last decade or so, a shift that is seen by many as the solution to maximizing human resources. But even here, resistance in the form of improper implementation constrains many firms from realizing the full potential of teamwork. Chapter 7 looks at the history of teamwork and discusses its successes and failures. Firms that have used new organizational structures to better integrate their employees have often met with success, but making the transition from a compliance model of management to one that creates commitment among workers can be difficult. It requires a specific type of leadership that encourages the growth of trust, engenders loyalty, provides a challenging work environment, and inspires hard work.

In Chapter 8 we provide a case study of a firm that accomplished this when leadership was used to release the latent talents and creativity of the workforce and achieve successful bottom line results.

Finally, in Chapter 9, we outline the key features of communication that arise when firms successfully make the shift to a horizontally structured organization. Research studies have consistently shown that when people are hired for their heads and not just their hands, creativity, innovation, and commitment increase dramatically. Tapping into this talent pool with cutting-edge communications technology to enhance bottom-up communication from what are increasingly "knowledge workers" opens a largely underutilized corporate asset. Strategic advantage will increasingly lie in firms that use the digital economy to make their workers more knowledgeable and then capitalize upon that knowledge.

6

The Changing Perception of Work

Information technology is doing what previous managers found difficult to do with the tools they had. Future oriented firms are building a digital nervous system that makes data flow—through departments, among employees, out to partners and suppliers, and between the firm and its customers. The twentieth century has brought an incredible amount of technological innovation and progress. And yet business is forecast to change more in the next ten years than in the past fifty. Driven by the Internet, personal computers, innovative software, and new generations of digital devices, rapid technological change will continue as we enter the twenty-first century.

Despite technological innovation and decades of automation, organizations still need people to do the work. People are crucial to a firm's success. Yet these people, when they come to work each day, come with different motivations and intentions. For some, money is uppermost in their mind; for others, the intrinsic satisfaction that comes from the job itself might be just as important; for still others work is an escape from the drudgery of domestic life. One can appreciate the difficulties faced by managers and supervisors in dealing with these various individual orientations. While no two workers are alike, managers in the last century nonetheless organized work around certain assumptions regarding worker behavior. These assumptions are pervasive, embedded in our institutions and hard to change.

This chapter takes an historical perspective, looking at how workers have been viewed by managers. Until recent years, workers were hired for their hands, not their heads—as in the oil industry slogan "we hire good hands."

The fundamental assumption before the growth of the knowledge worker was that hands needed to be controlled, as though workers were children. In his book *The Human Side of Enterprise*, Douglas McGregor addresses the perception of the hired hand. He says, "In its *basic* conceptions of managing human resources . . . management appears to have concluded that the average human being is permanently arrested in his development in early childhood."[1] Since then many others have argued that we have created human resource strategies that are suited more for children than adults. Consequently, businesses end up with workers who are treated like juveniles and then, unsurprisingly, start behaving in that manner.

This way of viewing workers is best described as a parent-child relationship, and the best way to manage worker-children is to remove individual discretion; provide them with routine, often repetitive tasks; tell them what to do; and reward them monetarily for doing it efficiently. This approach, which came to be known as Taylorism or Fordism—after Henry Ford's famous early assembly lines—was the cornerstone of the mass production system that brought more sustained economic growth to the United States than other industrial nations for much of this century.[2] But in recent decades market changes and technological innovations have forced many firms to rethink this directive style of management and, with it, their attitudes toward their workforce. With demands for speed, flexibility, quality, and a customer focus, firms are forced to treat their employees as a resource rather than a cost. And yet many firms cling resolutely to the old system, tinkering with it rather than changing it. This chapter charts this bureaucratic legacy, explaining its logic and its implications for the organization of work.

ESTABLISHING CONTROL OF THE WORKPLACE

As the United States industrialized during the latter part of the nineteenth century, manager-worker relations became increasingly conflictual. The replacement of craft workers in factories by semiskilled workers performing routine and standardized tasks was part of the re-organization of the work process under continuous process innovations. Routine task performance was crucial to the new production systems, but employers had to socialize this new generation of workers into an acceptance of it. Such workers had to be disciplined, controlled, and encouraged to work—no mean task since the new work systems lacked many of the intrinsic benefits associated with skilled craft work. In addition, as firms grew larger, the physical oversight of workers by managers grew more difficult. No longer could the owner/manager supervise daily operations and rely upon a form of paternalism to oversee the workforce. New forms of coordination and control became necessary as management by intuition and experience was gradually replaced by more analytic and detached methods.[3]

The initial response to the oversight problem led to the creation of a supervisory group of workers. Lacking a developed managerial class from which to draw such people, firms promoted workers from their own labor force to fill these roles. Unfortunately, once in such a position, these new foremen were often unscrupulous and certainly not objective in their dealings with other workers. The historical literature is replete with stories of their nepotism, bullying, and arbitrary actions against other workers.[4] In fact much of the incipient union unrest that occurred during the 1880s seemed to be spawned by supervisory inequity rather than wage issues.

By the 1890s, employers in the large firms faced two related problems. First, the increased productivity drives to meet the demands of a growing mass market led to the introduction of labor-saving machinery and the further simplification of worker tasks. However, instead of improving performance such changes more likely resulted in "a loss of direction, a decrease in efficiency, and a basic need for much greater coordination of activities and operations."[5]

The second problem that employers faced with greater productivity demands was an erosion of worker motivation. The new production systems relied on increasingly simplified tasks that had no tangible mechanism for providing workers with a sense of final product ownership. Gone were the old ties between craft worker and his employer, the old basis of traditional authority. In their place a vacuum emerged from which unionization and working class consciousness were created. When problems arose—as they did with increasing frequency over wages, benefits, job safety, and supervision—workers were likely to seek redress in collective action. Using foremen to coordinate work activities had merely exacerbated an already simmering discontent that was further fueled by the new productivity pushes. As Mauro Guillen notes, "The new organizational practices seemed to erode rather than strengthen worker discipline and motivation to produce."[6]

The Assembly Line Reduces Inefficiencies

At the turn of the twentieth century, many American firms faced a dilemma. The continued growth of a mass market provided a huge demand for products. Technically, firms could satisfy this demand. Their problems lay in workplace tensions that were disrupting production. They needed an effective way to manage the people side of the organization. In the assembly line, and later in scientific management, they found a process innovation and an organizational framework that would prove beneficial.

The assembly line was borne out of attempts to reduce human inefficiencies. As factories had increased in size, more and more of the workers' time was spent unproductively moving around the factory to perform routine tasks on product assembly. Rather than have workers move to where the product is, employers began asking, why not bring the product to where the worker is? Gustavus Swift's meatpacking plants had already demonstrated the productivity gains associated with such a product flow. Now others began innovating with this "assembly line" type of operation. By keeping workers stationary, the product could move through the factory in a systematic fashion with each worker performing standardized tasks on the product as it came to him.

Such flow principles also allowed employers to further subdivide worker tasks, making them even more routine and standardized. This reduced the requisite skill levels of workers and minimized training time (and cost) for new hires. Once firms began experimenting with this system they realized it provided an answer to their problems of worker motivation. The machine or assembly line now dictated the pace of work, rather than a supervisor. Embedding supervision in what Richard Edwards refers to as the "technical control"[7] systems of the assembly line not only removed many of the social problems of human control, it also allowed firms to speed up production and improve productivity. Machines rather than humans controlled the work and workers were left with little recourse but to submit to the abstract dictates of machinery.

The assembly line became the standard operating norm for mass production. It allowed firms to dramatically lower their unit production costs and increase the speed of production. Its manifestation is best seen in the early automobile factories of Henry Ford. In 1911 the Highland Park plant turned out Model T Fords using such a production system which ever since has been known as "Fordism." For example, the labor time of car assembly went from twelve hours and eight minutes under the old system to just over one and a half hours in this plant. With lower production costs, firms such as Ford could lower the price of the finished product, thus further stimulating demand.

Fordism worked well providing standardized large volume production. It allowed firms to realize the benefits of economies of scale and appealed to the acquisitive instincts of workers by providing them with a reasonable wage. Admittedly, it took the institutionalization of collective bargaining and the growth of trade unions in the 1940s to secure higher wages for assembly line workers, but by that time the system had become the production norm in industrialized countries. Even Lenin in the newly formed USSR admired it for its practical efficiency.

The new assembly line was not, however, without its employee problems. Even Henry Ford recognized that the work tasks were intrinsically unsatisfying. His famous five-dollar-a-day wage was high for that time, but it was conditional upon punctual arrival at work and a six-month absence-free attendance record. This wage premium was a pragmatic response to high absentee rates and labor turnover that plagued many mass production industries of that time.

Incentive Wage System

Concurrent with the growth of the assembly line system, a more "scientific" approach to the study of work and management developed. Concerned about the gross inefficiency of many work sites at the turn of the century, the engineer Frederick Taylor argued that low productivity was not necessarily the fault of "lazy" workers. For him, the problems lie in the design of the workplace and work process. His scientific designs of how best to structure work involved workers working at a steady pace, performing routine tasks in a structure coordinated by managers to optimize efficiency.[8] He argued that if workers could learn how to do their jobs more effectively, the work would become easier for them and they would be paid more because ultimately they would be more productive.

His incentive wage system replaced contract labor and established a formalized role for managers. He also provided credibility for organizational changes within firms that were cementing the functional division between management's tasks (thinking) and labor's activities (doing). Workers were increasingly seen as a resource to be exploited. Managers, meanwhile, made all of the important decisions and oversaw production since they alone possessed the exact scientific knowledge to determine what was a fair day's work. While few firms formally adopted Taylor's complete principles, most subscribed to the idea of separating managers' and workers' tasks. They knew work was repetitive and boring but they claimed that workers were compensated accordingly. As long as mass production flourished and unit costs continued to fall while markets expanded, they could afford to pay reasonable wages to workers.

From time to time, managers expressed interest in the social and psychological well being of workers. The "human relations movement" arose, for example, because of concerns that further productivity increases might not be realized unless workers' noneconomic needs were addressed.[9] But while it was recognized that workers might be more motivated if they were more involved, few managers were prepared to abandon the authoritarian style of management that enshrined managerial prerogatives. The Great Depression and the attendant high levels of unemployment weakened workers' bargaining power, leaving managers virtually free to structure work however they saw fit. When the economy picked up after World War II, workers were more emboldened, but their embrace of unionism resulted in a further segmentation of the division between managers and workers.

Business Unionism and the Further Erosion of Trust

The late 1940s was a period of considerable industrial unrest. Workers were flexing their collective muscles as they sought to regain some of the losses that they had incurred in the prewar decade. Firms were profitable following the stimulus of wartime production and the postwar boom. But they had to ensure continuous production, which necessitated a committed workforce. More and more, this was not the case.

As workers in the burgeoning mass production industries struggled to find a collective voice to articulate their grievances (pay, conditions of work, seniority, etc.), they increasingly embraced unionism. The old craft unions (AFL) had largely ignored the mass production industries because the workers were unskilled and (often) immigrants; admitting such workers would have devalued the craft status of the unions. However, a new organization, the Committee for Industrial Organization (CIO) that was founded in 1935, saw the potential of organizing such a large body of the workforce and proceeded to do so. As workers in steel, automobiles, coal mining, and tire manufacturing became organized, they resorted to work stoppages to press their claims. Such disruptions, which were extensive in the late 1940s, brought many of these industries to a standstill. Firms were forced to negotiate and recognize the new unions and collective bargaining became institutionalized across a wide range of manufacturing industries.

The pattern of bargaining that was established was quite distinctive and became known as *business unionism*.[10] Workers were permitted to bargain, via their union, over wages and benefits. Once agreement was reached, a contract was signed and workers and managers were bound to uphold its terms. During the term of the agreement workers were not allowed to strike. Work stoppages could only occur (at least legally) when the agreement expired and while a new agreement was negotiated. In fact, it was incumbent upon the union to enforce the no-strike rule during the period of the agreement.

Issues having to do with control of the workplace and the coordination of work (except for seniority rights) remained managerial prerogatives. Managers refused to give away what they felt were their basic authority rights. This separation of noneconomic and economic issues became the cornerstone of the industrial relations system. One could argue that it is a legacy of the individualism that pervades American culture. Managerial rights are essentially property rights that deem control accompanies ownership. This is what most managers believed.

Workers accepted the system insofar as they could share in the profits of sustained economic growth—which is what they did during the 1950s and 1960s. Rarely did they argue for codetermination in the workplace, except when workplace health and safety became an issue. Their commitment to work was a function of the size of their paychecks, plus other residual benefits that accrued with seniority. Performance was determined by productivity, not product quality. If managers were not prepared to treat workers with dignity and respect why, they thought, should they (workers) bother expending effort on ensuring a "job well done?"

This work climate was firmly rooted by the late 1960s. Managers viewed workers as inherently lazy and subject to constant monitoring and discipline. Their input into any decisions about the nature of work or product idiosyncrasies was to be kept to the minimum since they could not be trusted. While many workers were skilled, most manufacturing work required at best semiskilled workers. Because of the bulk of semiskilled workers, many managers asked, "What could a worker possibly have to say or contribute that would be of any use?" Decisions were made at the top of the hierarchy and information flowed downwards in the form of directives.

For workers, meanwhile, a similar lack of trust was endemic. Relationships with managers and supervisors were adversarial. Since bargaining focused on economic issues (wages and benefits) workers were determined to get as much as possible in these areas. When they couldn't obtain what they wanted they would strike. Even though strikes were deemed illegal during the tenure of a contract, it didn't prevent workers from engaging in unauthorized work stoppages (wildcat strikes) and work slowdowns (overtime bans). Even at work many expressed their dissatisfaction with conditions through subtle forms of sabotage. During the 1960s and early 1970s, the GM plant at Lordstown, Ohio, for example, witnessed repeated and systematic disruptive acts such as workers breaking off keys in car ignitions, putting sugar in gas tanks, and other vandalisms. Such behavior indicated the increasing worker frustration with assembly line work and further revealed the gulf that had developed between managers and workers.

STABILITY AT THE EXPENSE OF CREATIVITY

The type of work system established in the manufacturing sector and described above became paradigmatic for other industrial sectors. Workers were assigned routine tasks in a bureaucratic organizational hierarchy. Managers saw their function as one of control and coordination in a system that endowed them with legitimacy provided they could deliver the goods at the end of the day. They treated workers as a replaceable cost, to be motivated by a combination of fear (fire them if they don't perform) and wage incentives. Because skilled workers weren't really needed, it was not deemed necessary to invest heavily in worker training. When such investment occurred, workers often capitalized upon their newly acquired skills and left for better paying jobs elsewhere. This provided further disincentives for managers to embark upon such costly, and in many cases, futile programs. It also reinforced the prevailing view of the workplace that workers were a disposable commodity, and it further contributed to an atmosphere of distrust.

The benefit of a bureaucratic system of work organization is that it provides predictability and consistency. As in mass production, work would be organized around similar precepts and workers treated accordingly. As long as mass production was the norm, and there was no serious challenge to U.S. economic hegemony, such a system would persist. Admittedly, there were flaws as people lower down in the system periodically protested their subordinate status. But when times were good they could be bought off. During times of recession and higher unemployment they could be cowed into submission. Standardization, not creativity, was the mantra of this period.

Growth of System Tensions Become Inevitable

Arguably the individualism that underlies American culture might have predisposed workers not to embrace such a workplace organization. And yet competition has been enshrined as the hallmark for success and individual effort the guiding principle. Those that fall behind have only themselves to blame, according to this institutionalized rhetoric. As a consequence, many workers continued to accept this "alienating" work system because they lacked a meaningful alternative. Most still believed that if they worked hard they could accumulate the material goods that were increasingly viewed as the measure of success in a capitalist society.

This does not mean that resistance was absent—far from it. The work place became a breeding ground for labor-management tension that would prove corrosive to the system as a whole. Managers wanted to preserve their individualism and so did workers. Those that managed clung to the prerogatives of control that they deemed necessary and inevitable given their position. Those in a more subordinate status worked as hard as they needed to earn sufficient incomes, but also resisted, whenever possible, attempts that were made to control them. The former invoked their authority and knowledge to maintain the command and control culture typical of so many firms. The latter nurtured a culture of resistance in which individual interests were pitted against those of the firm (and ipso facto managers). The result was a workplace where discontent simmered, sometimes boiling over into industrial unrest, at other times manifesting itself simply through production problems.

Integrating Workers into a Productive System

The inherent contradictions in such a system, together with its weaknesses, were finally exposed beginning in the 1970s and through the 1980s. During this time, many American firms faced increased competition from abroad. But the new challenges represented a departure from the old way of doing business. As Japanese imports flooded the country, they were not only cheap but had a quality that often surpassed locally U.S. manufactured goods. When they were followed by low-priced imports from other Asian countries, warning bells rang aloud in many U.S. firms.

It appeared that other countries had taken the easily replicable mass production system and modified it to lower costs, improve quality, and speed product throughput. They had achieved this, in part, through organizational changes that involved a treatment of workers different to that often found in the United States. A more collaborative and cooperative workplace was evident on the Japanese assembly lines than in the American industrial heartland. The much-vaunted lean production systems pioneered by Toyota had managers and workers sharing a similar orientation to work. Consensus was the engine of growth in such organizations and a common culture integrated workers in various facets of the organization. Even though tasks were rigidly scripted in such factories, workers nonetheless had the responsibility and capability to initiate changes when necessary.[11] This has given Toyota its flexibility and consistency up to the present day.

Whatever problems existed under such a system—and it would be naïve on our part to assume that there weren't any—were nonetheless overshadowed by the obvious successes that it produced. By harmonizing work relations and eliciting effort around common goals, such firms eliminated much of the destructive divisiveness of American firms. Their success was obvious. Despite attempts to attribute such gains to the distinctiveness of Asian culture, it was apparent that changes needed to be made in the United States if manufacturing was to survive. Pleas for tariffs and quotas on imported goods might temporarily stave off imports, but they could not be a permanent solution to the problem. So what happened?

Lay Off Workers, Ignore the Root Cause

The initial response by many firms to the increased competition and the resultant decline in profitability was to lay off workers and cut wages and benefits. Throughout the 1980s and into the early 1990s many manufacturing firms underwent retrenchment and restructuring. Typically this meant shutting plants, laying off workers, or renegotiating contracts to cut wages and benefits. Workers were convinced into believing that they were the problem because labor costs were too high and union job classifications were too rigid. Firms wanted flexibility, but this usually meant the freedom to cut back on what workers were earning. It seemed that every time one picked up a newspaper in the 1980s, it had a story of more layoffs and plant closings. The industrial heartland was devastated. Steel mills employing several thousand workers shut in the Youngstown, Ohio, area, for example. Flint, Michigan, home to several large automobile parts and manufacturing facilities, witnessed similar job losses.

In most instances, firms claimed it was cheaper to relocate offshore where labor costs were lower and workers more pliant. In other instances, the motive was more duplicitous. If firms announced a restructuring and closed factories, Wall Street responded favorably and share prices rose. Senior management felt secure and reassured because the value of the company increased. In fact, CEOs' pay and job security appeared not to suffer despite profitability crises and the fact that large swathes of their work force were being laid off. Needless to say, such action did not go unnoticed among workers who saw such behavior as yet further evidence of managerial indifference to their plight.

By the early 1990s even white-collar workers were suffering in these restructuring programs. Since reengineering was being peddled as a panacea for most problems, firms were eager to embrace its harsh medicine. If it meant firing loyal and dedicated white-collar workers as well as those from the blue-collar ranks, so be it. The result was that it undermined what trust there was among lower level managerial workers, placing them in the same subordinate category as blue-collar workers.[12] The message was clear. People are expendable, regardless of their skill, commitment, or service. All of this was happening despite no clear evidence that reengineering produced the sorts of gains advocated by its exponents.[13]

The mass production system that resulted in a hierarchical and inflexible organizational culture was ill-equipped to meet the challenges posed by lean manufacturing introduced by Japanese car manufacturers and the increase of what Joseph Pine calls "mass customization."[14] Simply laying off workers was a simple short-term solution to cost cutting but not a viable strategy for long-term success.

A LEGACY OF FEAR AND DISTRUST

Today, countless numbers of employees still work under a set of legacy assumptions about how to treat workers. Downsizing has only added to the problem. In these downsized companies, the fear and distrust continue. This is bad business, say Jeffrey Pfeffer and Robert Stutton, authors of *The Knowing-Doing Gap*. They cite a 1994 Princeton Survey Research poll of 2,400 employed adults that found that one in six workers claims to have withheld a suggestion about improving work out of fear that it would cost someone a job. Illustrating what they argue is "the pervasiveness of fear and distrust,"[15] another large company they studied in 1997 revealed that:

- Only 47 percent of employees felt they could challenge accepted practices.
- Only 46 percent said they were sure of their jobs even if they continued to perform well.
- Only 45 percent thought management was interested in their well-being.
- Only 37 percent said "innovative ideas can fail without penalty to the originating person of work unit."

Although this chapter focuses on the role and perceptions of workers, the real problem is with the system, as Part III demonstrates. In a command and control setting there is no way for people to work together to make a team-driven environment. There are still too many reasons to hold back, collect a paycheck, and keep a low profile. This is the legacy of the command-and-control system.

However, when the system changes, perceptions of work are slowly altered. What we have seen in the past decade is a gradual realization of not only the need for structural changes in the way organizations function, but also an acknowledgment that people will matter more and more in the new workplace. Companies like Southwest Airlines or computer software maker SAS Institute have squarely predicated their success on building commitment from the ground up. This has involved careful staff selection, training, and attractive work conditions. But their success has also been based on establishing routines that permit workers discretion and routinized input into decision making—thus maximizing their effectiveness as employees. This, and a form of interactive leadership, mark the break from the old system to a new, emergent system where workers' talents are encouraged to flourish.

SUMMARY

This chapter has charted the growth of the command-and-control system that has been pervasive in American firms and its implications for workers in those firms. We have shown how the growth of such a system was in part made possible by treating workers as a variable cost. For managers, their task was how to maximize effort from such workers. Their solution was to treat workers as any other input that was manipulable. Workers meanwhile resisted such a tendency when they could (through strikes and sabotage) and when they couldn't, they allowed themselves to be bought off. The results were tensions, discontent, and a virtually institutionalized commitment to mediocrity.

Even when the competitive environment changed, many firms responded very slowly or retreated into more extreme versions of the old system. The paradigm of mass production predisposes managers to treat workers (people) in ways that are increasingly inappropriate to the demands of the new marketplace. In the next chapter we explore some of the ways firms have experimented and attempted to break from this system.

NOTES

1. Douglas McGregor, *The Human Side of Enterprise* (New York: McGraw-Hill, 1960), 43.

2. See Michael Best, *The New Competition* (Cambridge, MA: Harvard University Press, 1990).

3. Mauro Guillen, *Models of Management* (Chicago: University of Chicago Press, 1994).

4. Richard Edwards, *Contested Terrain* (New York: Basic Books, 1979).

5. Joseph A. Litterer, "Systematic Management: The Search for Order and Integration," *Business History Review* 35 (Spring 1961): 372.

6. Guillen, op. cit., 37.

7. Edwards, op. cit., chap. 7.

8. See Stephen P. Waring, *Taylorism Transformed* (Chapel Hill: University of North Carolina Press, 1991) for a good discussion of Taylor and his legacy.

9. See Guillen, op. cit., 58–59.

10. Ian Taplin "The Contradictions of Business Unionism and the Decline of Organized Labor," *Economic and Industrial Democracy*, II (1990): 249–278.

11. For a good discussion of how this paradox of rigidity and flexibility has been resolved, see Steven Spear and H. Kent Bowen, "Decoding the DNA of the Toyota Production System," *Harvard Business Review* (September/October, 1999): 97–106.

12. See Charles Heckscher, *White Collar Blues* (New York: Basic Books, 1995) for a discussion of the corresponding decline on managerial loyalty.

13. For example the work of Michael Hammer and James Champy, *Reengineering the Corporation* (New York: HarperCollins, 1993).

14. Joseph Pine, *Mass Customization* (Cambridge, MA: Harvard Business School Press, 1993).

15. Jeffrey Pfeffer and Robert Sutton, *The Knowing-Doing Gap* (Cambridge, MA: Harvard Business School Press, 1999).

7

A History of Teamwork-Driven Environments

In this chapter we trace the growth of teamwork-driven structures. We focus on how managers came to realize the faults of the old system but were unwilling to embrace a new one that would give workers more autonomy. Despite compelling evidence of the benefits of such new work systems, many firms resist the introduction of such practices, or adopt weak versions of them that are destined to fail.

Research literature, contrary to the popular business press, highlights a number of factors impeding the progress of teamwork. By looking at the research evidence, as well as examples that are perhaps less widely documented, we outline what makes a team environment work. We also document why many team environments fail.

EVOLUTION OF TEAMS AND TEAMWORK CONCEPTS

The notion of teamwork is central to U.S. culture. It draws from our love of sports and the idea that performance can be enhanced when everybody works together. Even team managers are either commended for being team players or chastised for not being so. So it comes as something of a surprise that teams as a structural concept have only recently been embraced by business managers. As vertical hierarchies are gradually being displaced by end-to-end business process solutions, organizations are being forced to adopt teamwork structuring.

This has not always been the case. Chapter 4 described the American life cycle in broad terms. The last chapter detailed the changing perception of work as industrial society matured. One of the defining characteristics of America's industrial past has been the emergence of mass production that resulted in a work organization that was rigid and hierarchical. Since manufactured products were standardized and produced in large quantities, workers who produced them required little in the way of skills. Managers designed the work process, told workers what to do, and then assigned supervisors to the shopfloor to ensure that they did it correctly. The actual work tasks were fragmented, specialized, and repetitive. Workers had little or no discretion in deciding what or how tasks could be done. The work was boring but the productivity increases that such a system produced allowed workers to be paid a reasonable wage for what was essentially unskilled or at best semiskilled work.

While the system had always had its detractors, its functional efficiency was very appealing to most managers because they retained control. Its precision derived from the detailed procedures, duties, and functions that were laid down. Rational procedures, organized systematically in an administrative hierarchy, ensured smooth functioning and avoided the pitfalls of ambiguity found in favoritism and nepotism.

At a time when mass markets and the demand for standardized goods of reasonable quality was continuously expanding (the post–World War II boom), the success of such a system was ensured and spawned the likes of AT&T, GM, and Exxon. As management education exploded in the United States in the 1960s, it sustained a belief in the efficacy of professional management.[1] Managers were the ones making decisions in firms because they alone had the organizational skills (and educational credentials) necessary to do so.

Notwithstanding such widespread beliefs and acceptance of the system, some had always questioned its true effectiveness. In the 1920s and 1930s, researchers working at Western Electric had discovered that relations among workers could affect their performance. They found not only that technical issues were important in determining productivity, but also that how the workers actually felt and related to each other at the workplace influenced their effectiveness. In what has now become a classic, F.I. Roethlisberger and W.J. Dickson in 1939 argued that more research needed to be done on the informal organization of the group, particularly the satisfactions and dissatisfactions of members, to determine its impact on overall organizational effectiveness.[2] From then on, the "human relations" perspective became a significant research area but not necessarily one that was adopted by organizations.

THE HUMAN SIDE OF ENTERPRISE

Belief in the need to treat employees fairly and with respect—if productivity was to be truly maximized—led to an interest in viewing workers as a resource that could be developed. Perhaps the best known advocate of this "human resource" approach is D. McGregor who attempted to conceptualize the value of recognizing employee needs through his Theory Y perspective.[3] According to Theory Y, since workers would like to take more responsibility for their work, and would be more fulfilled (and ipso facto more productive) if doing so, then firms should recognize the value of employee initiative and structure work accordingly. This contrasts with a Theory X perspective, prevalent at the time and an integral part of Fordism, that workers dislike work, want little if no responsibility at work, and simply want pay for unthinking task performance. Whereas the latter had resulted in a rigid, hierarchical workplace with managers (and technical experts) firmly in control of decision making, the former recognized the need to make jobs more interesting so that workers were more fulfilled at work.

The human side of enterprise views were further elaborated in the 1970s when other researchers argued that workers could be trusted to make important decisions about production issues over which only they have firsthand knowledge. Instead of merely making jobs more interesting and acknowledging the potency of social relations at work, attention shifted to actually soliciting worker input. Companies acknowledged that it is impossible for engineers or managers to know all of the technical details pertaining to work, let alone understand the intricacies of human dynamics in the workplace. Further, if workers were allowed input into routine decisions, such participation could improve overall organizational effectiveness. Exactly how much "participation" should be allowed has been difficult to specify, with some arguing for mere consultation with workers and others favoring decentralizing most decision making.[4] But the end result, albeit grudgingly accepted, has been the recognition that workers are an underdeveloped resource that could be more fruitfully tapped in the future. As one manager is reputed to have said, "We hired a pair of hands and much to our surprise also obtained a brain."

Pressures to Change

By the early 1980s many U.S. organizations were experiencing declining market share and reduced profits. Since Fordism as a system was easily replicable, many newly developing countries adopted the basic production techniques in their export-led industrialization drives. With plentiful supplies of unskilled labor, but at a fraction of the cost of U.S. workers, they could easily develop manufacturing capacity and then compete in hitherto U.S.-dominated markets. American workers were still the most productive in the world, but increasingly found themselves at a comparative disadvantage to their low-waged counterparts overseas. For as E. Appelbaum and R. Batt succinctly state, "Cumulative gains in productivity and reductions in cost on the basis of high-volume production of standardized products is no longer a sufficient basis of competitive advantage for most firms in the advanced industrialized economies."[5] It is not that the old system was discredited; it was merely that too many organizations with far lower input costs were imitating it successfully. The gradual managerial response to these problems varied but generally involved one of two approaches.

The Human Relations Model

The first response was squarely based on behavioral science theories that emphasized issues such as employee satisfaction as a key motivational determinant. It presumed that all members of an organization should share common goals and that the interests of both managers and workers were congruent. This response is best classified as the American human resource (HR) model, which became commonplace in many firms after the 1970s. In part it was an attempt to redesign the organization and avoid the conflictual bargaining that characterized many unionized workplaces. Employees were given more varied tasks and compensated on the basis of differential task performance. By tapping employee motivation and designing work tasks that would facilitate greater worker involvement and interest, firms hoped to become more efficient. The HR model also provided them with greater levels of flexibility than that provided in the rigid Fordist system. This model, it was argued, would improve organizations' competitive performance in both old and new markets.

While such a system sounds good in theory, in practice the results have been mixed. Since many of the new HR systems have been put in place in greenfield sites (e.g., GM's Saturn plant built from the ground up in rural Tennessee), it is difficult to determine whether improved performance comes from new work systems or merely new technology. While much of the research evidence suggests that absenteeism is lower under such new practices and that workers have fewer grievances, productivity gains are less clear-cut. Some have argued in fact that many of the performance gains have been accompanied by a suppression of workers' voices. In other words, the HR model may covertly undermine the effectiveness of collective bargaining by appealing to worker self-interest.[6] By atomizing worker interests (the appeal to individual effort and pecuniary gain), some claim that the HR model has eroded collectivist interests that formed the basis of union legitimacy. From a managerial viewpoint, the resiliency of such a system lies in its ability to limit "me-they" feelings and the conflict that often ensues with that sentiment. Organizational control remains, therefore, firmly rooted in managerial hierarchies, with the latter manipulating worker interests.

Back to the Efficiency Model

The second approach in response to declining market value does nothing more than fall back upon existing systems, trying to make them work better—an attempt to revitalize Fordism. Cost cutting, productivity drives through work intensification, downsizing, and outsourcing work have all been used by many firms as they attempt to stay competitive. While some organizations have introduced new technology as a substitute for labor, improved skill levels among workers have rarely accompanied such improvements. Instead of the existing workers being given the training and knowledge that might add to their improved effectiveness, many firms remain obsessed with cost cutting and continue to compete on the basis of low price. The routinized work practices of semiskilled and unskilled workers persist, embedded in the old hierarchy of control. Flexibility comes from subcontracting or outsourcing specific activities, particularly those that are low value-added. While core workers do the core activities in-house, other less predictable needs are often met by an external labor force. After decades of sustained commitment to the benefits of vertical integration, many organizations now pursue this form of vertical disintegration. But the basic Fordist mentality of seeking productivity improvements through more efficient use of "a pair of hands" persists, preventing many firms from the pursuit of more effective work practices.

Despite the persistence of downsizing as a productivity-enhancing strategy adopted by many firms, the results often point to its ineffectiveness. A 1992 survey by the American Manufacturer's Association found that downsizing often results in lower profits and declining worker productivity—precisely the opposite to what many firms had hoped. Not surprisingly, the problem that accompanies downsizing is declining worker morale and a drop in motivation. Motivation is difficult to sustain in a workplace culture more notable for fear than trust. Unfortunately for worker morale, much of the motivation for downsizing is driven by senior management's attempts to manipulate stock prices. In an effort to demonstrate the appearance of proactive strategies, firms announce that they will downsize and Wall Street responds by purchasing that company's stock, thus pushing the price (and the net value of the company) up. Meanwhile, back on the shopfloor, little has changed—that is, except the morale of the workers who were not fired in this round but who are fearful for their security when the next lot of heads roll.

In the face of such dismal results associated with human relations and efficiency, some firms have once more begun to think of ways to more meaningfully involve their employees. As the competitive environment changes, it has further exposed the weaknesses of a rigid system of mass production. But how can organizations gain flexibility and improve their overall performance? The answer appears to lie once more in the resource that has most often been overlooked: the workers themselves.

Other Failed Innovative Work-Practices

The list of publications extolling the virtues of teams and teamwork is long indeed. The business press is full of success stories, anecdotal information, and miscellaneous tidbits on the virtues of teams. Since the early 1990s, firms have been promised a capitalist New Jerusalem if only they adopt the innovative work practices associated with teamwork. This followed an earlier flirtation with "quality circles," which many argued underlie the success of Japanese manufacturers.

Quality circles, however, were doomed to fail. In an attempt to mimic the success of Japanese firms, American managers tried to imitate various features of Japanese work practices. Quality circles were identified as one such feature and were seen as a way to involve employees more in decision making. The essential premise of quality circles was that a group of employees (generally 6–12 volunteers) who received training in problem solving and statistical quality control, could meet regularly as a group to solve problems or recommend solutions to them. When they were introduced in the 1980s, however, they were found to be ineffective. On paper they sounded good and many suggested they were a move towards a more participative work culture. In reality, their achievements were more modest, and in many cases, as E.E. Lawlor and S.A. Mohrman argue, were destined to self-destruct as resources for their maintenance dwindled and they became less and less productive.[7] While an attempt at developing teamwork, quality circles simply imposed another structure on the existing organization, and because they were outside of the chain of command, they were doomed to failure. In this respect they follow a history of failed suggestion systems, cost reduction programs, and worker involvement schemes. Most input in these failed attempts went into a black hole or became tied up in bureaucratic fights between competing departments.

Managers themselves were often responsible for the failure of quality circles as midlevel managers ended up sabotaging them. Middle management was often the group responsible for implementing quality circles and other forms of employee participation. Under quality circles, shopfloor workers were deemed capable of making suggestions that could improve many aspects of the production process. If workers provided input, their suggestions, it was assumed, would be articulated by supervisory managers to upper management. In turn, upper management would be responsible for implementing the suggested changes. Not surprisingly, managers approached such a system in a less than enthusiastic way. If workers, earning say ten dollars an hour, were providing most of the meaningful input into improved operating efficiency, what was management's job?

Middle managers did one of two things. They either ignored the suggestions of line workers or they co-opted such suggestions, claiming them to be their own. In either case, the end result was the same. Workers lost interest in such a system, seeing it as yet another management fad which would not be beneficial to them. Since their suggestions were ignored or not acknowledged, why should they bother?

Quality circles faded, but it was into this impasse that the concept of teamwork-driven structures was introduced. Since many firms had downsized, they had inevitably shed layers of management. If operations were to continue to be lean, a way had to be found that would enable organizations to continue functioning with less day-to-day oversight of workers. These same firms were also facing increased market volatility, which meant they had to become more flexible. Yet flexibility often meant more complicated coordination at precisely the time when there were fewer supervisory personnel to facilitate this. How could organizations obtain more (in production, productivity, etc.) with less (managers and workers)? The answer appeared to lie in the use of workers in *permanent* self-managed teams.

PERMANENT SELF-MANAGED TEAMS FOR COORDINATION

There are many instances of firms that have introduced some form of teamwork or made workplace innovations that involve giving more autonomy and decision-making powers to the workers themselves. Such practices are designed to enhance worker participation (which returns us to the motivation issue), break down the rigid work practices of mass production, and decentralize managerial tasks. To be successful, such efforts require goal clarity, adequate training for workers involved, clear task delineation, and appropriate rewards for such workers. Ideally, assignments should be flexible and broadly defined; there should be employment security and very clear mechanisms for dispute resolution. Management must support the endeavor with resources and personnel to facilitate communication, coordination, and collaboration within the team and between the team and its outside constituencies.[8] In sum, a different workplace culture must replace the traditional rigid and hierarchical one, with cooperation rather than conflict becoming the modus vivendi.

The driving force behind the above changes is the idea of treating workers as a primary resource rather than a secondary one meant simply to accomplish work. This is nothing new, since many of the ideas are grounded in the earlier assumptions about the human side of enterprise. Once again, though, managers have discovered that if work is challenging and requires using shopfloor knowledge, workers will work harder. If that work provides them with feedback, and they are given the necessary training to make good decisions, then they will work more efficiently.

To reiterate, the key issue in teamwork involves granting decision-making capabilities to workers and self-managing teams who usually are the most familiar with daily operating problems. Letting them decide on how best to solve problems is quicker and cheaper than having managers or supervisors do it for them. And finally, for permanent self-managed teams to be successful, organizations have found all of the innovative practices need bundling together with managers fully supporting and facilitating the endeavor. Successful change is systemic, not partial. Failure often comes when new work practices are only introduced in selected individual areas.

The Research Literature Sheds Light

Because innovative teamwork practices vary, the research literature can shed light on what works. In the last decade there have been a number of case studies of firms that have introduced some form of teamwork.[9] In most instances this has involved the introduction of teams and fewer job classifications. Generally speaking, the results of such changes have been positive, with firms reaping gains in productivity and quality. Although such programs are costly, productivity gains usually offset such investments and in some cases teams have enabled firms to dramatically reduce overall production costs. With higher sales per employee in other instances, such practices have also increased firm profitability.

In general, workers appear to like working in teams, preferring the increased autonomy and lack of omnipresent supervision. They indicate a higher level of motivation and a willingness and enthusiasm to tackle problems. However, some complain that they have not been adequately trained to deal with the new levels of decision making and in these instances report heightened levels of stress. But this indicates incomplete implementation of a team-driven operating philosophy. Those that report a high degree of job satisfaction have received additional training. They are also able to increase their own earnings capacity and therefore perceive a tangible benefit from the changes. This is important since many previous innovations provided gains for the organization but little in the way of rewards for individual workers.

In addition, with self-managed work teams, the reduction in the number of supervisors needed for task coordination has not only cut costs but also removed an often contentious feature of the supervisory process. Under cross-functional teams, workers coordinate their own activities—with internal upstream suppliers and downstream internal customers—and meet pre-established commitments. Although workers generally work harder in team-based structures, they report feeling more "liberated" and enthusiastic about work.

How Widespread Are Innovative Work Practices?

In a recent summary article, Paul Osterman used data from a 1992 survey of U.S. manufacturing establishments to examine the incidence of innovative work practices (teams, quality circles, job rotation, and total quality management).[10] He found that the majority of firms sampled have adopted at least one of these new work practices. Firms that are most likely to innovate are those that are in internationally competitive markets or that have technologically sophisticated production processes that require a high level of worker skill. Additionally, those firms that compete on a broad basis (for example in service and quality) are more likely to innovate than those who pursue low-cost competitive strategies. Finally, improved financial performance is associated with firms that have introduced a bundle of innovative work practices.

Osterman, however, also notes that few firms have introduced an integrated set of new practices. An integrated system is more than just a few new practices since it attempts to align the people, process, and purpose of a firm in an interdependent relation. Failed change programs usually address only one element, such as reengineering (process), but ignore the impact on people or purpose. New strategies are often put in place in an attempt to help a floundering change program, but failed implementation limits their effectiveness. In order to reap the extensive gains promised by such innovations, firms must adopt an integrated approach and not rely upon piecemeal changes. Most firms, it seems, try the latter—known as "flavor of the month" initiatives—but are reluctant to embark on the former. An integrated approach means dealing with the "sacred cows": tradition, culture, and an ingrained mind-set of "this is how we have always done it."

Limits of the Research Findings

How effective are innovative practices when implemented? Despite the plethora of journalistic commentary on teams and the new workplace and the occasional academic study such as that listed above, reliable data are lacking. What is conspicuously lacking are rigorous studies evaluating the long-term impacts of such innovations and the extent to which they have been comprehensively implemented. Even the "scientific" studies are fraught with methodological problems, often because a control group is not available against which to measure innovations. The following are some of the major problems:

• First of all, it is not clear whether the firms that have introduced such practices have better quality/trained workers than those that don't. Likewise, one could make the same argument for quality of management. In other words, explaining

the success of teamwork in an innovative firm might have more to do with the
characteristics of the workers and managers than the new system itself.

- Second, if the performance benefits of teamwork are low, how much of that can
  be attributed to the fact that the firm was already in trouble? Since troubled firms
  are more likely to innovate than successful ones, an otherwise successful new team
  system might appear to be a failure. In seems as if many firms innovate when all
  other attempts at efficiency gains have failed. Because of this, the larger sample
  of failed team systems has more to do with the tenuous position of the firms than
  the system effectiveness itself.
- Third, many firms partially implement team systems or go through the initial
  motions only to abandon them later. We don't know whether systemic problems
  or lack of managerial intent causes such inconclusiveness. Do teams fail to live
  up to their earlier goals because they are inappropriate to the setting (say for
  instance they don't really fit a particular type of manufacturing)? Or do they fail
  because the gains are longer term than management is prepared to wait, and they
  are dropped before realizing the long-term benefits?
- Fourth, do they fail because they have not been comprehensively introduced, with
  midlevel managers tinkering in ways that limit their effectiveness?

These are all difficult to deduce from the case study evidence. We know
that firms often abandon teamwork, claiming poor performance gains. But
what we don't know are the full range of reasons outside the actual functioning of the team system that might have contributed to that failure. Is
it a systemic problem or a cultural one? The resilience of the command and
control system suggests that many mangers might be extremely reticent
about introducing the full range of activities associated with permanent
cross-functional teams. In other words what is often the most contentious
issue is in fact the difficulty of changing workplace culture.

CHANGING THE WORKPLACE CULTURE

While the exact performance benefits of teams are difficult to estimate,
there are several widely cited problems that account for their non-
implementation in organizations.

First, the costs of implementation might outweigh the benefits of teamwork. Firms with high turnover rates, for example, are reluctant to invest
in the necessary training to make teams successful. In other cases, technological alternatives such as automation might result in greater gains than
those of teamwork. Relatedly, perhaps there are certain types of industries
or manufacturing processes that do not lend themselves to teamwork. Conceivably Fordist systems might continue to be most efficient, especially
when long runs of standardized products are the norm.

Second, many firms have such strong cultural heritages that any systemic change is extremely difficult. Strong cultures, often associated with strong leaders, are the most difficult to alter. Even incremental changes in such conditions are very difficult. Relatedly, many individuals who are powerful in an organization resist innovations because they might undermine upper level positions. Given a choice, managers not surprisingly would usually prefer to continue doing things in the same old ways.

Third, even when teamwork changes are implemented, workers sometimes resist them. The latter view such innovations with suspicion, believing that they might result in lost jobs or harder work. Without the support of workers, the entire system collapses from within. Workers also fear for their own security, which was well defined and systematized under the command and control hierarchy. Older workers tenaciously hold onto the seniority rights that teamwork often subverts. Even if it is apparent that the new system will improve not just productivity but also individual payment, many workers simply mistrust managers. A virtually institutionalized "me and they" culture of conflict is difficult to shake off.

Finally, there are many broader institutional factors that can impede innovation. Wall Street's commitment to short-term growth is seen by many senior managers as a disincentive to making investments for long-term growth and performance. For many it is easy to engage in short-term cost cutting that appeals to investors. The results are quite dramatic and such action is usually rewarded by increased share prices. In reality, there are few institutional market mechanisms that reward longer term thinking of the type necessitated by teamwork. A similar problem occurs with many reengineering efforts that were designed to be efficiency enhancing but in the long run proved to be costly programs. Furthermore, 80 percent of all reengineering efforts failed in the early 1990s because the human element was not adequately addressed in the implementation plans. And because of management-leadership's failure to align employees in ways that permit successful strategy execution, thirty-six CEOs from Fortune 500 companies were relieved of their jobs in the last ten years.[11]

SUMMARY

The mass production system that spawned the command-and-control approach to management at the turn of the last century was arguably necessary given the low skill levels of most workers. But it was also the product of the new profession of management and reflected the desire of newly minted managers to establish their authority (and control) in the workplace. Since quantity of production took precedence over quality, and standardization was the operating norm, managers embraced the emerging hierarchical system and used it to consolidate their status. Periodic attempts to recognize the value of employee's brains rather than just their hands had limited success. As long as the U.S. economic hegemony remained intact, there was little pressure to change the system.

That pressure to change came in the late 1970s, following the massive increase of imported manufactured goods into the United States and the emerging efficiency of countries such as Japan with different work place cultures. At first overseas manufacturers offered both low cost *and* quality for standardized goods. Then, they demonstrated an ability to produce more customized goods at favorable prices. Forced to respond to this new competitive challenge, many U.S. manufacturers rediscovered their human resource assets and set about ways to build more participative cultures in the work place.

The evolution to a team-driven culture is not clear-cut. The research data is spotty about what works, pointing to many variables that can derail the best of intentions. One factor that stands out above all others when firms attempt a transition to teamwork structures is top-management's failure to take a holistic approach to change. They put together piecemeal process elements, human resource initiatives, or changes in strategic direction. Rarely do they recognize and tackle all three as a system.

NOTES

1. Louis A. Allen, *Professional Management: New Concepts and Proven Practices* (New York: McGraw-Hill, 1973).

2. F.I. Roethlisberger and W.J. Dickson, *Management and the Worker* (Cambridge, MA: Harvard University Press, 1939).

3. D. McGregor, *The Human Side of Enterprise* (New York: McGraw Hill, 1960).

4. See E. Lawler, *High Involvement Management* (San Francisco: Jossey Bass, 1986) and D.I. Levine and L. D. Tyson, "Participation, Productivity and the Firm's Environment," in A. Blinder, ed., *Paying for Productivity* (Washinton, DC: Brookings Institution, 1990).

5. E. Appelbaum and R. Batt, *The New American Workplace* (Ithaca: ILR Press of Cornell University, 1994).

6. Ibid., 19–21.

7. E. E. Lawlor and S.A. Mohrman, "Quality Circles After the Fad," *Harvard Business Review* (January–February 1985): 65–71.

8. See D.E. Yeatts and C. Hyten, *High-Performance Self Managed Work Teams* (Thousand Oaks: Sage, 1998), 47–50.

9. See C. Ichniowski, T. C. Kochan, D. Levine, C. Olson, and G. Strauss, "What Works at Work: Overview and Assessment," in *Industrial Relations* (1996, 35/5): 299–333.

10. Paul Osterman, "How Common Is Workplace Transformation and Who Adopts It?" in *Industrial and Labor Relations Review* (1994, 47/4): 173–188.

11. Ram Charan and Geoffrey Colvin, "Why CEOs Fail," *Fortune*, 21 June 1999, 68.

8

From Compliance to Commitment:
A Case Study

Under the old command-and-control system, morale, commitment, and motivation were frequent problems in the workplace. Because workers were systematically denied any formal input into the decision-making process, they developed a "me-they" view of management that resulted in major conflicts between labor and management. In addition, the workers who knew the most about all of the intricate details that could result in company failures were discouraged from sharing their information. The system was one that did not encourage workers to take pride in what they produced. They were no longer craft workers, for whom intrinsic satisfaction in task performance resulted in quality production.

Yet there are some firms that have not only demonstrated a commitment to their workers but also flourished by squarely predicating their strategic goals around such an emphasis. The current list of "best companies to work for" is full of firms that have sought to unleash the huge potential of their workers. It has become increasingly evident that the new workplace requires flexibility and quality together with cost-effectiveness, neither of which is possible unless the worker has a more expansive involvement with his/her job than what occurred in the old command and control workplace. While the transition from one system to the other takes many routes and differing amounts of time, success tends to stick. In this chapter we document one of the many success stories that followed such a system shift. The story of this small boat company demonstrates the type of commitment building that will be crucial for the emerging workplace. This company was able to move workers from their simple compliance with company rules and authority to a true commitment toward the work they accomplished.

LEADERSHIP ON THE OCEAN WAVES

In 1989 a manufacturer of yachts in a medium-sized town in southwestern England was on the threshold of bankruptcy. It had been in business for almost eighty years and had employed as many as 220 workers. By 1989 the workforce had shrunk to 105. It was struggling to compete in a saturated market, facing competition from overseas that was far cheaper than each of the boats in its three lines. It also faced domestic competition that was far better in quality and in the speed in which new orders could be filled.

The owners were largely absent from the factory. Daily responsibility for running the production fell to a production manager and a plant manager. Each had been there for over fourteen years, and both subscribed to the classic command and control view of production. Workers were mistrusted even though many of the tasks were skilled and involved scrupulous attention to detail. Quality was poor, production inconsistent. A previous attempt to "restructure" production had resulted in some changes and managers calling for more participation (which usually meant more effort) from the workers. But the managers' idea of participation was to inform several of the supervisors who in turn told the workers how they should participate. Not surprisingly, workers saw the strategy as a sham and continued working and loafing in the same old way. Absenteeism was high and turnover among the younger recent hires was rampant.

When the owners decided to sell, the purchase price was equivalent to that found in a "bargain basement" sale. Even then, few were interested in such an obvious white elephant, despite the brand potential that was probably the company's major asset. When it was bought by two young sailing enthusiasts who in their own words "had more money than sense," even fewer thought the business would survive. The two owners had inherited some money and loved to sail and play around in boats, but they had no experience either in running a company of this size or manufacturing the boats they sailed.

Their first acts were to fire the managerial staff, reduce the production staff to seventy and concentrate on manufacturing two lines. They took over the daily managerial functions, sharing various tasks, and doing others individually according to their skills. The workers that were retained were older, established, and skilled. Many had worked for the company for most of their lives. These workers were disillusioned and skeptical about the new owners' ability to run the factory. They stayed because in many instances they were too old to get an equal paying job elsewhere.

After several months, during which time the hemorrhaging red ink had been somewhat stayed, the owners called a meeting of everyone in the factory. It was, as one of the workers said, "a memorable event." They told the workers that they loved to sail and wanted to build boats that they would enjoy sailing themselves. They went on to say that the people who knew most about the building of boats were assembled around them. All of those accumulated years of knowledge must, they said, be able to be put to good use to save the company. "Tell us how to build beautiful boats and what you need to do it," said one of the owners. "We have some great designs but they can only become marketable designs if they're built properly," he went on to add. They told them that they had a five-year plan in which time they hoped to be profitable. If by that time they were not, they would have to sell the company. During that time they needed to build better boats, market them more effectively, and find ways of making modifications as and when necessary. They had to incorporate design changes efficiently which meant the workers had to become part of a problem-solving network.

The workers were cautious. They understood what the new owners were saying, but wondered what was in it for them. They had heard all this before, albeit in a somewhat different form, from the previous management. How would this be different? How serious were the two owners about soliciting input from them? As one of the workers said, "we wanted actions not more gestures."

With employees' suggestions, production lines were rejigged, a form of quality circles was introduced, and pay-for-performance systems were recalibrated to take into account quality as well as productivity. A form of profit sharing was introduced but would not become operable for three years since there weren't any profits initially. The owners promised to share information with the workers, and said to them, "Tell us what you need and we will make sure you have it." Most workers remained skeptical, but two events proved to the workers that a new regime had truly arrived.

There are many perks associated with managerial work but few are typically available for workers. In the yachting industry, attending boat shows in big cities or glamorous locations is clearly one such benefit. But when the first big show was coming up, the owners asked the workers to elect two of their fellows whom they felt would be able to best represent the company at the show and talk about the boats. After some deliberation (and incredible confusion and excitement) two workers were duly elected and dispatched (along with two boats) to the show. Although new orders were not significantly higher than in previous years, the company was the talk of the trade for having done this. Other owners called to comment on the fact that these two representatives were always at the booth, working diligently and enthusiastically. As one said, "They worked far harder than our sales managers did and seemed to really know what they were talking about."

Other workers in a similar fashion attended subsequent shows. After a while a subtle competition developed between the workers, with each group trying to sell more boats than the previous groups. Orders increased after two years. Defects dropped and productivity increased. Even the two owners were surprised at the high level of commitment by the workers who went to the shows. The workers came back reporting on ways to improve the boats *and* ways to lower costs for the boat shows. Their hotel and food bills were 30 percent lower than those of a similar number of managers who had attended under the previous ownership.

In the third summer after their purchase the new owners made another proposal to the workforce. The demand for boats is seasonal, with spring and early summer often the busiest time for orders. The Mediterranean coast (particularly southern France, Italy, and the Greek Islands) is a prime area to market new boats. The owners decided to send one of their new designs down there, to try and build up some interest. They suggested to the workers that from May until July the boat should be crewed by two workers, on a two-week rotation. The firm would fly them out and back, and would pay for their basic expenses as long as they stayed in port as much as possible and did their best to market the new boat. Again, it was up the workers to decide who should go and what the daily schedule would be (the actual ports to be visited were determined by one of the owners following market analysis).

Although the move was not always popular with family members, it was a great success for the firm, and hugely enjoyed by the workers who went. The firm obtained a number of new orders and captured the attention of the yachting press. Several very flattering articles about the firm and its boats were subsequently published, which helped push up sales in the following two years. The workers loved the experience and admitted that they worked far harder on such an assignment than when back home in the factory. Most importantly, they commented on how much they felt part of the company. As one of them says: "We were talking with this wealthy businessman in Monaco, explaining the new features of the boat and took him out on it. I noticed that we kept talking about 'our' boat, and what 'we' were building. It's kind of stupid but for the first time in sixteen years since I've worked here, I actually felt pride in what we'd built. Me and the company, it's like the same thing."

For the first time they said they felt they were really trusted by the managers. They were given a huge amount of freedom and they took it with the utmost responsibility. The company has repeated this endeavor in subsequent years and sees it as a very useful marketing tool. The costs of flying the men back and forth and paying their expenses are offset by the marketing and sales benefits, as well as by the massive increase in commitment by the workers.

WHAT DOES THIS TELL US?

The lesson of this story is about how to utilize a workforce as a resource. People must be made a part of a firm's competitive advantage, very much as Jeffrey Pfeffer, in his book *Competitive Advantage through People*, has argued.[1] The boat company's story illustrated that if companies want to integrate their numerous activities, they need commitment, and to build commitment, they need leadership.

Trust Is a By-product of Leadership

If leaders are to escape the adversarial relationships that have characterized so much of the industrial sector, they have to find ways to build bridges between what managers do and what workers desire. To do this, managers have to treat workers as if they are capable of thinking *and* managers have to give them opportunities to be independent. The two new owners of the boat company were forced to do this because they had neither the skills nor the experience to do otherwise. But they recognized the importance of people in their organization. They knew the workers were the keys to their success but they also had to find a way to harness that accumulated knowledge. They did this by being honest with them up front, sharing information with them, being brutally frank about future potential, and then turning the decision making over to them.

Admittedly, not every worker liked this arrangement. Some quit, and more than a few were fired in the first few months. But since the two owners said they would share whatever information the workers requested about firm performance, most of the workers stayed and re-focused their efforts because they started to believe what the owners were saying. This was not just another reengineering effort, full of rhetoric, but short on benefits.

It took more than a few months for the boat company to build this trust. Day by day and week by week, actions cemented the intent of the owners. Gradually the workforce came around, but it took several years before the company began to reap the financial rewards. Only in the fourth year did they make a profit, but since then sales have increased at approximately 16 percent annually.

Empowerment Creates the Conditions for Participation

As the boat company example shows, the energy for change must come not from above but from the workers themselves. Working under a new system in which their activities were defined as interdependent rather than fragmented, and with a clear sense of the importance of their role in the finished product, their tasks became more fluid and dynamic. This is similar to what others have termed "task alignment," where the energy for change focuses upon the work itself rather than abstract conceptualizations such as "participation" or "culture."[2] Companies create new behaviors not by talking about them but by practicing them.

When there is a clear identification with organization *purpose*, workers tend to perceive what the situation requires and to do it whether management exerts influence to have it done or not. In fact, managers need not be present or even aware of the immediate circumstances. Workers could not help but participate because their survival, and that of the firm, depended on it. A willingness to trust the workforce has long-term implications, and for our boat company example, after the initial impetus for change came from above, its implementation and subsequent institutionalization was sustained from below. This is the concept of empowerment at work.

The boat company is an example of true participatory management. Workers were encouraged to make key decisions and when they did so they were fully accountable for their actions. Sometimes they made mistakes, but whenever this happened they were not punished or treated in a punitive fashion. One of the owners was adamant about telling them to experiment, take chances, and learn from mistakes ("but don't," as he said, "sink any of the **** boats in the Med!!").

Training and Knowledge Acquisition

Fortunately, the boat company had a core group of highly skilled workers. They were able to do what was required of them in most new assignments. However, whenever new skills were needed, workers self-selected for training programs. Some even took draftsmanship courses at a local college in the evenings (on their own time, but at company expense). The owners recognized that skill development should be ongoing and the firm showed a commitment to it by encouraging workers to become "learning centered." They created a management process that encouraged a group of younger new employees to apprentice themselves to older workers. The latter, in turn, were encouraged to mentor the recent hires. Such training is vital not just to establishing commitment but to sustaining it over the long run. It demonstrates a belief in workers as valuable assets that need to be continually developed.

Natural Work Groups Produce Positive Action

Once the boat company owners established trust, they concentrated on reinforcing it through task interdependency. Instead of treating workers in an atomistic fashion, typical of the hyper-individualism shown in many companies, natural work groups were constructed so that workers depended more and more on each other. They worked together on projects and took joint ownership of them. Not only did they acquire pride in the completed product, they began to conceptualize work not in discrete tasks but in a more holistic fashion. As individuals they worked together efficiently in order to maximize the effectiveness of the overall team processes. They thereby created the problem-solving networks that would be crucial to the company's attaining the requisite quality levels.

A Long-term Approach

Key to the whole undertaking at this company was the commitment by the owners to take a long-term approach. They recognized the difficulty of becoming profitable in the short term. Their goals would take time to accomplish. There would be no easy, short-term fixes that could miraculously turn the firm around. In fact they soon realized that they would have to take short-term losses in order to build a stronger and more competitive company for the long term.

Since they were a privately owned company they did not face short-term pressures so acutely experienced by managers in public companies. There were no institutional investors who needed to be placated by immediate earnings and hefty dividends. The company floated on the owners' money; as long as it lasted the company could survive. In that sense they were fortunate. But they also had to face the crisis of creativity/profitability and the stark reality of going bankrupt should they fail. Other managers might lose their jobs; these two stood to loose everything.

As the firm reapplied a directive style of management, they laid off the inefficient workers and cut costs. Many firms going through a restructuring stop there since it has a dramatic effect on the balance sheet. But the boat company owners went further and offered implicit guarantees of employment security to those that remained. Provided the firm stayed in business, they said everyone would have a job. Furthermore, worker pay would be the last to be cut. Once again, this perspective demonstrated the commitment that the owners had to the workers in the long run. Their example shows how workers reciprocated with their own commitments.

A Teamwork-Driven Community

Workers in the boat company clearly thought of themselves as being important and took pride in what they did. They felt as if they were in it with the owners for the long haul. They were treated with respect, their opinions were courted, and their input solicited. They believed in the firm because the firm believed in them. This is a form of what Pfeffer aptly calls "symbolic egalitarianism."[3] But it is more than a sense of equality that is pervasive and symbolic. It is different from just abolishing executive dining rooms or having everyone wear a blue smock. Here, *a community of intent* was created and it produced a teamwork-driven culture. As in any community, shared norms and values sustain the integrity of work that is done together.

This company is probably not unique in recognizing the importance of one of its major assets—its workforce. But in soliciting input it did something that many companies are reluctant to do. It didn't just try to keep the good jobs and eliminate the bad ones. It delegated much of the responsibility for decision making to the groups and individuals most capable of exercising it. By encouraging participation among the workers that stayed with the company, it created an environment in which they could express their concerns without feeling threatened. Likewise the managers did not feel their authority compromised. This is the sort of cooperative workplace that harnesses creative effort more effectively than the old command-and-control model ever could, no matter how many supervisors were on the shopfloor.

In a recent study, Richard Freeman and Joel Rogers conducted a survey of workers and managers in America to find out what sort of workplace they wanted.[4] Remarkably, both groups indicated similar preferences—for a workplace that is jointly run by managers and workers. It is perhaps not surprising that workers wanted to be able to share in problem solving and have cooperative relations with management; to have more responsibility (and training) in making decisions and participating more meaningfully in day-to-day operations; and still have some independence from management. What is remarkable is that a large number of managers expressed a similar set of preferences, with the major exception being that they opposed unions. Workers, for their part, believe that a firm's efficiency can be improved by such worker participation. And while managers still want to exercise final decision-making authority, many managers nonetheless believe that a firm's performance could be improved by allowing workers a greater say.

Not only do we find a situation where, as Freeman and Rogers state, "workers have consistent views on, and strong desires for, a workplace relations system quite different from what now exists,"[5] many managers are less and less inclined to display antipathy to such an ideal system. But for such a system to be implemented, both leadership vision and perhaps the sort of crisis that afflicted the boat company are needed.

While the boat company rebounded, its next task is to build a solid foundation of performance management—the bedrock upon which future growth depends. Natural leadership can take this company only so far. With sales increasing, hiring on the upswing, production volumes doubling, and a healthy marketplace for the company's boats, focus must shift internally to the company's infrastructure.

There are many firms, some well known like Maytag and Southwest Airlines, many small and anonymous as the boat company case we describe, that have built trust and commitment. Although there will always be people for whom such an environment is unacceptable, the important thing to note is that when firms report people problems they either have the wrong operating philosophy and the right people, or the right people-centered philosophy and the wrong people. Usually it is the former. People typically are not the problem; it's the system of control. In the next chapter we describe in detail the type of system needed not only by the boat company, but by any company making the transition to a teamwork-driven structure. We also describe how to make such a system—a performance management system—run.

SUMMARY

This chapter describes how people-centered management requires a different organizational structure. Instead of a rigid structure delimiting individual activity and consigning employees to routine and repetitive tasks, it needs a fluid framework that allows for creativity and networking between groups. Gone is the machine imagery that is the antithesis of flexibility and commitment. In its place—as this case describes—is a hierarchy of respect. Authority is embedded in an organizational culture that thrives on commitment, with decision making residing in the hands of those deemed most capable of exercising it. Instead of expending effort and resources to control employees, dynamic organizations such as the one described above endeavor to reenergize such a resource and capitalize upon its potential. The surface benefits gained by tinkering with the old systems are not solutions to long-term competitive problems.

NOTES

1. Jeffrey Pfeffer, *Competitive Advantage through People* (Boston: Harvard Business School Press, 1994).
2. Michael Beer, Russell Eisenstat, and Bert Spector, "Why Change Programs Don't Produce Change," *Harvard Business Review* (November–December 1990): 158–67.
3. Pfeffer, op. cit., pp. 48–50.
4. Richard Freeman and Joel Rogers, *What Workers Want* (Ithaca, NY: Cornell University Press, 1999). This book reports on the results of a "Worker Representation and Participation Survey" that they conducted in the mid-1990s in the U.S.
5. Freeman and Rogers, op. cit., p. 8.

9

When Span of Control Becomes Span of Communication

The technology life cycle trends identified in Chapter 2 and graphically depicted in Figure 2.3 predict the 55-year embryonic beginnings of the Internet. This technology with its Web-based links is connecting millions of people and organizations. As Part I discussed, organizations today are being networked at an increasing pace. Their functions are intricately tied to and dependent on other organizations. The organization itself is composed of components that function like mini-organizations within the larger framework.

Not surprisingly, a premier challenge faced by such externally and internally networked organizations is communication across all the teams and functions. How can all the diverse yet related components of an organization talk to one another? How can communication successfully turn the organization into an efficient forward-thinking organism? This chapter addresses these questions in the context of the explosion of technological advances in communication that continues today. It also addresses how companies have dealt with the massive shift in the availability and use of information that have come with increases in communication technology and the growth of supply-chain management.

In the 1990s, global companies instituted major changes to become and remain competitive internationally. They restructured their organizations by downsizing bloated hierarchies to achieve a horizontal, more efficient organization. By reengineering enterprise processes and aligning them with strategic goals, they streamlined so they could work more efficiently with fewer resources. To support the new organizational structures, they in-

Figure 9.1
The Supply Chain in a Performance Management System

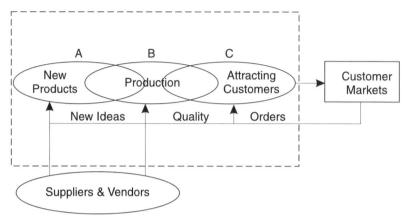

vested heavily in all kinds of technology infrastructures, from hardware and databases to enterprise planning software and other strategic initiatives—ranging from customer management to distribution and vendor procurement systems.

All these changes in organizational structure have fundamentally altered the role of remaining managers. The "span of control" of the command-and-control model has given way to "communication spans"—this is the number of people that can stay in touch with one another through e-mail, teleconferencing, and a good information system. However, such a communication system is only as effective as the management system that underlies it. Figure 9.1 illustrates a horizontal view of a company functioning within a performance management system. It provides several advantages over the traditional vertical organization in that it focuses on three key elements: the process flow of work, supplier inputs, and the customer. Critical interfaces, which occur in the "white spaces" on a traditional organization chart, become visible in the horizontal view. Notice that the lateral view documents how work actually gets done. It indicates the external and internal customer-supplier relationships through which results are produced. The lateral view also clarifies the critical importance of communication between elements. Clear and efficient communication is crucial to the efficient production of work.

The company boundary in Figure 9.1 is designated by dashed lines. The figure indicates that function B is an internal customer of function A and an internal supplier of function C. To maximize efficiencies, a good process management system is needed to optimize the hand-offs between these different entities. Business value-chain software assists in this job by increasing communication. Horizontal functions are integrated with new software tools that track performance, turning operating data into monthly operating statistics and financials that can be quickly communicated across functions.

CHANGES IN MANAGEMENT STYLE

The horizontal organization is front-loaded with a multitude of suppliers and vendors who assist in new product development in addition to supplying parts. They, like customers, are outside company boundaries. As supply-chain management works its way into corporate America, communication is increasingly needed to strengthen ties with outsiders. From automobiles to personal computers to fashion retailing, global competition is restructuring how organizations communicate. As companies focus on their core competencies and outsource the rest, their success rests on their ability to stay in touch with parts of the supply chain over which they have no command authority. To do this job, managers must develop a different system of relationships and learn to manage a new set of realities. Throughout the history of supply-chain management, the nature of communication has increasingly diversified—from talking with suppliers to integrating operating systems and customizing customer interfaces.

In the 1980s, arms-length relationships were the norm with suppliers. Partnerships formed primarily to improve cost and quality. In today's faster paced markets, the focus has shifted to innovation, flexibility, and speed with ever closer strategic alliances. In essence, supply-chain management is about working with suppliers as team members, letting them design components, and together shortening the delivery cycle. Supply-chain management requires "reaching into the suppliers" to ensure that things happen on time and at the right quality level. Managing a network of suppliers is very different from managing workers over which managers have command authority. For example, it requires management-leadership not to grind the vendor for cost reductions. Old style management can't force things to happen in this new age of vendor partnerships. But the good news is that work redesign and the digital revolution have combined to make the job easier. Product managers, production teams, and buyers are all able to peer into one another's production schedule to coordinate, share data, and to make decisions in real time.

ELECTRONS AND NETWORKING

Two high profile companies, Cisco Systems and General Electric, have created vast electronic networks linking their internal operations with those of suppliers—reaping substantial savings of time and inventory costs.[1] Not surprisingly, these types of benefits do not come without a lot of hard work. For example, Xerox, together with the help of Oracle, began mapping business and supply-chain processes in an attempt to cut costs and stay in business. Both soon realized they had more than 50 strategy systems, 100 planning systems, 100 different supplies acquisition systems, 50 building systems, 50 configuring systems, 50 inventory systems, and 150 material-moving systems. After the investigation phase, it was clear that in order to survive Xerox needed to move these multiple legacy systems to a common integrated digitized software suite for enterprise-wide resource planning.

However, computer software isn't always the first step necessary to improving supply-chain management. For example, a company may get by with little sophisticated computer software as it works out the process. For instance, Li & Fung is Hong Kong's largest export trading company. It has only 50 buyers making hundreds of individual transactions flipping data between 350 customers and 7,500 suppliers around the world. Li & Fung has perfected supply-chain management by focusing on the high value-added tasks such as design and quality control, while subcontracting the lower value-added tasks of production to small suppliers. They do not have bricks and mortar on their balance sheet, but instead invest in building personal relationships with suppliers and customers. They pride themselves on coordinating and synchronizing other companies in their supply network. What's more, Li & Fung accomplishes these complex tasks with little support from information technology. For them, customized customer solutions and hands-on managing are what create value.[2]

On the other hand, Dell Computer is a digital pioneer that has used computer software significantly. Dell has deftly translated its direct approach to selling the end user by using the Internet. Instead of designing, handling its own orders, and manufacturing, it has decided to off-load this work either to software automation or to suppliers, concentrating on the marketing of its brand franchise. The resulting structure is a virtual organization knitted together through digital communication links.

SUPPLY-CHAIN MANAGEMENT'S RELIANCE ON KNOWLEDGE

With the growth of supply-chain management over the last fifty years, the world's economies have undergone a significant transformation from an almost pure production-based structure to one based on skill and the requirement that employees think while doing their work. In the United States, production workers as a percentage of the total workforce are declining while output continues to increase. In 1900 over 75 percent of the population was employed in production jobs. In 1940, the number dropped to 57 percent. By 1980, the percentage was 34 percent.[3] In the last 100 years while production jobs have steadily declined, output and productivity, especially in the last ten years, have consistently increased. This trend is epitomized by Li & Fung's example discussed above.

In addition, businesses have seen decreasing returns from investments in reengineering production processes, Total Quality Management (TQM), Just-in-Time (JIT), and Activity-Based Costing. These management methods are now widely used in mature organizations, but they are no longer the precursor for a world-class production enterprise. Instead, world-class firms are defined by how connected they are to their suppliers and customers, the speed at which they can create customized products, and their return on knowledge.

Finally, technology itself has created an *imperative* for efficient communication through supply-chain management. The explosion of databases, the Internet, Extranets, and technology to capture data, information, and knowledge, have far outstripped people's ability to absorb and analyze the content. Therefore, it is becoming even more critical that organizations use available approaches to maximize communication and minimize data and information overload.

TERMS OF COMMUNICATION

With the increasing importance of communication in the horizontal organization has come a distinction in the types of communication circulating through the organization. As employees contact internal and external suppliers, review performance and production resources, and develop new ideas, they are working with data, information, knowledge, and innovations.

Data is characterized as a set of discrete facts about events and the world. Most organizations capture significant amounts of data from operations, sales, quality assurance, distribution, and their business processes, all of which feeds monthly financials. Most of this data resides in company computers. In addition, most firms subscribe to external data sources that provide demographics, competitive statistics, and other market information. Thinking skills are required to analyze, synthesize, and then transform this data into information.

Information is created when a decision is made. Decisions are codified into policies, procedures, manuals, standards, mathematical expressions, specifications, and quantifiable ways of doing things. Information is also the semistructured content such as written documents, e-mails, and even voice mail. For example, typical questions answered with information are, "what is my job?", "how do we solve this problem?", or "what is the best way to make this product or obtain venture capital?"

Knowledge is the tacit experiences, ideas, insights, values, and judgments of individuals. It is personal, hard to articulate, and is accessed through direct collaboration with experts.

Innovations—new knowledge—are created from highly interactive dialogues where other elements, such as data, information, and knowledge are put together into new combinations to solve problems or plan for the future.

Data, information, knowledge, and innovations all come into play when managing an outsourced supply chain. In some companies, the number of employees working on the company's behalf may be huge, exponentionally increasing the importance of communication. Companies that outsource and delegate decision-making authority to suppliers still deal with as many arms of the organization pyramid, but these arms no longer report directly to the firm. The firm can outsource 10,000 jobs but is still accountable to manage the results—data, information, knowledge, and innovations of its suppliers. The lesson for management is to appreciate the value of employees under its direct control, but to continually communicate with and monitor the growing numbers of employees outside the span of control, but within the span of communication.

They do this through the efficient managing of data, information, and knowledge assets in order to ensure a dynamic, innovative, and agile organization. Without properly implementing supply-chain management techniques, it is predicted that in the Internet age a company will not grow effectively—information is lost, knowledge walks out the door, lessons are unlearned, work is prolonged, tasks are repeated, trends go unnoticed, and completed job insights are reinvented.

THE EMERGENCE OF LEARNING ORGANIZATIONS AND KNOWLEDGE MANAGEMENT

The growth of supply chain management emphasizes the importance of having an organization that focuses on the creation and use of information—the information central to the successes of any supply-chain communication. An organization that smoothly communicates both internally and externally is one that continually produces information and knows what to do with it—it is an organization of knowledge creation and knowledge management.

Such an organization constantly creates new knowledge and makes it available as information, which gets embedded in processes, products, services, and systems. An underlying tenet of such an organization is an operating philosophy that supports, encourages, and rewards learning behavior. Without this support, knowledge management becomes just another passing management fad, never fully implemented and with poor results to show for the effort. Relatively few Western firms have attempted the kind of thoroughgoing cultural and organizational restructuring that would lead to dramatic improvements in knowledge creation and transmission, in part because of the massive amount of communication such a shift entails.

KNOWLEDGE BECOMES DISCRETE

A forward looking vision of knowledge creation is captured by Ikujiro Nonaka and Hirotaka Takeuchi in their path-breaking book, *The*

Knowledge-Creating Company.[4] One example of the authors' insights concerns how adults learn. An underlying assumption widely held in the West is that knowledge can be taught through education, training, manuals, books, or lectures. This may be a partially valid assumption, but the opposite seems equally likely—that knowledge can neither be taught nor passed on, and that learning comes from direct experience and through trial and error. Nonaka and Takeuchi's theory of learning refocuses attention on the individual.

In organizations today, new knowledge begins with the individual. It germinates from highly subjective insights, intuitions, and hunches. For example, a marketing manager's sense of market trends could become the catalyst for important new product categories. A shopfloor worker could draw on years of experience to come up with a new production process. A project team could complete its work and afterwards analyze what worked and what didn't. In each of these cases, "creating new knowledge is not simply a matter of learning from others or acquiring knowledge from the outside."[5]

The key to building knowledge is intensive group interaction and communicating among team members. In a team, data, information, knowledge, and innovations are amplified and crystallized through dialogue, discussion, and experience sharing. Such an atmosphere brings consensus. Insights are then internalized—that is, they are translated to fit the company's way of doing things. When the group communicates through both analytical and intuitive approaches it allows for both linear thinkers and those that see things conceptually to contribute to any knowledge gleaned. Intensive interaction between people tends to create positive tension as people are confronted with demonstrating how their points of view support the common goal. The whole process energizes the group to move off in new directions and innovate. This is the essence of a learning organization.

Making personal knowledge available to others is the central activity of the knowledge-creating company. As the following example from *The Knowledge-Creating Company* suggests, sometimes it can take unexpected twists and turns.

In 1985, product developers at Osaka-based Matsushita Electric were hard at work on a new home bread-making machine. But they were having trouble getting the machine to knead dough correctly. Despite their efforts, the crust of the bread was overcooked while the inside was hardly done at all. Employees exhaustively analyzed the problem. They even compared X-rays of dough kneaded by the machine and dough kneaded by professional bakers. But they were unable to obtain any meaningful data. Finally, software developer Ikuko Tanaka proposed a creative solution. The Osaka International Hotel had a reputation for making the best bread in Osaka. Why not use it as a model? Tanaka trained with the hotel's head baker to study his kneading technique. She observed that the baker had a distinctive way of stretching the dough. After a year of trial and error, working closely with the project's engineers, Tanaka came up with product specifications—including the addition of special ribs inside the machine—that successfully reproduced the baker's stretching technique and the quality of the bread she had learned to make at the hotel. The result: Matsushita's unique "twist dough" method and a product that in its first year set a record for sales of a new kitchen appliance.[6]

Tanaka's innovation illustrates a movement between two very different approaches to product development—rational and intuitive knowledge. The final product was documented and turned into *information* with a set of specifications for manufacturing a bread-making machine. However, the starting point relied on the *tacit knowledge* of the chief baker. To ensure a steady stream of innovations, management's responsibility is to ensure cross-functional communication where employees share their expert knowledge and value a diversity of ideas and approaches to problem solving.

THE COMING OF AGE OF THE INTERNET MODEL

The late 1990s saw the introduction of the Internet economy with enterprises operating globally and increasingly relying on a virtual presence on the Internet. As a result, the bedrock of business—strong distribution channels, customer loyalty, and reliable service relationships—have been cast in a new light. The Internet model, with fewer hard assets, a direct pipeline to customers, and freedom from hierarchical structures, offers a new level of speed and operational efficiency for those who master it—and huge dislocations for those who don't. Jack Welch says of its impact, "I don't think there's been anything more important or more widespread in all my years at GE."[7] With the Internet economy, not only have physical assets been replaced with intangibles—knowledge, experience, and relationships—these intangible assets also depend on a solid base of efficient communication.

Another result of the growth of the Internet economy has been the increased importance of individual communications to the end user. This new economy is about treating every customer uniquely. It is about establishing one-on-one relationships. In their 1993 book, *The One to One Future: Building Relationships One Customer at a Time*, Don Peppers and Martha Rogers predict that companies will find themselves "competing for business one customer at a time."[8] This is surely the case with the exploding Internet with its interactive flavor, customer dialogue, and feedback. The nature of this relationship suggests customer relations are moving into a new era.

Like the supplier, the end user is outside the physical boundaries of the corporation. In this new economy, the "boundaryless organization" sees end-user interaction as a vital link to understanding new product requirements. From electronic customer communications, net-based companies are building databases that allow them to learn the interests, demographics, and credit histories of consumers, whereas most traditional businesses follow time-honored mass-marketing rules of pitching their products to the greatest number of people. Selling more goods to fewer people is more efficient and more profitable. The Internet Economy has created a world of one-on-one marketing, mass customization, and end-user communication—a system in which the marketing paradigm has shifted from share of market to share of customer, one customer at a time.

THE GROWING IMPORTANCE OF E-COMMERCE—THE FRICTIONLESS EXCHANGE

Interaction costs are rapidly declining as supply-chain, enterprise-planning, and customer-relationship software tools help management improve business processes and customer communication. No company has done more with the technology in this area than networking equipment giant Cisco Systems. It handles 78 percent of its orders over the Internet. Half of that, or $4 billion, go directly to contract manufacturers. This method saves them between $500 million and $800 a year million over legacy systems.[9]

In total e-commerce revenue, Intel ranks number one in the world.[10] Intel averages $1 billion worth of online orders every month from customers in forty-six countries. Customers check product specifications, pricing, availability, order status, and delivery dates in real time. All information is personalized for every company and for every type of user. In 1999, close to half of Intel's direct customer business was happening online through a set of Internet applications built in just a few short months. That's how fast the Internet is changing the way companies do business. To take full advantage of frictionless exchange, companies must challenge the way they transact business.

Any communication among groups and any exchange of goods, services, or ideas have an associated cost. E-commerce focuses on significantly reducing *interaction costs*, or the friction and inefficiencies in each transaction. Because Internet transaction costs with suppliers and the end user are decreasing dramatically and communications are instantaneous, specialized suppliers and distributors are offering services once thought central to a company. As a result, those central services—primarily product innovation (R&D), production (operations and customer relations/sales)—are being outsourced. The authors of *Unbundling the Corporation* predict that, "As the interaction costs fall, companies will come under pressure to unbundle their core processes, each of which has very different economics, culture, and competitive imperatives."[11] Their conclusion is that traditional corporations will realign themselves into separate large production and customer relationship businesses and small and nimble product innovation companies.

This is exactly what has happened in the computer business. In the late 1970s, companies like IBM, Digital Equipment, and Burroughs dominated the computer business. With their huge-scale and vertical integration, they seemed unbeatable. Just ten years later, these giants were struggling to survive and the small and nimble innovators were thriving. Apple Computer launched the Apple II personal computer to compete with these giants, and the rest is history. Others followed. Software component sales flourished, allowing the entry of many other specialized products. The advent of the Internet heralded a similar movement. Opportunities of the future are going to rely on creativity, where speed to market counts, and where flexibility is the sword of the specialist.

BUSINESS INTELLIGENCE TOOLS PROLIFERATE

If organizations choose to dive into the possibilities offered by the Internet, proprietary data becomes critical to coordinate the production of goods and services. With fewer people, a flatter organization is more dependent on the "right" information to ensure that processes operate effectively and that strategic initiatives produce the planned-for return on investment. Corporations have growing stores of data in millions of records in multiple formats in disparate systems. Most of this data is transaction-based. What corporations need is enterprise intelligence to easily turn that data into information that's meaningful because it is customer-or vendor-specific and can help employees and others make decisions that control costs or take advantage of new business opportunities. By delivering the right data at the right time, corporations have a greater chance of achieving their strategic goals. Enterprise intelligence is the invisible asset. Corporations need to reengineer their data to store, find, and effectively use it.

THE DATA EXPLOSION

Bill Gates argues in *Business @ the Speed of Thought* that in the corporate world it is only by collecting the correct data and storing and distributing it broadly throughout the corporation that employees can have access to what they need to make specific proposals to improve performance.[12] This is not a new concept; what's new is the technology that makes it a reality.

One of the most common complaints heard on the shopfloor or in the executive suite is that data is so important but so difficult to access. In many cases, the data exists but getting at it in a useful form is hard. This is why in nondigital companies staff groups often resort to calling line managers for additional facts even though the requested data is in monthly reports. It's often easier to call the source than go digging for data when that data is poorly managed.

One reason useful data is hard to come by is that, as computers are used more in all job applications, the amount of data being generated is enormous. Software applications for manufacturing, supply-chain management suites, and e-commerce systems are rapidly being installed as companies seek to reduce costs, enhance productivity, and improve customer service. All of these applications have a common output: data. Every time someone hits SEND or ENTER, data is generated. Data courses through the veins of software systems, but where does it go? Hidden and inaccessible is often the answer.

DATA MINING GOLD

There is an alternative. To get at the gold deposits buried deep within the firm, companies must do a better job of "data mining." Imagine a company has a database packed with more than 10 million detailed customer records, yet it cannot extract and use the market intelligence it contains. Staples, the office-supply chain, found out how frustrating this could be when a simple query—for example, identifying customers who had purchased a computer but not software—would take hours of computer time as every customer's record was searched.[13]

Although the Staples story is not uncommon, in the last few years technology has improved to the point where database management is quite good. Companies can now tap into these resources to extract the data they need to make decisions.

Companies using new and powerful data storage and retrieval systems have fared well.[14] Storage has been the invisible giant of Information Technology (IT), and it is forecast to be a huge growth area because of its importance. Given the fast pace and volatility of the marketplace, investments in electronic data storage and instant data retrieval, along with data mining and diagnostics, are paramount in order for cross-functional teams and others to make real-time decisions and plans.

The general result of the growth of the Internet Economy, in its changing the concept of supply-chain management, its establishment of the Internet as a model, and its emphasis one-commerce and data management and storage, is an explosion of the span of communication. Corporate information can no longer be viewed as isolated islands of data disbursed throughout the enterprise; it needs to be viewed as a separate and manageable entity.

EFFICIENT COMMUNICATION ACROSS THE WHITE SPACES

Identifying and mapping internal and external business processes is the first step towards digitizing and automating horizontal process management. Geary Ummler and Alan Brache did their seminal research in this area in the late 1980s. They argue, in *Managing the White Spaces*, that the greatest opportunities for reducing costs and improving performance lie in the interfaces—those points at which a baton is being passed from one group to another.[15] These interfaces are the "no man's land" between suppliers and the manufacturer, from one internal department to another, and within the external distribution systems. These spaces are "white" because typically no one is accountable for them; communication is not managed between them. These macro transfer points are where transaction costs are potentially the greatest. For example, the passing of new product ideas from marketing to engineering, the involvement of component suppliers in design requirements, the hand-off of a new product from R&D to production, the transfer of customer billing information from sales to accounting—all of these hand-offs create potential white space inefficiency costs. Most of the ineffectiveness of vertical structures is management's failure to recognize what goes on in the white space.

In the horizontal organization, permanent cross-functional teams become the building blocks of the organization. These cross-functional teams exist across departments or functions, and form around core business processes such as new product development, order entry, and customer relations. When multidisciplinary teams begin to manage separate business processes, they serve as the communication links tying the organization together. In Figure 9.1 it is precisely those spaces between A and B and between B and C in which these linking teams perform. The resulting horizontal organization eliminates the white spaces, lowers cost, reduces finger pointing, and improves quality, productivity, and most importantly communication.

SLOWING THE CHANGE

The biggest problem facing corporations today is the "drag of the past." In other words, too many managers view their organizations through the lens of past practices. Ask managers even in progressive companies to draw a picture of their firm and you'll get something that looks like the traditional organization chart. You will see boxes, levels, and lines connecting the pyramid together into a hierarchy. This graphic does not show the horizontal connections. Furthermore, it often leaves out customers and suppliers. There is no sense of how the work flows or how communication links function. Such a picture reinforces the military model of management.

When managers see their organizations as a collection of vertical functions (exploration here, production there, accounting down the hall), they manage them on an individual basis. Upper management reinforces outdated operating philosophies when performance measures, budgets, and goals are separately negotiated with each function. As a result, departments fail to establish the communication links crucial to productivity and efficiency. For example, in an oil company managed by vertically thinking superiors, drilling can achieve its goals and look good by coming in under budget. If the well doesn't produce adequately, that's seen as a problem for production; drilling did its job. Or, for example, the R&D department in a consumer products company can look good by designing technically sophisticated products. If they can't be sold, that's marketing's headache. If it can't be made at a profit, that's manufacturing's problem. During monthly reviews, management in such vertically structured organizations often demand to know why the organization failed to produce on time or up to specifications. The predictable response is, "It's not my fault." Finger-pointing shifts the blame to a black hole and the group agrees to meet again next week to hopefully resolve the problem, but it is lacking the fundamental basis of communication that serves to remedy those problems.

Under this scenario, individual departments tend to perceive other functions as enemies, rather than as partners. Walls are built, turf battles erupt, and each department attempts to keep its affairs inside and everyone else's affairs out, closing off communication rather than opening it. This condition prevents interdepartmental issues from being resolved. Conflicts are pushed to the next highest level. And that's not the worst-case scenario. Sometimes department heads are so at odds with one another that cross-functional issues don't get resolved at all. Things start "falling through the cracks" or "disappearing into a black hole."

Top management's resistance to change often comes from an inadequate understanding of the digital revolution, possibly because it arrived after many of the "gray hairs" rose to a position of power. It resists the huge investment needed to manage with sophisticated end-to-end business software and e-commerce communication links. Bill Gates didn't see the Internet coming in the early 1990s but when Microsoft realized the potential impact of the Internet, it shifted gears quickly. However, the average employee age in Microsoft is under 45.

Symptoms like these abound in bureaucratic cultures where there is resistance to change. Chapter 2, describing the "corridor of crisis," documents these symptoms in detail. There is a way out of this crisis, but it necessitates managing the organization differently and shifting attention from vertical process to horizontal communication.

SUMMARY

Information technology is accelerating the trend toward the horizontal corporation, replacing span of control with span of communication. Managers still want to know in real time "how they are doing" and "that they are in control," but they get that knowledge through an increased emphasis on communication. Huge data storage systems and intelligent software agents are becoming more and more crucial to the day-to-day running of an organization. Cutting-edge firms will need to integrate data from disparate sources, analyze the data consistently across business, and deliver personalized, timely insights to a wide range of corporate consumers via PCs, Web portals, cell phones, or a Personal Digital Assistant (PDA).

To move forward in the emerging economy, top management needs to ask how digital its company is and how it can create corporate value by utilizing forward-thinking communication technologies to build a horizontal corporation.[16] A new understanding of customer satisfaction is driving the digital imperative. The business value chain isn't just being transformed; it is being reinvented. Those companies wishing to jump the curve will reinvent their data-gathering infrastructure, product conception, development, manufacturing, distribution, and system of communication to be customer-driven. Whether the business is autos, oil, or financial services, what counts is having real-time answers to questions about how the business is doing in the marketplace. A firm's strategic advantage lies in spotting trends and reacting quickly.

NOTES

1. Steve Hamm, "Chairman Bill's Guide to the E-Business Age," *Business Week*, 5 April 1999, 20.

2. Joan Magretta, "Fast, Global, and Entrepreneurial: Supply Chain Management, Hong Kong Style," *Harvard Business Review* (September–October 1998): 103–114.

3. Thomas A. Stewart, *Intellectual Capital* (New York: Doubleday/Currency, 1997), 40.

4. Ikujiro Nonaka and Hirotaka Takeuchi, *The Knowledge-Creating Company* (New York: Oxford University Press, 1995).

5. Ibid., p. 10.

6. Ikujiro Nonaka, "The Knowledge-Creating Company," *Harvard Business Review* (November–December 1991): 98.

7. Nanette Byrnes and Paul C. Judge, "Internet Anxiety," *Business Week*, 28 June 1999, 80.

8. Don Peppers and Martha Rogers, *The One to One Future: Building Relationships One Customer at a Time* (New York: Doubleday/Currency, 1993), 15.

9. Robert D. Hof, "A New Era of Bright Hopes and Terrible Fears," *Business Week*, 4 October 1999, 84.

10. Source: *PC Computing*, July 1999.

11. John Hagel III and Marc Singer, "Unbundling the Corporation," *Harvard Business Review* (March–April 1999): 133.

12. Bill Gates, *Business @ the Speed of Thought* (New York: Warner Books, 1999).

13. Peter Jacobs, "Data Mining: What General Managers Need to Know," *Harvard Management Update* (October 1999): 8.

14. Nelson D. Schwartz, "The Tech Boom Will Keep on Rocking," *Fortune*, 15 April 1999, 72.

15. Geary Ummler and Alan Brache, "Managing the White Spaces," *Training* (January 1991): 55.

16. Adrian Slywotzky, "How Digital Is Your Company?" *Fast Company* (February–March 1999): 94–113.

PART III

THE FUNCTIONING OF PERFORMANCE MANAGEMENT TODAY

In Part II we detailed the historical trends that lie behind much of the way managers think about organizing work systems. In Part III we will examine the nuts and bolts of "what could and should be" as the organization leaves the entrepreneurial and directive phase of its evolution and enters the "corridor of crisis." In this critical phase, the organization must change the *control system* and install a *performance management* system so it can move to an appropriate network structure that is internally consistent as well as horizontally aligned with suppliers and customers.

While many "faddish" programs have been introduced to accomplish this end with varying degrees of success in recent decades, technological innovation is the real driver of change. To make the transition to a technologically competent Internet economy, a firm first needs tight *process controls*, one of which is the management process that is adopted throughout the firm. Installing a performance management system requires the establishment of performance measures, the clarification of delegated decision-making authority, and a clear articulation of how individuals (and teams) review results. This system means managers must learn a new set of skills in the evolving teamwork environments of business today.

Chapter 10 explores the functioning of an organizational "team." Workers need to have answers to such questions as "where are we going?," "what's my job?," "what's expected of me?," and "how am I doing?" Ensuring answers to these questions is the job of performance management. Sports teams have measures and statistics to tell them how well they play a game. Each player knows precisely what his or her job entails, how each player fits into the whole structure, and how well he or she is doing at an assigned task. However, in many organizations clearly defined performance expectations and systematic, accurate feedback are missing. This chapter details how to create measures for each job and how to create continued growth. It presents the "tools" of performance management: the use of purpose statements (PSs), major areas of responsibility (MARs), performance measures (PMs), action plans, and performance reviews to achieve carefully planned commitments. These tools, the building blocks of an integrated management system, build a foundation for speed and continuous improvement in a connected economy.

Chapter 11 looks at how a decentralized model of control might work. This chapter discusses the art of delegation and how to cascade responsibility, authority, and create vertical accountability to align the horizontal business structure. In doing this, managers can build and sustain the worker commitment that is necessary for any decentralized firm's success.

In chapter 12, we examine the features that characterize the new leadership patterns in performance management systems. Leadership has often been confused with managing. But leadership is really about people, vision, establishing an emotional connection through shared values, and the ability to communicate widely to all levels. It is a much more expansive view of the senior executive's role than past practices envisioned. Managers typically have concerned themselves with efficiencies; letting leaders focus on effectiveness. We discuss the differences between old and new versions of management-leadership and how the evolving organization needs a radically different type of leader than in the past. Inspirational leaders of past eras will only take a firm so far. Now a form of interactive-management-leadership is necessary. It entails skills of listening, supporting, and creating an environment in which different viewpoints have a serious voice. In other words, it is the ability to create a web of inclusion in which people feel valued, heard, and committed to a common purpose.

10

Establishing a Performance
Management System

As Chapter 9 made clear, the first role of performance management in a horizontal organization is communication. When managers communicate, they usually talk about either the results they want or the results they are not getting. Using these two categories, we first explore the management process of defining the results a firm wants—it's called performance *planning*. To communicate regarding results they are not getting, professional managers formalize the process of performance *reviewing* through the operating review meeting.

Together, these two processes describe how organizations communicate their purpose and link individual and team goals to a corporate direction. A performance management system serves as a framework for defining accountability, assessing performance, providing performance feedback, addressing personal improvement and development needs, measuring results, and linking performance to the organization's pay and reward system.

The performance management system is a system of processes. It lays a structure of processes which is actually *vertical*, but which must be in place for the *horizontal* organization to work. Because performance management is a system of processes, it must be understood by and developed with input from all levels of the organization. A performance management system allows for and creates a common concept of management. It serves an organization like a music score serves a conductor and instruments alike—it's the structure that the organization follows. Just as the conductor draws together the score and focuses players' skills and knowledge, the good manager of a performance-based system defines a set of unified levels of performance, which clearly state expectations and focus team members on achieving those commitments.

A quick way to determine the extent to which a performance management system has been implemented is to ask how well its parts communicate. The questions workers most commonly ask are questions for which management must have definite and satisfying answers. How well an organization can answer these questions determines its movement towards a performance-based culture. These most common questions, along with the areas that should provide the answers, are:

TYPICAL QUESTIONS	ANSWERED BY:
Where are we going?	Strategic Planning
What is the job?	Position Planning
How does my job contribute?	Position Planning
What is expected of me/us?	Period Planning
How are we doing?	Operating Review Meeting
How am I doing?	Personal Performance Review
What's in it for me?	Reward System

See Appendix A for a survey instrument appropriate for any organization that measures these areas and Appendix B, Figure B.1 for an expanded definition of common planning terms.

PERFORMANCE PLANNING

Strategic Planning—*Where Are We Going?*

A performance management system starts with a vision and an articulated strategy. Too often managers focus on the past, going forward by looking in a rearview mirror. They spend vast amounts of time monitoring activities rather than spending equal time looking toward the future.

Planning terms such as strategy, operating philosophy, and mission statements give direction to the firm and help to define its *purpose*. They establish why the firm is in business and why people are asked do things. They tell employees where the company is going. Workers want to share in the vision. They—especially younger generations—want to know if they are with the right organization to fulfill their personal visions. They want to know where they are going.

Position Planning—*What Is the Job?*

Once a firm's strategy is clear, lower levels need to define why their groups exist. Each function or cross-functional team within an organization needs a *position plan*. Managers and subordinates need to define on paper the ongoing measures of results expected from each job. Once these are clear, desired levels of performance, as defined by standards and goals, can be set. Authority to make decisions can be delegated within certain control limits, and employees can be held accountable for results after action plans are finalized. The key difference between the styles of the entrepreneur or directive leader and the technique of the professional manager is the position plan. It allows managers truly to control results rather than people. The professional manager's job is to put together a position plan that, like a blueprint, shows relationships between components, input and output values, and the tolerance limits of each subsystem system. Engineers wouldn't think of producing a product without first documenting the desired performance. Composers wouldn't write music without indicating who is to play what in the score. How products are built or how the music is played is left up to the specialist. The professional manager needs to do the same for workers.

A position plan is a step above a job description. Job descriptions define responsibilities or the tasks of the job, and are used for wage and salary administration and in the hiring process, but they do not define the end result with measures of performance. This is a huge distinction. The position plan, on the other hand, is not interested in tasks or the way the work is performed, but rather with the yardsticks that will be used to measure results. How those results are achieved is left up to the accountable person. With position plans, creativity and innovation are encouraged because workers have freedom within defined boundaries to do the work their way. Such a plan consists of purpose statements (PSs), a list of the major areas of responsibility (MARs) for the position, and applicable performance measures (PMs).

Purpose Statement (PS). This is a written statement of why resources are being allocated to a position, team, or group. It defines the mission of the unit, what customers or clients (either internal or external) it serves, what product or services are rendered, and where the work is carried out. It also articulates the unit's operating philosophy. To ensure alignment, it is a subset of the corporate purpose statement. It flows from and is linked to the firm's *theory of the business*. Peter F. Drucker defines this as the "assumptions that shape any organization's behavior, dictates its decisions about what to do and what not to do, and defines what the organization considers meaningful results. These assumptions are about what a company [or business unit] gets paid for. They are what I call a company's theory of business."[1]

Major Areas of Responsibility (MARs). These are the areas in which time, talent, and money are allocated. They define the major blocks of work that must be accomplished if the unit or team is to achieve its purpose. In a sense, they are the basic design specifications of the unit. For a symphony orchestra, MARs define what instruments are to be used. When building a house, for example, the first step is to lay out a commitment to floor space, such as the number of bedrooms, whether or not to have a family room or dining room, the size of the kitchen, and the like. An organizational unit requires the same kind of planning. Managers need to answer questions such as, "What do I want this particular unit or team to do? What is the work they are expected to perform?" MARs answer the question "What is the job?"

Performance Measures (PMs). Once the MARs are in place, the next position requirement is to define the measures, or yardsticks, by which job performance is determined. These are often referred to as key performance indicators (KPIs). A KPI might be "department operating cost in dollars" or "sales expense as a percent of sales." KPIs deal with quality, quantity, cost, timeliness, or a ratio of these. Ratios, for example, are used to document productivity. KPIs measure the results of *operating* processes and *project* commitments. Staff or service functions mainly responsible for projects (e.g., engineering and personnel) need to track their progress. These areas deal with cost, time, and customer requirements. Project KPIs are "actual" versus "estimated outcomes" for cost and time and "customer satisfaction" for quality. For MARs, managers need measures of quality, cost, time, and quantity. Combinations of these in ratios create productivity, financial, and business process measures. For example, the quantity of work produced divided by some resource such as hours gives a performance measure of output per hour.

Many managers fail to recognize that traditional financial measures may help them monitor the performance of the business as a whole, but are inadequate at lower levels where individuals and multifunctional teams need to monitor operating results to constantly improve performance. In an article in *Harvard Business Review*, "How the Right Measures Help Teams Excel," Christopher Meyer suggests that one job of the performance manager is to ensure that lower levels understand how their work fits into corporate goals and then train workers to jointly develop their own work measures to track results.[2] (See Appendix C for an in-depth discussion of performance measures).

Once managers have negotiated a purpose statement, MARs, and PMs, the job blueprint has been defined. It is important to remember that a position plan is ongoing. Unlike goals and action plans, which are discussed next under period planning, the position plan is not time-limited.

Period Planning—*What's Expected of Me/Us?*

Period planning is about time-limited commitments. One method of reducing firefighting (or banishing management by crisis) and focusing on the future is to define in each MAR what is meant by "good work." The way

Establishing a Performance Management System

to do this is with a *period plan*. The period plan defines acceptable levels of performance for the next time-limited period. It also requires setting control limits to define the area within which accountable employees have the authority to make decisions affecting their results. These limits create an opportunity for exception reporting. There are two kinds of period plans; one deals with operating goals, the other with project plans.

Period Plan for Operations. The first period plan performance managers need is called the *Period Plan for Operations*. For each PM, a goal needs to be negotiated. Goals are predetermined levels of performance and represent commitments for the coming period. They address operating results, not activities such as projects or action plans. These can be for one week, one month, or one quarter. With operating goals in place, upper management can be assured their financial commitments have integrity.

Here's a three-step process for setting goals:

1. **In what PM area is there a need for improvement?** KPIs may include sales volume, margin per sale, cost per unit, past-due accounts, turnaround time, quality acceptance rate, schedule adherence rate, market penetration percentage, or net profit contribution.
2. **How good is performance?** A sales manager might indicate, for example, that monthly sales have been $5,000 per month over the last six months. This can be compared with previous periods and benchmarked accordingly.
3. **What improvement is reasonable for the coming period?** The period plan for operations might reflect, for example, a goal of increased sales volume by 5 percent above the last six-month average within the next sixty-day period.

Period Plan for Projects. The other period plan performance managers must have reflects project commitments. It is called the *Period Plan for Projects*. To give meaning to the project, a project objective needs to reflect why the project is being undertaken. Very often projects exist and the people working on them either don't know how the project creates value for the firm or why it is being undertaken. Without this understanding, work becomes just work, without a connection to business results. Workers can *comply* with decisions regarding the work but they can't become *committed*.

Here's a three-step process for defining projects:

1. **What is the task?** For example, the activity could be to clean out the mess in the parts stockroom.
2. **Why is the project being requested? What PM needs to be improved?** In the stockroom example above, these questions could be answered in two parts. *The facts*: because of the mess in the stockroom, inventory turns are below standard. *The period plan* goal: increase parts inventory turns from the last six-month

average of eight per year to fourteen—exceeding the standard by two—within six months.

3. **What is the project objective?** Reorganize the stockroom next month at a cost not to exceed $300 in labor and materials. All major projects need to be tied to improving an operating goal area. Then the connection between a project and the operating goal is clear. When such rigor is not practiced, organizations can fall into the "activity trap" in which it is action-oriented, but people are in the dark about why they are doing things. Objectives such as "improve cross-functional communication" or "gain a better understanding of customer needs" are activities. They don't say why the project is requested. Activities are worthwhile only if they serve to improve clearly defined MARs and their corresponding PMs. In the activities "improve cross-functional communication" and "gain a better understanding of customer needs," the goals might be to improve the employee communication satisfaction index and shortening the cycle time to introduce new products.

Focusing first on the goal for each project forces managers and workers to articulate why a given activity is important. It also helps workers see the connection between what they do every day and what the organization intends to achieve. Period planning is a formalized way to clear up any confusion, and it gets all levels of the organization making commitments for the coming period. When this type of planning is done routinely at upper levels it cascades to lower levels and turns performance review into a forward-looking activity.

PERFORMANCE REVIEWING

Operating Review Meeting—*How are We Doing?*

The operating review meeting (ORM) answers the question, "how are we doing?" Because the ORM is so important to the smooth function of an organization, it is covered in detail at the end of this chapter. This is a brief summary.

The ORM is the heart of any short-term planning and control system and so should take place often. Review and commitment cycles should take place at least quarterly, preferably monthly, and at first-line supervision, it is often done weekly. The purpose of these review cycles is to plan for the next cycle. This is period planning but within the context of review. In this meeting, new goals are negotiated for substandard results. Behind schedule or overbudget projects are reported as exceptions and are discussed with corrective action plans. Through this process, team members are able to renegotiate realistic goals and project commitments for results that have slipped. Since all members of a team are interdependent on one another, any decision affects all team members, so all participate in approving suggested recovery plans.

Personal Performance Review—*How am I Doing?*

If operating review meetings are held frequently, workers should have clear and expected indications of how they are doing. Monci J. Williams in an article entitled "Performance Appraisal Is Dead. Long Live Performance Management," suggests a continuous process of observation, conversation, thinking, planning, and coaching that occurs throughout the year to track and tabulate results as work is done.[3] To assist in this dialogue, managers have a way of keeping score of any exceptions noted by individuals or teams. With the ORM in place, they can look back over operating goals and project commitments for sets of data.

Once a year an organization needs to formally review the performance of individuals. At this time, they can also review technical, management, and interpersonal skills by measuring against predefined descriptors of the behaviors. Traditionally, these skill areas are measured on a 1 to 5 rating scale. Present day 360-degree feedback techniques help in this process by gathering data from peers, subordinates, managing supervisors, and others.

A final element in a performance review should be an evaluation of each position. The employee and the supervising manager need to revisit the MARs and PMs to see if they are still applicable. Together, they keep the expectations of the position clear and update the measures of performance.

Note that with the review process, the elements of performance management have come full circle. By helping employees answer the question, "how am I doing?," management comes around to individual planning which ties into the larger question, "where are we going?" Performance review, therefore, is fundamentally tied to *planning*. With operating results at their fingertips and with the knowledge of what they committed to, workers themselves can set the date for reviews, lead the discussion of plans for the future, and engage the boss not as the boss but rather as a coach. The manager's role becomes setting up and overseeing the review and planning processes and negotiating new commitments.

Rewards System—*What's in It for Me?*

For individuals, revisiting the question, "what's in it for me?," is often difficult because it requires that they review what motivates them. Further, it requires management to understand and give an answer that motivates. The old motivator, fear, has no place in a professionally managed firm today. Motivation must instead come intrinsically from job satisfaction, doing "cool stuff," and of feeling a sense of accomplishment.

When it comes to money or bonuses, most compensation issues are in fact rooted in performance management issues. Compensation delivery mechanisms such as base salary, short-term incentives, equity-based compensation, benefits, and retirement programs must be based on sound performance management processes and their resultant measures to create a fair and equitable management tool.

As we've repeatedly said, continuous communication is vital to maintaining employee motivation. To keep talent, employees want to know they are part of a successful enterprise. They want solid answers to all of the questions discussed. They want to know, "where are we going?," "what is the job?," "what is expected of me/us?," "how are we doing?," and "how am I doing?" Answering the question "what's in it for me?" forces management to constantly redefine and communicate answers to each of these questions.

Operating Review Meeting Procedure

When reviewing operating results, each worker in a firm must understand his or her role in the operating review meeting, the purpose of the meeting, the problem solving of exceptions, and the requirement to set new levels of performance. To accomplish these things, workers need to agree on the procedure for the meeting and the format for reporting results, discussing performance improvement, and recording action items.

It's a known fact that meetings can consume up to 40 percent of the time people spend at work. Most meetings waste valuable time. Having a formal procedure or format, as provided in the operating review meeting, enables individual workers and larger teams to function effectively. Below we document several elements necessary for a successful operating review meeting.

Hold Regular Meetings. Organizations that put together annual plans but have no intermediate mechanism to track performance often find themselves in crisis. Short-term planning and review are what ensure that annual commitments are achieved. This is one purpose of the operating review meeting. Meetings must be held regularly, at least quarterly at the top of the organization, monthly at some middle-management levels, and, in some cases, on a weekly basis for process team members to coordinate activities. No meeting is more important for getting things done, being decisive, and delivering on results.

At the middle-management level, the operating review meeting requires no more than one to two hours per month, twelve times a year, and less at lower levels. Once a month seems to be the most appropriate frequency. For most organizations, one month is the shortest time period for which financial data are available. Team members annually block out predetermined dates in their calendars a year ahead of time and plan their vacations, conventions, and other trips around these meeting dates. They are the most important events in the year because they are when team commitments are reviewed and new plans are made.

When functioning fully, these reviews reduce the need for weekly staff

Figure 10.1
A Typical Team Meeting Agenda

AGENDA

1. Agree on length of meeting and agenda times.
2. Discuss new items to be added to agenda.
3. Discuss old "open" action items.
4. Review KPI results by function or business unit.
   a. Review preceding month's commitments.
      • Discuss successes.
      • Discuss exceptions.
   b. Buy-off next month's commitments.
   c. Record action items that come up during the meeting.
5. Discuss policy issues.
6. Communicate information of interest to entire team.

---

meetings, monthly reports, technical reviews by staff specialists, and numerous other mechanisms that management uses in trying to maintain appropriate levels of control from the top

Set an Established Agenda. The agenda provides a structure for a smooth operating review meeting. If possible, it should be published ahead of time. At the beginning of the meeting, a team typically determines approximately how much time will be spent on each agenda item. Figure 10.1 shows a typical agenda.

Review Exceptions to Goals and Project Plans. Since the operating review meeting looks toward future plans, little time is spent discussing past successes. Instead, only exceptions to goals and project plans are discussed. Team members review data before the operating review meetings and prepare themselves to present any failures in their past period's performance. Sample forms for project plan exceptions and reviewing goals are shown in Figures 10.2 and 10.3. Goals are renegotiated for agreed upon KPIs. Only the *exceptions*, both positive and negative—for example, being 20 percent under budget or 25 percent ahead of the sales forecast—are discussed. Positive exceptions are as important as negative ones, for results can be "too good" and may adversely affect another team or department. For instance, if sales are 25 percent ahead of forecast, production is affected negatively.

Reviewing goal and project exceptions enables team members not only to document their performance, but also to be acknowledged in a meaningful manner for on target results.

Discuss Performance Improvement Plans. When a team member reports

Figure 10.2
Sample Form for Project Exception Review

Department:						Month:	
PROJECT EXCEPTION REVIEW							
		Completion Date					
Project Description	Who	Forecast	Revised Forecast	% Complete	Actual	Status Comments / Exceptions	

Figure 10.3
Sample Form for Reviewing Goals

Department:					Month:	
EXCEPTION REVIEW AND GOAL COMMITMENTS						
Key Performance Indicators	Standard	Last Month's Goal	Exceptions	This Month's Goal	Next Month's Goal	
KPI	(+/−)	____	____	____	____	
KPI	(+/−)	____	____	____	____	
KPI	(+/−)	____	____	____	____	
KPI	(+/−)	____	____	____	____	
KPI	(+/−)	____	____	____	____	
KPI	(+/−)	____	____	____	____	
KPI	(+/−)	____	____	____	____	
KPI	(+/−)	____	____	____	____	

Figure 10.4
Performance Improvement Plan Format

Department:		Date:	
PERFORMANCE IMPROVEMENT PLAN			
Situation			
Goal			
Most Probable Cause			
Action Plan			

Action Steps	Who	When

on commitments that have not been met, that is, those outside control limits, the team buys off on his or her performance improvement plan. It is helpful if the accountable team member creates a draft prior to the meeting. A suggested format is shown in Figure 10.4.

Performance improvement plans are broken down into four problem-solving steps:

1. **Analyze the current situation.** "Excuses" are listed under this heading. But excuses are also facts, and the job is to define them clearly and concisely so all team members get a picture of the situation. These facts answer questions such as: When did the process stop producing? Where did the trouble start? What were the conditions leading to the change? Who was involved? Is it always the same person?

2. **Identify the goal.** This is the revised level of performance that is forecast. With this, the team has a gap analysis between the desired condition and the present condition. Questions to ask are: Is the gap big enough to warrant action? Why did the gap develop? What stands in the way of closing the gap?

3. **Analyze the most probable cause.** The team member reporting the exception describes the barriers standing in the way of achieving the desired result. These are weaknesses to overcome or constraints still needing attention. Team members need to ask what must be done so the problem doesn't recur. Some problems, such as the *Challenger* disaster discussed in Chapter 2, should never happen again. In determining probable causes for the failure of *Challenger*'s "O" rings, scientists probe the root of the problem. They also ask questions such as:

Why didn't management know? At this step, there are no more Band-Aids for symptoms. This is the step that gets at the heart of the problem.

4. **Agree on action steps.** For each root cause obstacle, there is a corresponding set of action steps. Employees are required to present the data in this sequence. This procedure makes them think the problem through and gives others a chance to review their thinking. When the exception has been thoroughly analyzed, corrective actions often become self-evident. Finally, team members agree on the action plan by defining by whom and when the work is to be accomplished.

As the team solves problems, duplication and overlap of responsibilities often surface. A key element in performance improvement is fixing accountability. Who can make the performance improvement? If it is a cross-functional problem, who owns the process? Holding subordinates accountable for results helps resolve duplication and overlap and creates a sense of group ownership of commitments.

Setting performance improvement plan deadlines and adhering to them establishes a climate of trust between team members. Sometimes, completion dates are unrealistic, set without knowledge of all the facts, and under peer pressure. The team members must test each commitment to assure that it is realistic. Holding each other accountable builds trust and establishes integrity within the group. By reviewing each exception and corrective action plans together, the team members serve as consultants to one another.

Review Commitments for the Coming Period

Since the purpose of review is planning, any area not covered by exceptions is up for discussion. Typically, period plans cover quarters and yearly commitments. If budgeted numbers have changed, this is the time they are reviewed, changed, and agreed to by all. The important activity is to obtain a firm understanding and buyoff on next month's commitments.

Document Meeting Action Items. Too often in business today, members attend meetings that have a lot of discussion, but no specific individual is held accountable for what he or she presents or suggests. People leave the meeting not sure who is going to do what, certain only that there will be another meeting next week. To avoid this kind of nonaction meeting, decisions and policy items must be recorded as they come up. Meeting minutes are not necessary, however, because action items replace these documents. Action items represent the critical few issues coming out of the meeting. They are the assignments that team members have agreed to accomplish within some time period. A format for recording action items is shown in Figure 10.5.

Before the end of the meeting to ensure the understanding and acceptance

Figure 10.5
Team Meeting Action Items

Department:	Date:
TEAM MEETING ACTION ITEMS	

Members Present:		
Next Meeting Date:		

Action Items	Who	When
1.		
2.		
3.		
Policy Decisions:		

of all the team members, the action list is read aloud. Later, it is published and routed to each of the affected team members.

Anticipating Meeting Traps. Knowing what a good operating review meeting is and actually getting one going in an organization are two different things. While a team leader must convince team members of the importance of their tasks, the value of their input, and the interdependence of their actions, he or she must watch out for common mistakes in facilitating an operating review meeting. To be successful, the leader must anticipate, recognize, and address several obstacles that are common to the establishment and productive functioning of meetings. Below are some traps to avoid.

Lack of performance measures. One of the first barriers teams often encounter is the lack of relevant KPIs for team processes and measures of customer satisfaction. Although there may be plenty of procedures explaining what to do for routine jobs, translating these into the "desired levels of performance" is sometimes difficult. Since the evolution of control moves from inspecting tasks to monitoring exceptions, identifying the right KPIs takes time. Historical data are needed to help determine what is important.

Performance measures for line departments are fairly easy to identify because of the routine and repetitious nature of the jobs. Here, almost any job lends itself to hard productivity indicators, such as "advertising cost per retail gallon sold," "lifting cost per barrel," and "on-time percentage."

An area where staff spends time is in project work. Here, the hard measures are "actual" versus "estimated outcomes." The percent of projects that come in on time, below budget, and meeting client specifications are the performance measures of a project department. Without good KPIs against which to set project goals, staff functions like human resources, quality departments, and planning groups are let off the hook all too easily. Often these departments grow unchecked, and their contribution to the organization becomes harder to measure.

Much harder to measure are staff jobs in which performance criteria are often determined by the customer. Soft measures of perceptions that can be used to evaluate staff or service departments include the "timeliness of response," the "quality of work performed," and the "courtesy of personnel." These measures need to be quantified through periodic customer surveys.

Getting sidetracked. Another obstacle to successful operating review meetings is the tendency members have to get sidetracked. Discussions of technical issues or operating problems, rather than sticking to discussions of results, usually indicate that the meeting is running off course. Technical talk normally comes up in the course of discussing operating results. However, given an opportunity to discuss operating results or technical problems in the same time period, team members often prefer to talk about technical issues, which can lead the group off on lengthy technical rabbit trails. The meeting facilitator must remain alert to this tendency. When this happens, the leader must step in and record an action item to be handled by the accountable individual or in another meeting.

Boredom and pace. If the team leader fails to review results at a brisk pace, he or she may lose control and boredom may set in. Further, wandering down blind alleys, indulging in personal issues, blowing up minor problems, and beating dead horses also serve no purpose; they only waste time.

Reviewing too much data and too many activities. One of the traps of the operating review meeting is the desire to review all the data. This is a natural tendency. People are proud of their results. In companies that require written monthly activity reports, the transition to operating review meetings can be frustrating because past meetings focused on presenting data. Unfortunately, there is not enough time in a team-based organization to review all the data carefully; that is why only exceptions are reviewed.

Not having the right data. Teams often find that only 20 percent of the data they need to manage their team is available. Initially, this data comes from the financial information system. The financial tracking device is set up primarily to capture data for the accountants, not teams. The remaining 80 percent of the data comes from performance measures the team identifies. Without the benefit of hard numbers, early operating review meetings sometimes can't do much more than go through the motions of reviewing activities. This is frustrating, of course, but the long-term rewards associated with tracking performance offset this initial inconvenience.

Poor attendance. When competing pressures are accepted as legitimate excuses for skipping team meetings, the feeling of obligation to attend regularly will break down. The first sign of tardiness or absence is just cause for a firm directive that no excuses will he accepted and that competing time pressures are an indication of poor planning.

Looking in the rear view mirror. As stressed above, the purpose of review is planning. In the poor operating review meeting, the meeting is for the benefit of the manager, not the team. Its focus is activity reporting and the manager's intent is to look at the data. A clear sign of this tendency is an increasing percentage of meeting time spent on past performance with little time devoted to future team commitments.

Managers and team leaders who have a hard time giving up the old command-and-control model may use the operating review meeting as a way to be more in control and "on top of their jobs." This is a serious trap, as it is hard to change techniques that were successful in the past. Therefore, in a successful teamwork organization, senior managers must lead a cultural change in which old ways of managing are penalized and new approaches are rewarded.

Loss of decisiveness. The art of excuse making undercuts productive action and destroys integrity. Weak team members show their lack of decisiveness by avoiding accountability for their commitments. The team leader must, therefore, be alert to any tendency of the team to lose its decisiveness and he or she must constantly apply pressure and insist on written performance improvement plans.

Lack of coaching. Some teams may be unable to operate effectively without training or coaching. However, it is the responsibility of the next higher level of management to make sure lower-level operating review meetings are running effectively. This can be done by coaching subordinates as they facilitate their meetings. Higher-level managers can also audit lower-level team meetings and act as consultants, monitoring the exceptions and performance improvement plans, looking for evidence that the systems and procedures for commitment and control are present.

Too much paperwork. The new forms for the operating review meeting procedures are often seen as an increase in paperwork. It is quite true that parallel control systems exist for awhile—the old system and the new—so there *will* be too much paperwork for a short period. However, in time, a new agreed-upon set of forms will emerge. The old paperwork and lengthy monthly reports eventually fade away and the paperwork for the new standardized procedures actually diminishes the total paperwork load.

Unchallenging meetings. A problem common to operating review meetings is that they can easily lose their challenge and become routine. For example, the challenge will no longer be there for team members who continue to select the same goal commitments month after month. In this instance, management needs to help this team set new goals for its members. It might, for example, negotiate higher monthly goals or rework its goals for continuous improvement. At other times, team meetings may become shorter and shorter and lose their initial excitement when the data begin to flow smoothly and results are within control limits. When this happens, the remedy is again to shift to what could be done to continuously improve results. Emphasis needs to be placed on benchmarking against the best and setting goals to be in the industry's top quartile. The group assesses the impact of these targets and discusses new methods, with a focus on creativity and imagination. When the group moves into this phase of its evolution, crisis management is left behind and team members begin to affect and control their environment. Besides enhancing teamwork, the operating review meeting is the final step in the evolution of self-control at the point of control. With delegated authority pushed down to teams, PMs tracking performance, and a formalized process to review operating and project results, the knowledge worker has the ability to flourish under these conditions.

SUMMARY

To make a performance management structure work, management must do the hard work of clearly communicating where the firm is going, specifying the measures by which employees are to be held accountable, and providing team or individual performance feedback. Management must not abdicate its responsibility in this area, nor be unwilling to trust teams with decision-making authority.

The primary process tools of performance management are planning strategy, establishing major areas of responsibility (MARs), defining clear performance measures (PMs), gaining commitments to goals and projects, and setting up operating and personal performance review meetings to verify planned commitments. These tools represent the building blocks of a firm's management system and are the foundation on which cross-functional teams and network alliances can be managed.

The operating review meeting is a powerful tool to monitor results. It gives managers and workers at all levels the ability to review results and plan for the next period using goal-setting that forces the organization to utilize problem-solving skills. By linking teams at all levels of the organization to its shared strategic goals, promoting open communications among the various departments, and nurturing the logical evolution of high-performance standards, the operating review meeting becomes the cornerstone of a performance management process.

NOTES

1. Peter F. Drucker, "The Theory of the Business," *Harvard Business Review* (September–October 1994): 95.

2. Christopher Meyer, "How the Right Measures Help Teams Excel," *Harvard Business Review* (May–June 1994): 95.

3. Monci J. Williams, "Performance Appraisal Is Dead. Long Live Performance Management," *Harvard Management Update* 1 (February 1997).

11

The Art of Delegation

Firms today feel increased pressure to learn the art of delegation. With the advent of teams, downsizing, and fewer levels and increased numbers of direct reports, the kind of work that managers are being asked to do is changing. In the past, the command-and-control style of management fostered top-down task assignments in hierarchical organizations. Assigning tasks, however, is not delegation. Today, lateral coordination among cross-functional teams is accelerating. This requires upper management to delegate decision-making authority to these teams.

The biggest challenge to delegation is getting people to let go, especially when they get promoted. For example, Bob Baker, an employee in production at Jackson International (not the real company name), an airbag manufacturer based in California, was promoted to a manufacturing process coordinator as a team leader and had difficulty relinquishing his former responsibilities. If he saw his eight-member team slipping behind schedule, his first instinct was to jump in and do the work himself. But the more work he did, the less work seemed to get done—and the less motivated his team became. They'd return late from breaks and wait for specific instructions before tackling obvious problems. Why? Baker's *help* was offending his colleagues. He thought he was helping and would hurry and pack some parts for them. But his employees thought he was telling them they weren't working fast enough. His nonverbal actions sent the message that he could do the work faster than they could.

After reviewing performance carefully, Baker learned that his job was not to do the work his team is supposed to do. As any team leader learns, he understood that his job was to provide the tools, delegation, and coaching the team needed to do the work itself. The lesson is simple, and all too easy to ignore: never do what could and should be delegated.

Anne Donnellon, a professor at Babson College, and author of *Team Talk*, urges managers to manage the process rather than the content. The real work of a manager involves priorities and information flows, she suggests. Too many technical experts try to control the details of work. They think of themselves as doers, which encourages team members to assume less responsibility.[1]

One of our consulting assignments uncovered this example. Bill Archer, a new manager at LapPro for Windows (not the real company name), discovered that managing content as well as process can do more than drain a team's motivation. It can be downright exhausting. There simply weren't enough hours in the day to attend to his new responsibilities and keep his hand in the details of software code. "As project manager I'm responsible for getting the product scoped out, launched, positioned, and targeted," he said. "My biggest challenge is prioritizing all the things coming at me: What can I say no to? What can I delegate down? What am I doing that I have no decision-making authority over? How can I tell my boss he is accountable? What needs to be decided today?"

Archer applied an engineering mind-set to his challenge. He identified the factors most critical to the success of LapPro. Then every morning, as he reviewed his to-do list, he'd decide which action items contributed to those success factors and which didn't. He worked on those that did and delegated the others to one of his fifteen engineers. "I was spending an excessive amount of time on little things that didn't relate to my major goals. I had to ask myself: How do I meet the needs of people on the team who want help without spending my own time on it?" By figuring out how to spend his own time more efficiently, Archer learned how to let go from the do-it-yourself model of most beginning project managers to *leveraging the work of managing*. This is a lesson firms leaving the directive phase have to learn.

DIFFERENT KINDS OF WORK

To delegate work effectively managers need to understand what types of work their organization needs. They need to break work down into its component parts and clearly define each part so employees can make sense out of the different activities that they perform. There are four categories into which all work of the firm can be slotted:

1. **Technical Work.** The person in the job must do this work; it cannot be delegated to others. Since it is discipline-specific, like engineering, marketing, and accounting, this work requires that *the person doing the technical work make the final*

technical decision. All positions from the most senior to the shopfloor have a technical component. Obviously, the amount of technical work is less at the top and increases at lower levels. As we have seen, the entrepreneur, the newly promoted supervisor, and the technical expert all resist delegating technical decision making until they either burn out, get fired, or learn the art of delegation.

2. **Operating Work.** When technical work is delegated it becomes the "operating work" of a lower level. As the size and complexity of a business increase, the need to delegate operating decisions, which could and should be made at lower levels, becomes vital to leverage and sustain growth. For example, day-to-day operating decisions about what needs to be done and problems that need resolution can and should be pushed down to the teams of people actually doing the work. For example, pricing decisions, who gets what office and what furniture, and staffing decisions are typical of operating work, and should be pushed downwards.

3. **Management Work.** Management must be careful not to let operating work get displaced by slowly drifting upwards. Managers could do everything themselves, and they usually do when starting a business or taking over a new position. But as the business grows, both the technical work of the unit and the management of others require delegation. When this is done, decision making is pushed to lower levels and becomes the operating work of the unit. Managers leverage their effectiveness by doing management work—planning, coaching, and reviewing the work of others. Ultimately, their job is to get work done through and with others.

4. **Teamwork.** This has become increasingly important as alliances, partnerships, and task force assignments occupy more of a manager's time. The interpersonal skills of leadership and facilitation are critical skills that team members need. Chapter 12 covers the art of leadership. What the work teams do is no different than what occurred in an old command-and-control structure, except for one major difference—everyone is a peer of the other. What was done at the top is now done at lower levels among peers. Teams have to plan and review the work they agree to do. Further, solving problems require process skills in problem analysis and decision making.

It is important to understand the difference between these four categories because the perception of what work is has been changing. There has been a steady shift over the last century from hand to headwork. The emergence of "knowledge workers" brought about by a massive shift to the New Economy, driven by the digital revolution, is having a profound effect on what employees are being asked to do. Much of what used to be the domain of upper management is now being delegated to lower levels. Delegation is a process to transfer accountability.

ELEMENTS OF DELEGATION

Delegation is the work a manager does to *entrust responsibility, provide authority to others, and to create new accountability for results.* Through a performance management system, new accountability is created at lower levels. Recognizing that upper levels are still ultimately accountable, delegation is not the abdication of decision making, nor is it the assignment of tasks. Neither is it synonymous with empowerment, which comes from leaders (see Chapter 12). Delegation comes from managers. However, both techniques motivate subordinates to solve problems and take action. Delegation is a *process* that ensures people can carry out the concept of empowerment. To be successful, managers must entrust others with the responsibility to do their work and the authority to make any necessary decisions, thereby making them accountable for delivering the desired results. The key word in delegation is *trust*.

As the boat company example in Chapter 8 makes clear, establishing such trust takes time. Even when a sound basis of trust is established, however, delegation is not easy. In fact, one of the primary dangers in delegation is that of confusing employees. Often top management says it wants to delegate authority, but then it rejects employee initiatives. A typical example of this is GE's effort to de-bureaucratize, when employees were encouraged to become more "self-confident." This effort, called "workout," was introduced by Jack Welch in the 1980s. At one plant site, GE Silicone, a steering committee organized problem-solving teams and delegated authority to them. However, when team decisions were in conflict with prior management decisions, management prevailed and employees became confused about what their "authority" meant.[2]

The reason for GE's delegation failure was that management abdicated its responsibility to do the hard work of defining both the responsibility (the work) and the amount of authority (decision making). As long as managers talk delegation but don't clearly define who is accountable to make final decisions, the organization can quickly fall back into the command-and-control model of management, with employees making only what Chris Argyris calls "external commitments"—think of it as contractual compliance.[3] The elements of the delegation process—responsibility, authority, and accountability—must be carefully nurtured for delegation to be successful.

Responsibility for the Work

When people don't know what to do, they do whatever makes most sense to them. Mature organizations need more structure than that. This is why it is critical to define any job. To clarify the delegation of responsibility, the first requirement is to distinguish between assigning work to a *person* and assigning work to a *position*. During the early stages of organizational growth, companies organize around people. They tend to assign work to the people they trust and to who can get the job done. Further, they permit trusted employees to take on the work they prefer and, as a result, the content of the position tends to grow around the person doing the work.

As organizations mature, a better approach is to assign work to the position. Whoever fills the position assumes the obligation to do that work. In the delegative phase, it is typical to find a succession of highly capable people marching in and out of positions over the years, with little change in the basic responsibilities of the position. Assigning work to a position increases efficiency and reduces friction. If carried to an extreme, of course, suggesting people to do just what the position requires can stifle individual creativity. Organization review meetings monitor positions to ensure continual challenges and opportunity for growth.

To summarize, **responsibility** *is the work, job, tasks, and activities assigned to and made a continuing part of a position.* A typical job description is a list of these tasks under the heading "duties and responsibilities." To define the work more accurately, these tasks need to be organized under applicable MARs dealing with technical, operating, managerial, and teamwork.

Authority to Make Decisions

People will not perform much work unless they can make decisions related to it. For example, if team leaders must check with the quality control manager every time they want to make a decision regarding product quality or with the plant manager to get approval for a change in the production schedule, they will spend most of their time checking, and no one involved will get much done. Again, if machine operators must go to the foreman every time they want to start or stop their machines or reposition their work, they will spend most of their time talking with the foreman. The solution in each case is for the people doing the work to make as many decisions related to that work as they are willing and able to make.

The more leeway (within certain control limits) people have to get work done—including making decisions—the more efficiently they will work. In addition, those doing the work will demand much less of upper-management's time. As an added bonus, they are more likely to be motivated and get more personal satisfaction from doing the work, ensuring optimum job satisfaction.

Delegating authority works best when limits are placed on decision-making abilities. For example, a worker or team could have the authority within limits on results such as goals for expenses, completion dates, expected quality, or standards. With predetermined control limits, team leaders and teams don't check with others before taking action if that operating result is within authority limits. **Authority** *is the amount of decision making assigned to a person, position, or team within defined limits.*

Accountability for Results

Here is how one entrepreneur jump-started his business and shortened a trip through the corridor of crisis. To combat poor motivation and a lack of commitment and bridge the gap between performance and potential, the owner of Johnsonville Sausage in Sheboygan, Wisconsin, completely changed his directive style and redirected the operating philosophy of his company. By delegating much of his decision making and getting his employees to take full accountability for decisions on production, personnel, quality control, and company expansion, he was able to significantly increase performance and market share.[4] Under this new operating philosophy, individual employees and teams schedule work, hire and fire team members, and track budget commitments, quality levels, and overtime.

Through the delegation process, managers create new accountability, but they are still ultimately accountable, just as boards of directors and CEOs—as in Harry Truman's saying, "The buck stops here"—are ultimately accountable. For people, positions, and teams, however, accountability is the obligation to deliver the desired end results in exchange for decision-making authority.

THE SIX PRINCIPLES OF DELEGATION

There is more to delegating than assigning work and authority. To be effective delegaters, managers must plan, coach, and review the workers to whom they have delegated. To that end, they must understand the six basic principles of delegation.

1. **The more people to whom a person reports, the less accountable he or she becomes.** This is especially true in matrix organizations, in which a person is assigned to a team yet maintains ties to a functional department. If a team member is accountable to two different entities, they often face confusion, contradiction, and inefficiency. Workers who report to two different entities, such as the team and a functional manager, are never quite sure of what priority each job has. Worse still, the direction from the two different sources may conflict. Too often, the solution is to play off one against the other so that the individual has enough freedom to get the job done. This first principle of delegation, however, is not applicable in young and emerging organizations experiencing rapid growth. Here, people do whatever needs to be done, taking direction from multiple sources in a frantic effort to stay ahead of growth. It's only as the organization grows and positions become more set that cross-report confusion occurs.

2. **The willingness and ability of people to do the work and make the decisions required limit the effectiveness of delegation.** Managers often assume that once delegated, work will be carried out effectively. But people can limit delegation by their unwillingness or lack of knowledge to do the work or to make the required decisions.

People are willing if they look forward to the challenge. Willingness is a can-do attitude. It consists of desire, confidence, and incentive. The proof of willingness is "putting out the effort." To make delegation work managers must ask: Do they want to do the task? What about their confidence? Do they see an incentive for performing the work? Do they understand what is expected? A person's ability is tied to learning skills. It consists of experience, training, and understanding priorities. The only true test of ability is proven performance, not potential. Managers must ask: Do workers have the knowledge and skill necessary to perform the task successfully? Do they have the tools to do the work?

3. **The less authority people have, the more difficult it is for them to assume their responsibilities.** Although the degree of authority conferred on subordinates depends on their competence, too often delegated authority is not commensurate with responsibility. That is, individuals or teams are not given the authority to make decisions related to the work they do. When this is the case, the manager inevitably ends up making many of their decisions. This not only overloads the manager, but also devalues the jobs of lower level workers and saps the motivation of employees. It is only natural that if people are not allowed to make decisions, their interest in their work will be reduced. Putting someone else's ideas into effect is not motivating. Indeed, most people find it more difficult to do things the way somebody else requires rather than in a way they themselves think best. Individuals or teams that are given commensurate authority make and carry out their own decisions. In the process, they secure an emotional ownership in what is being done. This is one of the best ways to maintain interest, develop skills, and ensure productive effort. This principle establishes the importance of delegating authority as close to the operating level as possible. The closer to the point of action a decision is made, the more effective the decision making tends to be. Successful delegation results in self-control at the point of control.

4. **The more complete the accountability, the more effective the focus of control.** This means managers must be able to hold individuals accountable for discipline-specific results and the team accountable for process results. To delegate effectively, managers must understand they are accountable for everything that occurs under their supervision even though they have created new accountability through the delegation process. They will do this only if they know that they are responsible for coaching and developing people to reach their core competencies. Getting help and service from the corporate training department or from outside consultants is appropriate, but final accountability rests with managers.

5. **Delegation is limited by the availability of effective controls.** Managers can assign work and authority only if they have a means of making sure that the work is done properly and that decisions are carried out within agreed upon commitments. Negotiating operating goals and getting a commitment on project time and cost estimates is essential. This principle reinforces the importance of establishing effective measures and having a formal mechanism to review operating results. The operating review meeting is the primary vehicle for ensuring results. The most effective control is to have predetermined performance standards and goals with control limits. The area within the control limits defines where the

person doing the work is to make decisions. Results outside the control limits are called exceptions. In these situations, decision-making authority reverts back to the next higher level, which is ultimately accountable anyway. Managers can use control limits as guardrails; workers can use them to track their own performance. Chapter 5 discussed the types of controls needed at different stages in an organization's evolution. Before an organization can successfully make the transition to a team structure it must first implement the elements of good delegation. This pushes accountability downward and conditions employees to take on decision-making responsibilities.

6. **Offering constructive disagreement builds two-way communication and better decisions.** If people are to do the best possible job for the person or team to whom they report, they may have to disagree occasionally. The person actually doing the work can see the work more clearly than others and will thus have better defined views of immediate operating needs. Because of the inevitable differences in viewpoints about how to do the job and the decisions to be made, such disagreements should be seen as opportunities to constructively criticize, but to still offer loyal support of any final decision. This can be described as loyal opposition.

WHAT TO DELEGATE AND WHAT NOT TO DELEGATE

As we've said above, there is some work that can and should be delegated, and other work that should not be delegated. How can managers make such a distinction? Here are some tips covering most of the delegation decisions managers must make.

Operating Work

Most nonmanagement work can be delegated. This is the work subordinates are paid to perform. Sales managers, for example, delegate all possible selling to salespeople, while continuing to plan, coach, and review the sales effort and lead the salespeople. Since managers are often specialists in the technical work they supervise, they may be the only ones in a given group qualified to perform certain aspects of operating work. The purchasing manager, for example, may be an expert in value analysis, or the industrial engineer in cycle time analysis. When this is the case, the manager does the technical work for as long as necessary, but should always be ready to delegate the work. This, however, can be difficult to do in a downsized organization where there are few middle-management positions to delegate to. In this case, the manager might consider outsourcing. When managers outsource, they must remember they are managing these vendors. In effect, they delegate to them and, therefore, must plan and review their work the same way they would an employee's.

Routine and Detail

Managers should spend half of their time on the unique technical work required of their position and the other half managing others. If they do not consciously delegate the routine and detail work, those tasks can easily monopolize their time and crowd out their more important work. This again is work that is delegated once a firm reaches a large enough size. Entrepreneurs are used to opening the mail looking for checks. They carry this habit often into their growing companies. It is not uncommon to observe CEOs also opening the mail in anticipation of purchase orders, approving outgoing purchase orders, making final decisions on furniture or what production equipment to buy.

Certain Management Tasks

Teams may be able to handle the detail, routine, and repetitive portions of planning and reviewing as well as or better than managers. Further, staff groups can handle such things as preliminary budgets, cost analysis, and cash-flow projections. And, for example, in selecting people, the human resources department can do most of the preliminary recruiting and interviewing for the manager. The general rule is to delegate everything possible relating to management work except the initiation of work—that is, seeing to it that the work gets under way and is carried through with the necessary rigor—and the final review of results.

Final Management Decisions

Managers can safely delegate everything but the work and authority of their position. Managers should never delegate final management decisions, decisions on overall operating problems, and technical work that subordinates cannot perform effectively. They can never safely delegate decisions on the overall plans of the unit. They also must reserve for themselves final decisions on overall controls, organization structure, and strategic direction. If they permit others to make these decisions for them, they abdicate the responsibility of their position.

Making final decisions does not mean doing the day-to-day work. Managers should require the accountable individuals or teams to develop their own recommendations to the point where the managers must only study prepared alternatives and make final decisions. If they wish to test individual viewpoints, they can do this through discussion. If managers find themselves deeply involved in collecting information, sifting through data, or screening facts relating to final management decisions, they should search out subordinates or staff agencies to handle these responsibilities.

Integrating Business Units

Firms working out the delegation of authority often find themselves facing problems concerning the work being carried out by different divisions, functions, departments, teams, or direct reports. When these problems involve two or more units or the team as a whole, the manager needs to reserve the right to make final decisions after trying to achieve consensus. By reserving these larger problems for him- or herself to ultimately solve, the top manager can consider all points of view and the requirements and prior decisions of higher levels of management and of staff groups with which only the manager may have had contact.

Upper management must encourage teams to coordinate operating as well as management problems to the point of final decision. But when relying so heavily on others, the manager must anticipate that personal preferences and even bias may color others' recommendations. The manager's best safeguard is to test the validity of both facts and assumptions by careful questioning.

Work That Subordinates Cannot Perform Effectively

If people do not have the ability or are not trained to do the work, delegation will not be successful. Particularly when new work is introduced, managers must do the work themselves, have it done by staff groups, or see to it that subordinates are trained. The most common approach is for managers to do the new work the first time. As soon as they become familiar with it, they train and coach others who could and should do the work. This has the advantage of making managerial supervision more effective. Managers must be always on the alert for reverse delegation—when subordinates fearful of making decisions try to put the "monkey" back on the boss, who is often too willing to take it.

STEPS TO EFFECTIVE DELEGATION

Knowing what can and cannot be delegated, and having the six delegation principles in mind, managers who want to delegate effectively can start by following these nine logical steps:

1. **Provide the proper climate for delegation.** Have the concept of delegation articulated as empowerment and a part of the organization's strategic plan. Delegation must begin at the top. Upper managers must remember that at one time somebody demonstrated faith in their ability by giving them their first opportunity to learn how to do the work and make decisions. Every manager should be willing to give others a chance to fail. When people are delegated challenging work and are given broad authority to make decisions, they have a sense of

guiding their own performance and can enjoy a feeling of real accomplishment when efforts are successful. People who are given authority are certain to make mistakes. Some of these will be unimportant, others will be significant. Keep in mind that the best way for an intelligent person to learn is to make mistakes and profit from the experience. Patience is the key word here. Managed discovery is the best kind of learning. Operating review meetings provide a formal process to discuss performance problems and to figure out how to prevent them in the future. After shortfalls in performance are gone over, workers should be given back their authority. For serious exceptions to plans, authority may have to be recalled for a time, but managers have to remember that they will have to train subordinates or end up doing much of their work for them.

2. **Recognize and deal with the barriers to delegation.** Managers often fail to delegate because of psychological and organizational barriers. Psychological hurdles arise when managers are afraid to delegate. They may fear that subordinates will not do the job properly and, as a result, the manager will look bad. Although this fear is justified if subordinates are untrained or poorly motivated, the manager's responsibility is to take positive action to overcome such deficiencies. Managers may also be reluctant to delegate because they expect subordinates to do their work and make decisions precisely as they, the managers, would. Managers must recognize the fact that, given the proper encouragement and training, people can develop many different ways of doing the same job effectively. On the flip side, managers may balk at delegation because they worry that subordinates may do their work too well and outshine them. Good managers realize that the most valuable skill a manager can possess is the ability to develop people who are more capable than the manager. Good coaches are one of the rarest and most valuable assets to any organization. Organizational barriers, such as failure to define responsibility and authority, also may block delegation. If managers do not know what work to perform and do not understand the degree of their authority, they will not be able to delegate parts of this responsibility and authority. Corrective action here involves clear and precise definition of the managerial position's responsibility and authority.

3. **Define responsibility, authority, and accountability.** The responsibility, authority, and accountability of each position should be defined with MARs, PMs, standards, goals, and control limits. This helps to answer the twin questions, "what's my job" and "what's expected of me?" It helps clarify for the manager, team member, peer, staff person, or the subordinate the work to be done, the decisions that are to be made, and the results to be accomplished. Doing this management work enables managers to determine whether the workload is properly balanced—that is, whether one individual or component has too much work, another too little. It is also a way to eliminate unnecessary work and is an important means of control; when managers specifically know what results people or teams are expected to accomplish, they can best hold them accountable for achieving them. Also, it helps clarify each person's responsibilities, making it possible for individuals to develop their own area of work and authority as fully as they are capable, while preventing subordinate's work from overlapping with the work assigned to others. Most delegation difficulties arise from the attempt to define how a job is to be performed. A better approach is to negotiate

the tolerance bands around commitments for key performance measures. Instead of attempting to pin down each decision a worker can make, it is much better to outline the limits of authority within which the accountable person or team can make any decisions necessary.

4. **Establish a formal method of review.** To be effective, accountability must be based on clear, understandable, and measurable performance indicators. These are the areas where work is repetitive, ongoing, and the outcomes affect the success of the business. If managers have not developed project plans or goals that are understood and accepted by the people who report to them, it will be difficult to get those individuals to account efficiently for their work. Focus only on exceptions that are outside the agreed-upon control limits. Remember, the role of management is to focus only on the critical few problems. Therefore, select that 20 percent of problems which affects 80 percent of the operating results. Require corrective action plans for this 20 percent to ensure that reverse delegation does not creep back, trapping upper management into making decisions that could easily be handled at lower levels. In Chapter 10, we detailed this formal review process, discussing how to conduct the meetings as well as suggest formats to present data.

5. **Create a training development plan.** In a decentralized organization functional department managers often become more like "homeroom teachers" responsible for training and development, career planning, and recommending transfers or promotions, but not for overseeing the performance of daily duties. In this capacity they assess the competency level of workers, concentrating on their skill level and ability to make final decisions. This provides a gap analysis and training needs assessment to train individuals thereby ensuring that competency levels are maintained.

6. **Enlarge jobs in depth as well as breadth.** Individuals' capacity increases as they become more proficient in their jobs, making them able to take on more complex and demanding work. When this happens, managers should delegate new work to the most capable people. They should also encourage improvement in depth. Everybody can think of new and better ways of doing their jobs, reducing costs, and increasing efficiency. Encouraging people to take on more decision-making authority increases the creative and innovative opportunities of the job.

7. **Reward outstanding performance.** People who do a good job want to be told about it, and they want others to know. The best source of this recognition is the manager. By giving credit freely, managers encourage repeat performance of the kind of outstanding work they want. Increased delegation can also build morale among dissatisfied team members. Giving people more important work to do and letting them make more important decisions clearly shows confidence in them and helps them feel important. Both intrinsic and external rewards help answer workers' desire to know "what's in it for me?"

8. **Know when to recall delegation.** When the ability to perform diminishes, delegated authority and responsibility should be temporarily withdrawn until the situation improves. For example, when a new person comes into a position, the manager should withdraw certain aspects of responsibility and authority until the new worker has shown that he or she has the skill and ability to do the job.

As the manager becomes confident of the new person's ability, the manager redelegates the responsibility and authority. A withdrawal of delegated responsibility and authority may also occur in cases of emergency, when new units are formed, or when a new manager enters a position. The ebb and flow of responsibility and authority are to be expected. However, the manager should be aware of the human tendency to retain authority. Once the need for recalling authority has passed, the supervising manager should redelegate the power to make decisions as completely as possible.

9. **Continue coaching the organization toward a culture of delegation.** For delegation to be effective, it must be part of a strategic intent. Therefore, top managers must articulate where the organization is currently and what it wants to evolve to. Moving from a top-down command-and-control style to one emphasizing empowerment and requiring delegation of decision-making authority to lower levels is a conscious decision on the part of upper management. To have piecemeal delegation in parts of the organization and not in others confuses employees and reveals the lack of an overall and consistent management philosophy. By consciously extending delegation, organizations can evolve to excellence in a predictable manner.

SUMMARY

To be able to delegate effectively, managers first have to understand that all work is not the same. It must be broken down into its component parts. Separating out the technical, managerial, operating, and teamwork components is the first step. Determining what ideally should be delegated to lower levels is second. Next, the terms and processes to be used in delegation require that they be fully understood. For example, the words *responsibility* and *accountability* are often used inappropriately and interchangeably by the press and managers alike. Finally, delegation takes time. The six principles of delegation help managers guide the process of delegation and keep it running smoothly.

The reason for a delegation process is to ensure commitment. Compliance, coercion, and even consensus mask true commitment. What management strives for are individuals and teams that pride themselves on doing what they commit themselves to do. To ensure results, management's role is to be supportive with the tools, resources, coaching, and encouragement after authority is delegated. When decision-making authority is in place at lower levels, teams and team leaders become something akin to real entrepreneurs. They become responsible for running their own chunks of the company. This is motivating and puts energy back into the organization. At the next level up, middle-management's job is to coach, support, and ensure that units are coordinated. At the top, senior executives are accountable for providing the context and culture within which delegation can happen.

NOTES

1. Reveals teams in their own words. Anne Donnellon, *Team Talk* (Boston: Harvard Business School Press, 1996).

2. Todd D. Jick, *Nigel Andrews and General Electric Plastic* (Cambridge, MA: Harvard Business School Case Studies, 1992).

3. Chris Argyris, "Empowerment: The Emperor's New Clothes," *Harvard Business Review* (May–June 1998): 99.

4. Ralph Stayer, "How I Learned to Let My Workers Lead," *Harvard Business Review* (November–December 1990).

12

The Art of Leadership—The Human Side of Enterprise

Since work patterns are undergoing a slow but steady shift to the knowledge worker, supervision, while lagging behind, nevertheless must change to reflect this new reality. Interactive leadership is a required skill for creating commitment in the emerging network organization. It implies a genuine concern for people. When all the rhetoric and preoccupation with leadership traits are boiled down, leadership is just about one thing—establishing an *emotional connection with people*. There are two skill sets that foster this. The first is an ability to create a shared vision between what the organization requires and what employees want out of the work experience. The second is the ability to get people working together by resolving conflicts and finding the acceptable middle ground. Underlying both abilities is the skill to communicate effectively. With good communication, employees work in a system of both freedom and control.

FREEDOM AND CONTROL—STRANGE BEDFELLOWS

A firm's performance management structure actually creates the conditions for empowering employees, but that empowerment requires leaders to lead well. Leaders get people to follow them because people want to; people are motivated because they feel they are supported and respected. A blend of management and leadership produces better results than either could alone. Strong leadership encourages freedom of creativity within the structural bounds of the performance management system. Leadership coupled with a system of performance and process management is crucial to the long-term success of any organization. Analogies in nature give a clue to understanding this apparently paradoxical approach. Take the quartz crystal, for example. Its structure is the same around the world, yet no two quartz crystals are identical in color, shape, or size. Nature abhors sameness; it loves creativity, differences, and innovation. Just as it does with people, plants, stars, and even grains of sand, nature gives quartz crystals unlimited opportunities for individuality and creativity within a clearly defined molecular structure.

Organizations need to do the same with their systems to manage and lead people. They need not to tell people how to do their work, but instead provide them with vision, clearly defined boundaries (business DNA), and then allow creativity to flow. Organizations must precisely define desired results, delegate authority, and then give people freedom within boundaries to obtain results. Typical top-down organizations tend to stifle rather than promote innovation because they install policies and procedures to produce work in a standardized way. They centralize creativity rather than opening up the creative potential of workers at lower levels. Organizations that balance management-leadership practices release worker creativity and demonstrate that workers truly are an organization's most valuable asset.

An interest in worker creativity has been around for a long time. In 1982, John Naisbitt in his book, *Megatrends*, coined the phrase "high tech-high touch." It recognized that as automation and technology accelerate, people need more interaction and involvement in their work. Two decades earlier, in 1960, Douglas McGregor wrote *The Human Side of Enterprise*, a seminal book on the importance of people and the need to recognize them as a human asset. Although Naisbitt, McGregor, and others have been talking about the human side of enterprise for some time, only just now are firms viewing their employees not as replaceable parts in a machinized organization, but as knowledge workers with much to contribute.

As firms become large and complex and attempt to move out of their corridor of crisis, *management* practices coupled with *interactive leadership* become increasingly important. These terms are often used interchangeably by people in business, top executives, and the media, but each has its own definition. Distinguishing between the two clarifies how each supports the other.

LEADERSHIP IS NOT MANAGEMENT—MANAGEMENT IS NOT LEADERSHIP

Managers *predict* the future; leaders *create* it. Management is about process; leadership is about people. Management control results through people; leadership motivates them by satisfying evolving human needs. While there are differences between them, these two concepts and their constellations of abilities are not polar opposites. Firms need both to function. As in the quartz crystal analogy above, firms need both structure and freedom to produce creativity and innovation in today's network organizations. Both leadership and management skills can be learned; both evolve as the organization itself evolves. Chapter 11 discussed the delegation skills most crucial to any managerial position. Below is a discussion of the evolution of leadership skills; both are vital to any organization that intends to succeed in the twenty-first century.

Differing leadership skills, not management techniques, are needed at different stages of a firm's growth. Chapter 5 summarized the required skills as an organization evolves through its evolutionary stages. Look again at Figure 5.2. It depicts the gradual shift from entrepreneurial to alliance-oriented leadership. Interestingly, the style of leadership in the first phase is similar to the leadership style of the last phase. Both phases require highly interactive styles. The directive leader of the past was a doer. Getting results—that is making money and ensuring shareholder value—was the requirement for success. These often larger-than-life titans of industry were directive decision makers and were operationally savvy. Tomorrow's leaders are predicted to be of a different cut. They are not as involved in the day-to-day operating details, but rather focus their attention on ensuring "the right people are talking to one another about the right things and have the right tools to what they decide needs doing."[1]

The shift in leadership for firms going through the "corridor of crisis" is from a focus on efficiency to one on effectiveness. This means that when an infrastructure of good management controls are in place to align vision and purpose, then attention needs to be paid to how to make the firm more effective—that is make sure it's doing the *right* things. That takes leadership. An impressive study created through hundreds of interviews by Anderson Consulting called "The Evolving Role of Executive Leadership" tried to create a profile of the global leader of the future.[2] Their conclusion was that vision, values, and setting priorities top the list, but emerging requirements called for building alliances with other organizations, building partnerships across the company, and treating people with respect.

The leader who fails to recognize the differences between leadership—qualitative skills—and management, and thus never learns to use them in parallel, may never give the outstanding performance he or she is capable of giving. Simply put, managers typically excel at planning, organizing, delegating, and reviewing. They focus on "what is" and rely on financials, hard numbers, facts, rules, schedules, and past experience as the basis of decision making. Good management controls complexity; effective leadership produces change. Leaders visualize larger possibilities for their organizations, emphasizing "what could be" and relying on the present for help in making future-oriented decisions. They inspire others through their own high commitment to their beliefs, encourage others through coaching and mentoring, and communicate with others constantly, enrolling others in a shared vision. Another way to describe this distinction is that *things* are managed, but *people* are led; managers are concerned with doing things *efficiently* and well, while leaders look into the future, doing the right things that enable their firms to be more *effective*.

Obviously, the ideal is a *combination* of both, or a management-leader. These individuals are practical and risk takers, analytical and intuitive, planners and visionaries. In any phase of organizational evolution, management-leadership requires high physical contact with people and high participation. It also requires good skills of influencing people. To influence others, management leaders must find a shared vision existing of mutual respect and support for other people's views.

THE EMERGENCE OF THE MANAGEMENT-LEADER

As we discussed in Part II, it makes economic sense today to be people-centered, with leadership being a key underpinning of commitment, but this was not always the case. It is much easier now to look back and understand that Henry Ford's notion of mass production was a soul-ignoring *efficiency* model employing standardized techniques. Alfred Sloan, who took over GM in 1923, did for upper management what Ford did on the shopfloor. Sloan formalized management techniques into a set of machine-like processes to achieve reliability, decision-making consistency, and control in the management of GM.

An article in *The Economist* succinctly states, "For Sloan, top managers had three clearly defined jobs: to determine a firm's *strategy*, to design its *structure*, and to select its information and control *systems*."[3] People, how-ever, were left out of the design criterion. This business strategy helped companies build multinational organizations, it created global empires, and it established the American model as the one to emulate. While it worked for decades, Jack Welch, chairman of GE, argues, "It was right for the 1970s, a growing handicap in the 1980s, and it would have been a ticket to the bone-yard in the 1990s."[4]

In a series of two *Harvard Business Review* articles, Sumantra Ghoshal of London Business School and Christopher A. Bartlett of Harvard Business School track this change. They document the role shift of top management from being the company's chief strategist, its structural architect, and the developer of its information and control systems to being the developer of people.[5] The first shift they document is from a top-down functional struc-ture to cross-functional business processes that attempt to manage the white spaces between functions and divisions. The functional model of manage-ment, they argue, fragments companies' resources and creates vertical com-munication channels hampering the development of cross-functional relationships. The bottom line is that the whole of the top-down organi-zation is often less than the sum of its functional parts. Furthermore, this model of management kept the responsibility for entrepreneurship with top managers. This shift from functional structure to crossfunctional processes, as described in Chapter 9, facilitated the emergence of the horizontal corporation. The shift is dealing a blow to hierarchy, bureaucracy, and the white spaces of yesterday.

Moving from vertical structures to business processes is a big leap. It is a leap from corporate control systems to letting people make operating decisions. This is the second major tectonic shift Bartlett and Ghoshal chronicle. It is the movement towards the people side of work. This trend has been underway for the last ten years but is forecast to mature in the twenty-first century. Bartlett and Ghoshal see this shift as a more personalized approach that encourages a diversity of views and stimulates employees to develop their own ideas. They see companies building operating philosophies that replace a top-down management style with what they describe as "the individualized corporation,"[6] a corporation built on the pillars of purpose and process but also including a people element. It is a shift from strategy to building corporate purpose, from framing structure to developing organizational processes, and from systems designed to control human nature to ones that create environments that enable people to take initiative, to cooperate, and to learn. The most basic task of postindustrial managers, they argue, is to unleash the human spirit; to recapture those valuable human traits that too long have been suppressed by a machine mentality of organization. Simply put, the shifting role of top management in the twenty-first century is towards more leadership.

The Management-Leadership Links

In Chapter 10 we identified questions for which all employees want answers. Figure 12.1 places these questions into two spheres—those related to a concern for *people*, and therefore falling under the province of *leadership*, and those related to a concern for production, and falling under the province of *management*. The bottom category is labeled concern for production, the second and top constellation of questions deal with people as human beings.

As Chapter 10 explained, questions dealing with management and production identify how the firm links individual and team goals to corporate direction. Further, they serve as a framework for defining accountability, assessing performance, measuring results, providing performance feedback, addressing corrective action, uncovering personal development needs, and linking performance to the organization's pay and reward system. Those questions answered through leadership show just how crucial emotional conditions, clear communication, mutual respect, and motivation are to employees' job satisfaction. Figure 12.1 demonstrates the need for a

Figure 12.1
Concern for Production and People

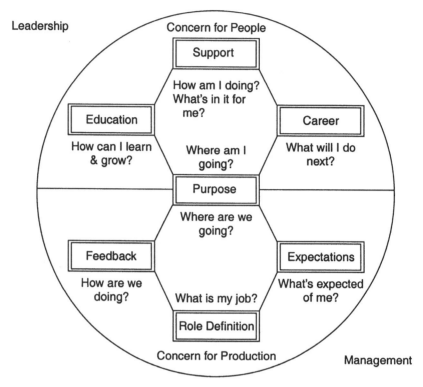

management-leadership balance between the needs of businesses and of the people who work in them.

To describe the importance of leadership in the traditional management-centered organization, McGregor articulated his Theory Y. It urges an integration of company and individual goals in a shared vision of purpose. McGregor says leaders need to "seek that degree of integration in which the individual can achieve his goals *best* by directing his efforts towards the success of the organization."[7] Therefore, the first requirement of a leader is getting this alignment. It starts with a clear vision of the firm's purpose. A leader is the drum major, the conductor of an orchestra, the person who keeps a vision out in front of employees. People want to be about good things. They want to believe that the work they do has some meaning, some purpose beyond just giving them a paycheck. Leaders help to remind people what they are about. In the process, they answer the most basic question—where am I going?—while relying on management's structural answer to the question, where are we going?

Global firms who make *Fortune*'s list of the 100 most admired companies are people-centered and answer these questions well. Almost all admired companies address the human side of enterprise. If companies expect truly exceptional results, their leaders must be willing to embark on a journey to secure an alignment between individual aspirations and company goals. As Figure 12.1 depicts, getting such alignment starts with clarifying *purpose* from two very different points of view.

Why Aren't Leaders Better at Being Leaders?

Leaders' most common failing is not understanding how they must use management and leadership together. When called upon to be a manager-leader, executives often assume that "the challenges of leadership are rational and tactical, rather than emotional and conversational."[8] They act as a manager and assume that if they just pull the right levers the organization will move in the right direction. The technique may have worked for them in the past, but it becomes a liability as the firm matures. Failing leaders also often frame their communications within a marketplace logic. Unfortunately, people don't tend to resonate with marketplace logic; they listen for personal significance and an emotional connection.

A Personal and Emotional Connection. A review of the research literature reveals that the underlying theme running through all the discussions around leadership boils down to creating a personal and emotional connection with people. This requirement is in stark contrast to the command-and-control paradigm where managers were told not to get too personal or too involved with their employees; doing so would reduce their effectiveness. People who become great interactive leaders understand intuitively that running a business is not a series of mechanical tasks but a set of human interactions. For them, leadership is a supremely human activity where an emotional connection is created, trust is fostered, and loyalty is strong. Leaders understand and resonate with the emotional needs and desires of people who follow them.

There is no single set of characteristics that describe a good leader. They come in all sizes and shapes, have different backgrounds and personalities, and emerge when the situation calls for them. In fact, leadership is not the property of an individual but is a complex relationship between a leader, the needs of followers, the organizational purpose, and the external environment.

Like many political and religious leaders, corporate leaders need to emotionally invest in people by supporting, nurturing, coaching, and respecting people's uniqueness and diversity. One hallmark of a corporate leader is belonging to a people-oriented company that shuns hiring a huge base of contingent or part-time labor. While contingent and part-time labor may be an economic fad, people-oriented companies realize they cannot build a strong corporate culture when people are just passing through and are not attached psychologically to the company's goals. They view people as a capital asset. Levi-Strauss, Gillette, Southwest Airlines, and PepsiCo use this human-asset approach.[9] Others falling into this category may total only 10 to 12 percent of all companies in the United States, but they are out there. Studies from Jeffrey Pfeffer's book *The Human Equation: Building Profits by Putting People First* indicate that people-oriented companies do 30 to 40 percent better financially than their competitors.[10] Companies falling into this group emphasize teamwork, decision making at lower levels, and developing other leaders, but always on a solid foundation of performance management.

Communicating by Walking Around and Differing. Leaders create a shared vision and an emotional connection with people by communicating. From his classic study, "What Effective General Managers Really Do," originally published in 1982 and updated in 1999, John P. Kotter of the Harvard Business School finds a consistent theme in how leaders communicate.[11] Those who limit their interactions to orderly management meetings and formal reviews of performance often cut themselves off from the very data and relationships they need in order to inspire people. Leaders need flexible agendas and broad networks of relationships. These networks allow them to have quick and pointed conversations that give them influence well beyond their formal chain of command. Kotter suggests that seemingly wasteful activities like chatting in hallways and having impromptu meetings are, in fact, quiet efficient. This approach sounds a lot like what *directive leaders* do as described in Chapter 1. This is true, but interactive leaders have a different agenda—they have a genuine concern for people, not just for production. Leaders like to stir the pot, rely on personal networks, build small relationships, and create growing pockets of trust. As we explained earlier, GE Jack Welch spends more than "50 percent of his time on people issues and considers his greatest achievement the care and feeding of talent."[12] He urges corporate executives to adopt the people-oriented model of managing people. "Above all else . . . good leaders are open. They go up, down, and around their organization to reach people. . . . It is all about human beings coming to see and accept things through a constant interactive process aimed at consensus."[13]

For any leader, three communication tools are essential: listening to others, supporting different points of view, and creating dialogue to see how each point of view helps achieve a common goal.

Much of the literature on leadership identifies *listening* as a key leader characteristic. This listening is empathic. The listener listens to understand from the speaker's point of view. It is what natural leaders do instinctively and what others can learn.

Supporting is a hard concept for some to understand. People usually think that supporting another's point of view means agreeing with it. This is not the case. Supporting means acknowledging the specific merits of others' ideas. It is a mind-set that acknowledges that each person is right from his or her point of view. Supporting means accepting differing views and allowing the disparity between opposite points of view to build creative tension so people can constructively differ.

To move people forward, creating dialogue is the skill. When people support each other's views by constructively *differing*, they avoid the polarizing effects of arguing, saying, "I'm right and you're wrong." When two people differ, both need to assume the other person has a valid point, and is right from his or her point of view. However, through discussion, options for action can be examined against how they help achieve the common goal.

Rather than resolving tension by coming to a decision quickly this process of communication allows people to experience both sides (or even more) of an issue. It teaches people to allow opposite points of view to exist with equal dignity and worth. The energy of the tension opens up the space for mutual respect and dialogue. A culture without such creative tension tends to let economic rationalism rule. A concern for production can then override people and their ideas. However, leaders must keep in mind that the opposite is also true. When companies let an overriding concern for people dominate their thinking they can dangerously take management's eye off of business. The Levi-Strauss example at the end of this chapter illustrates that when this happens someone else can quietly steal the company's market share.

Leaders at All Levels

There are three basic levels of leaders:

1. *Executive leaders* (CEOs) are responsible for articulating the vision and direction of a firm. CEOs make speeches and reorganize, but have very little impact on the day-to-day operation of any kind of business. This is the job of *line leaders*.
2. *Line leaders* are the lynch pins connecting lower levels to the top. They have a great deal of influence on what is important. They can act as filters or amplify the message executive leaders want communicated. Through their actions and even their nonverbal behavior they communicate what they think is important. They can kill any changed program or they can take a leadership position and promote change. Unfortunately, this group of leaders can possess a mind-set conditioned by years of adversarial relationships and can be wary of using interactive leadership techniques. Changed programs often fail because of this group's lack of effective leadership skills.
3. *Network leaders* are the third type. They are the invisible force behind how a firm really operates. Whether union representatives or a covey of technical experts, these individuals create a web of relationships and alliances that penetrate departmental walls. Often they represent communities having similar interests. They typically come together voluntarily, drawn by a common social and professional force. There are no bosses, diverse agendas, and no expected results.

The egalitarian nature of these groups promotes openness to exchange knowledge, to listen, and to support disagreement. These natural work groupings with their network leaders need identification and their networks formalized. Accepting and legitimizing these communities of interest is formalizing the informal organization. This is where "tribal knowledge" is created. In order to promote new leaders, change, and innovation, these communities must be strengthened to leverage the benefits in today's network organization.

WOMEN RISING IN PEOPLE-CENTERED CULTURES

Faith Popcorn of BrainReserve tracks business and personal trends for Fortune 500 companies. In the 1996 book *Clicking*, she and Lys Marigold identify one of these trends to be the growing importance of women in business. They label this trend "FemaleThink."[14] In business it manifests itself as a change from traditional, goal-oriented, and hierarchical models of interaction to more caring and familial ones. Since women tend to think differently than men, they interact with employees differently, in what has been called a more people-centered way.

Researchers Raquel and Ruben Gur at the University of Pennsylvania have concluded that the typical female manages information, emotions, and relationships differently than the typical male.[15] Their research concludes, "Where cross-functional collaboration is the medium for managing innovations, then individuals most comfortable with facilitating discussion and smoothing conflicts may be [women]." The Gurs' peer-reviewed research suggests that because female managers typically display those virtues best, project team leadership will shift more and more to women. When this prediction is coupled with the fact that for the first time—as we leave the twentieth century behind—women between the ages of 25 and 35 will have more education than their male counterparts, it appears that women may just have the right skills for the evolving New Economy.[16]

Similarly, in her book *The Female Advantage: Women's Ways of Leadership*, Sally Helgesen's findings reveal that organizations run by women do not take the form of the traditional hierarchical pyramid, but more closely resemble a web, where leaders reach out, not down, to form an interrelating matrix built around a central purpose.[17] A later book, *The Web of Inclusion*, takes her spider web analogy further and gives the reader a glimpse of the postindustrial organization: it is fluid, technology-driven, and based on creativity and relationships.[18] As an analogy, webs of inclusion perfectly mesh with the ever-changing demands of the information age, diversity, and strategic alliances. Women, more so than men, seem to function well in this environment. The women Helgesen studied in her research "had built profoundly integrated and organic organizations, in which the focus was on nurturing good relationships; and in which the niceties of hierarchical rank and distinction played little part; and in which lines of communication were multiplicitous, open, and diffuse."[19]

One of the nation's leading experts on the subject of women in business is Judith B. Rosner, at the Graduate School of Management, University of California, Irvine. Her 1990 *Harvard Business Review* article, "Ways Women Lead," suggests that generally men view job performance as a series of individual transactions with subordinates, with rewards given for good work and punishment meted out for substandard performance.[20] Women, on the other hand, encourage employees to align their self-interests by identifying with the group. In exchange, these leaders share power, encourage participation, and allow for what employees want out of the job. This people-centered way favored by women stems from a belief that allowing employees to contribute and to feel important is a win-win situation.

New studies find that women managers outshine their male counterparts in almost every management performance measure.[21] A recent *Business Week* article documents that out of thirty-one measures of performance, women ranked higher on twenty-eight of them. The researchers weren't looking to ferret out gender differences. While gender differences were small, and men sometimes received higher scores in some critical areas, such as strategic planning and technical problem solving, "female executives were judged more effective than their male counterparts."[22] The researchers stumbled on this finding while compiling hundreds of routine corporate performance appraisals.

One of the reasons women are better leaders is that the essence of what women leaders do is to interact with people. They do all the things that good leaders do, men or women, but women seem to actively work harder to make their interactions with associates positive for everyone involved. More specifically, they share power and information, enhance other people's self-worth by listening, and get others excited about the task at hand. These characteristics sound a lot like "participative management," or McGregor's Theory Y.

Women at the Top

The number of women in business, especially at the top, is exploding. In the next few years, according to the U.S. Department of Labor, half of all businesses will have a female owner.[23] Most women-based businesses are small-sized, where women's people-centered leadership is not only appropriate, it is a significant factor in attracting and retaining key employees, with the economy strong and unemployment low. It is also appropriate because, as noted in Chapter 1, entrepreneurs use their natural leadership to build the business.

A positive sign that women are making it to the top with their interactive leadership style is the outside selection of Carleton "Cindy" Fiorina for the top job at the high-tech firm Hewlett-Packard. At least two out of the four finalists for the top job at HP were women. In other words, not only was a woman chosen, but the odds favored that result. Among the candidates Fiorina had the clearest grasp of the "HP Way"—referring to the company's value system and its emphasis on the people side of business. She joins an elite group of women heading Fortune 500 companies. This is a first, since the biggest and best known high-tech firms—such as IBM, AOL, Intel, and Microsoft—are run by men.[24]

Two of the most important factors propelling women into positions of corporate power are the two giant forces that are shaping the economy itself—rapid technological change and the shift to the horizontal corporation with its ethos of meritocracy. The resulting culture favors workers who excel at influencing others and are team players.

CO-LEADERSHIP: THE POWER OF GREAT PARTNERSHIPS

In large complex organizations, one person may not have the requisite skills to be both a professional manager and an inspiring leader. In such a difficult role, manager-leaders tend to leave their leadership skills aside. Kotter, in fact, claims that "most U.S. corporations today are overmanaged and underled."[25] But the opposite is also true. Being overled and undermanaged is just as dangerous—as Apple Computer found out under its founder, Steve Jobs. Because the abilities to lead and manage are so different, aptitude for both roles is rarely found in one larger-than-life individual. Jack Welch, Chairman of GE, is the poster boy of this dual role. Another corporate chief falling into this category was Sam Walton of Wal-Mart. Both Welch and Walton excelled at being leaders and managers. But because their kind is so hard to find, corporate America is witnessing the emergence of co-leaders. In this new model, the boss and subordinate act more like peers. With leadership partners, one often excels as the interactive leader while the other's focus is management. David A. Heenan and Warren G. Bennis, in their book *Co-Leaders: The Power of Great Partnerships*, make the point that power sharing can work if the chemistry is right.[26] From Bud Abbott and Lou Costello to the short-lived duo of Orvitz and Eisner, or the long-term relationship between Bill Gates and Steve Ballmer, differing skills and a willingness to share power are fundamental to any such successful partnership.

Remaking Microsoft

Chapter 3 describes Microsoft as an example of a company smart enough to reinvent itself, jump the curve, and realize its need for co-leaders at the top. As we've described, Microsoft had hit its own corridor of crisis. Steve A. Ballmer, the new president, was convinced he had to reinvent the company.[27] Ballmer and his boss, Chairman Bill Gates, have come up with a sweeping overhaul of the thinking and structure of Microsoft. This is leadership at its best. The Internet changed everything for Microsoft. They had to take a leadership position and jump the technological curve or face the prospects of organizational decline. Their "DNA strategy" as it is called, sets a new direction and organization structure for the firm.[28]

Gates and Ballmer realized that they themselves were the bottleneck. Decisions large and small were being funneled to the top. Typical of this centralized control was a practice of reviewing key features of soon to be released software and the response records from the company's customer support lines. This undermined the confidence of managers below—they didn't feel as though they were in control of their own destiny. To achieve the new vision, Microsoft is now decentralizing into eight separate entities.

The roles at the top change too. While Gates envisions the technology of the future, Ballmer's job is tending to the performance management of the business. He is the nuts and bolts guy; Gates is the leader. That is not to say that Balmer's job isn't leadership. Microsoft of the future will need lots of leaders as it manages its network of internal groups and external alliances. As Ballmer says, "I have to grow from being a leader to being a leader of leaders"[29] as he manages the business.

The Larry and Ray Show

When it comes to famous co-leaders, Larry Ellinson and Ray Lane certainly qualify. Ellinson and Lane together ran Oracle, the world's second-largest software company, for many years. Ellinson is a promoter of grand new strategies, the consummate leader. Lane looked after day-to-day operations while he painstakingly built the organization. He was Mr. Process. While Ellinson tries to change the computing world, Lane's focus is on changing Oracle. As Bill Marshall, an Oracle consulting manager, says, "As a combination, they're much stronger than they are as individuals."[30] Both Oracle and Microsoft provide examples of the interesting openness in high-tech companies to share power.

The Two-Headed Manager

A very young Internet consultancy uses a CO-CEO approach. Neither has anything in common with the other, yet that helps explain why it works. Sapient's Jerry Greenberg is Mr. Outside. He heads up sales and marketing. He facilitates board meetings, talks to Wall Street—traditional CEO stuff. On the other hand, Stuart Moore is Mr. Inside. His focus is how to make the firm a great place to work, and hiring talent. He is the one who can relate to the technical experts in their own language and be sympathetic to their needs—COO stuff.[31]

Is This Marriage Working?

While co-leaders are often complementary, power sharing can get sticky. Ray Lane and Larry Ellinson parted company in 2000 when Ellinson wanted to improve operations, cut costs, and fatten the bottom line. When mergers take place co-leadership is often structured for the two surviving CEOs. When Weill of Travelers and Reed of Citicorp finally put their merger together, they were appointed CO-CEOs. A 1999 *Business Week* article entitled "Is This Marriage Working?" pointed out the tension paradox created at the top of Citigroup. Both Weill and Reed are good at what they do, but couldn't share power. Even though joint leadership appeared to be the best solution, old-line managers had too much difficulty with the new arrangement. Eventually Weill got the top job and Reed quit.

However, the time-honored notion that all great organizations are the lengthened shadows of a great man or woman is drawing to a close. It will be the maturity of partnerships like that of Gates and Ballmer, the co-stewardship of Greenberg and Moore, or the hundreds of alliances being formed around the world that determine if teamwork at the top is viewed as a key component of corporate strategy. Neither flipping a coin nor selecting one CEO over the other is a viable solution. Can organizations expect teamwork at lower levels if the very concepts of teamwork aren't practiced at the top?

Integration Needs to Replace Either/or Thinking

One of the reasons for the emergence of co-leaders and power sharing is a reduction in either/or thinking. When picking an operating philosophy—the balance between a concern for production and a concern for people—there is a tendency among business people to fall into the trap of relying on one approach at the expense of the other. The dilemmas of bigger or smaller, controlling versus delegating, planning or spontaneous creativity, leading with vision or encouraging entrepreneurism, being self sufficient or out-sourcing, downsizing or building trust with employees are typical of those facing management-leaders. As more and more successful co-leadership companies are established, the drawbacks of either/or thinking are becoming clearer.

For example, Levi Strauss fell into either/or thinking and lost its way in the late 1990s. Family heir Robert Haas' decision in the mid-1990s to focus on vague (touchy-feely) people techniques at the expense of hard nosed performance requirements led the once ever-cool Levi's jean manufacturer to lose half its men's market share. No question, Levi Strauss was renowned as one of the best places to work. It made *Fortune*'s top ten lists many times, but in an editorial, *Fortune* editors laid much of the blame for loss of market share on Haas for mismanagement. Haas, they said, lost sight of Levi's main management goal: "To sell as many jeans as possible by keeping brand fresh."[32]

Either/or thinking creates an imbalance. Purpose (maintaining or increasing market share) can't take a backseat to people (and their needs). Both requirements must be fulfilled at the same time. While this creates tension, resolving what appears to be mutually exclusive approaches precipitates a new set of solutions. High-performance organizations—whether they have co-leaders or larger-than-life individuals like Jack Welch—seem to deftly balance the tension between pairs of opposites. The good ones allow these tensions to exist. They understand that tensions generated by work-related differences are the source of creative ideas that add value. Instead of arguing which ways are best, successful companies and their management-leaders strive to integrate different points of view. They use their pragmatism and influencing skills to defuse polarization.

MANAGING INTELLECTUAL CAPITAL

The other skill management-leaders will need to master is effectively utilizing intellectual capital. As we discussed earlier, today's worker is no different from his or her counterpart of fifty years ago. He or she wants the same things out of a job; the only problem is that fifty years ago the perception of work was radically different than it is today. However, over the past half-century, survey results about what motivates workers and what makes a company a great place to work have been very consistent. Time and time again, the results come back that challenging work and opportunity to continually grow in the job are what produce job satisfaction. Pay and employee benefits are fundamental to job satisfaction, but they are not key motivators. So, what's the great workplace secret?

CREATING SELF-ORGANIZING NETWORKS

Developing human capital—and converting it into useful products and services—is fast becoming the critical executive skill of the age. A developed human capital yields a professional intellect that creates most of the value in the New Economy, in both service and manufacturing industries alike. But few managers have systematic answers to even these basic questions: What is professional intellect? How can we develop it? How can we leverage it? This chapter has provided answers to these questions. Managers that understand these answers know that the secret to a great workplace is to create self-organizing networks.

These networks draw on all aspects of a knowledge worker's activity. According to James Brian Quinn, one of the first authors to write about intellectual capital, an organization's knowledge workers operate on four levels within a networked organization: tribal knowledge; advanced technical skills; an understanding of business process; and self-motivated cre-ativity.[33] Tribal knowledge speaks to how things are done in the organization, how people are expected to relate and communicate to one another, and ways developed to get the work out the door. Doing a job well means that technical skills must be constantly upgraded. Investing in formal technical skill development is good both for the firm and for the individual. Knowledge workers know this for it is what creates their value.

Understanding end-to-end business processes provides the rationale for why work needs to be done in a certain sequence. Having this macro view provides knowledge workers with the big picture and demonstrates how their job contributes to the customer satisfaction. Finally, when decision-making authority is coupled with peer collaboration, managers find an in-crease in self-motivated creativity.

Quinn and his coauthors argue that organizations that nurture self-motivated creativity are more likely to thrive in the face of today's rapid changes. They illustrate how organizations as diverse as Merrill Lynch and NovaCare have leveraged professional intellect by providing analytic soft-ware tools, incentive systems, and organizational redesigns. The authors contend that organizations can tailor themselves to the particular way their professional intellect creates value by creating self-organizing networks.

When a few technical experts team up to meet a specific challenge, they create a temporary team. These webs of inclusion tap the talent and the knowledge scattered around the company. For example, when major oil companies have an exploration problem and knowledge is dispersed among many specialists scattered around the world, like British Petroleum, they assemble a virtual team. Because telecommunications and Intranets are widely available throughout the world, communication in real time helps workers share their knowledge. The more technical experts assembled for a discussion the better. As Quinn and his co-authors claim, "A basic tenet of communications theory states that a network's potential benefits grow exponentially as the nodes it can successfully interconnect expand numer-ically."[34]

Managing intellectual capital requires a long view. It takes leaders with a vision about what the future holds. Managing a network organization, where knowledge is a strategic advantage, means that how workers are viewed and how they are developed will be the key to long-term corporate success.

SUMMARY

Running a business well, like any other human activity, requires a bal-ance between two different and often contradictory approaches: manage-ment and leadership. In ever more turbulent environments, executive leadership matters more than ever before. Speed, flexibility, and the ability to manage discontinuous change require excellent leadership skills. Leadership's job is to articulate vision. Leaders need to communicate a shared picture of the future that fosters genuine commitment and motivation. Leadership must be augmented through attention to details on roles, performance measures, and reviews, but always with an eye on strategy. Management charts a course for control, stability, and practicality; with the other eye on the day-to-day operations, the customer, and market share. Balancing these two requirements is what the management-leader is asked to do.

Interactive leadership relies heavily on communication skills. It is about creating the space for dialogue and thinking together for the common good. It requires a level of maturity in which you-plus-me equals let us work together. By listening, supporting, and encouraging people to differ, leaders ensure a constant dialogue over future directions and resolving the tensions between competing and often opposing ideas. These leaders have a sensitivity to others and respect their ideas, feelings, and emotions.

Interactive leadership is all about creating *an emotional connection with people.* One of the reasons why women are finding their way into more and more leadership jobs is that they tend to know better how to create webs of inclusion and environments for open communication. While these skills may come more naturally to women, they may be the most important ingredients for success in the twenty-first century as male-dominated organizations struggle to find a new "touchstone" to release the talent locked within their diverse workforce.

NOTES

1. Thomas A. Stewart, "Have You Got What It Takes?" *Fortune*, 11 October 1999, 322.
2. Ibid., 318.
3. "The Changing Nature of Leadership," *The Economist* 10 (June 1995): 57.
4. Ibid., 57.
5. Sumantra Ghoshal and Christopher A. Bartlett, "Changing the Role of Top Management: Beyond Structure to Processes," *Harvard Business Review* (January–February 1995): 87–96, and "Changing the Role of Top Management: Beyond Systems to People," *Harvard Business Review* (May–June 1995): 133–142.
6. Ibid., 135.
7. Douglas McGregor, *The Human Side of Enterprise* (New York: McGraw-Hill, 1985), 55.
8. Jill Rosenfeld, "Want to Lead Better? It's Simple," *Fast Company* (March 2000): 58.
9. Charles M. Farkas and Phillippe De Backer, "There Are Only Five Ways to Lead," *Fortune*, 15 January 1996, 109.
10. "Walking the Talk of People-Centered Management," an interview with Jeffrey Pfeffer, from *Harvard Management Update* 3, no. 2 (Cambridge, MA: Harvard Business School Publishing, February 1998), 7.

11. John P. Kotter, "What Effective General Managers Really Do," *Harvard Business Review* (March–April 1999): 145.

12. John A. Byrne, "How Jack Welch Runs GE," *Business Week*, 8 June 1998, 105.

13. Ghosal and Bartlett, op. cit., 142.

14. Faith Popcorn and Lys Marigold, *Clicking: 16 Trends to Future Fit Your Life, Your Work, and Your Business* (New York: HarperCollins, 1996), 159.

15. Michael Schrage, "Why Can't a Woman Be More Like a Man?" *Fortune*, 16 August 1999, 184.

16. Christopher Farrell, "Women in the Workplace: Is Parity Finally in Sight?" *Business Week*, 9 August 1999, 35.

17. Sally Helgesen, *The Female Advantage: Women's Ways of Leadership* (New York: Currency/Doubleday, 1995).

18. Sally Helgesen, *The Web of Inclusion* (New York: Currency/Doubleday, 1995).

19. Ibid., 10.

20. Judy B. Rosner, "Ways Women Lead," *Harvard Business Review* (November–December 1990): 120.

21. Rochelle Sharpe, "As Leaders, Women Rule," *Business Week*, 20 November 2000, 78.

22. Ibid., 75.

23. Kedric Francis, "Women CEOs: Leading Business to the Future," *OC Metro*, 15 July 1999, 34.

24. Joseph Menn, "First Woman Named to Lead Blue-Chip Firm," *Los Angeles Times*, 20 July 1999, p A1.

25. John P. Kotter, "What Leaders Really Do," *Harvard Business Review* (May–June 1990): 104.

26. David A. Heenan and Warren G. Bennis, *Co-Leaders: The Power of Great Partnerships* (New York: John Wiley, 1999).

27. "Remaking Microsoft," Cover Story, *Business Week*, 17 May 1999, 106.

28. Charles Piller, "Microsoft Shifts Its Emphasis to the Web with 'DNA' Strategy," *Los Angeles Times: Orange County Edition*, 14 September 1999, C1.

29. "Remaking Microsoft," op. cit., 109.

30. Steve Hamm, "Behind the Larry & Ray Show," *Business Week*, 3 August 1999, 88.

31. David Whitford, "The Two-Headed Manager," *Fortune*, 24 January 2000, 147.

32. Amy Kover, "Levi's Gets a New Boss," *Fortune*, 11 October 1999, 55.

33. James Brian Quinn, Philip Anderson, and Sydney Finkelstein, "Making the Most of the Best," *Harvard Business Review* (March–April 1996): 71–80.

34. Ibid., p. 75.

PART IV

MAKING IT HAPPEN

As Part III explained, shifting from a top-down, command-and-control model to allowing control at the point of control requires a formalized management system. In trying to make all this happen, there are several major obstacles facing management. Resultant issues and questions that beg for answers are:

- How can managers deal with ineffective organizational structures?
- How can managers deal with the loss of traditional control they have exercised in the past?
- How can managers motivate, compensate, and reward "knowledge workers," especially when they are part of many cross-functional teams?
- What do career paths look like in organizations where promotions up the corporate ladder are limited by flatter structures?
- Where can managers get the specialized and highly educated lower-level work force they need?
- Where are the managers of the future going to come from?
- Can top management sustain the interest and long-term focus to accomplish change in its existing organization cultures?

As Chapter 13 discusses, answers to these questions must carefully address all three "legs" of any business—*purpose, processes,* and *people.* It is difficult to change an organization without a well-conceived plan for all three elements. This chapter looks at some of the most common obstacles to change, obstacles typically resulting from plans that aren't comprehensive.

The book concludes with Chapter 14 where we re-examine the key issues of organizational change as firms are forced to respond to external pressures. We also highlight the important internal issues that can make such changes successful. New technology and increased globalization are powerful forces as we enter the twenty-first century. Most managers recognize these forces but often pay only lip service to their impact. At best their response might be to alter a few parts of the organization in a reactive fashion. We argue for a total holistic approach to change.

In the second half of Chapter 14 we outline and reiterate the three principal components of a successful change program. What is required is an integrated approach that resolves the tension created by the competing demands from *purpose, processes*, and *people*. Handling what are often tension paradoxes managers face every day in their attempt to reconcile these components is becoming an increasingly important skill as the life cycle of products, industry, and technology continues to speed up. When properly aligned and integrated, however, the three components make up the strategies and structure of a successful twenty-first century firm.

13

Why Change Programs Fail

In Part I we showed that change has become an imperative for most companies as their size and complexity increase in a fast-paced global economy. Yet in the face of what is often compelling evidence for the necessity of change, why do some companies not embrace it or do so in a half-hearted fashion? Even when tensions signal the importance of change, many firms resist altering established practices. Why? In some cases it's easy to dismiss such behavior as simply inertia or bad leadership. Similarly, some companies have introduced change only to abandon the new programs before they can really take hold. Why make the initial effort if it is not sustained? In other cases there appears to have been active resistance to change, whether through sabotage at the worker level or systematic opposition among midlevel managers.

In this first chapter of Part IV we bring together the major issues behind the failure of change programs. We also examine the reasons many firms don't innovate in the first place. We look at patterns behind such intransigence. In highlighting the problems that many firms face in implementing change, we note the issues that need addressing for change programs to be successful. We document this framework with references from academic studies as well as anecdotal examples of failures and successes.

OPPOSITION TO CHANGE

Here are the comments of a plant manager in an apparel company where one of the authors conducted a case study in 1999:

The CEO attended an executive education program at Harvard Business School and came back full of ideas about how we needed to change our old way of working. He was particularly enthusiastic about teams and immediately set up a working group of staff people to figure out a way to implement teamwork in the plants. Shortly thereafter, we had visits from senior management to explain the team concept and what it could do for our numbers. We were told to start figuring out how to change various aspects of production and to work closely with the consultants who were coming to explain what needed to be done. This is typical of the sort of stuff that comes down from head office. The CEO discovers something new, tells everyone that we need to use it, explains what happens if we don't, calls in some outsiders to show us how to set it up, then expects us to do the rest.

This is typically how many companies introduce change. It's imposed from the top down, generally by a CEO who has "seen the light." New ideas abound in management circles so it's not surprising that when senior managers talk with friends, attend seminars, or even read the business press, often they will come away with something new that they want to try in their firms. In some instances they think it will improve their overall performance; in other cases they see it as being necessary if they are to survive. Sometimes they adopt changes because they discover that others in their industry are doing so, and they don't want to lag behind. One senior manager of a steel mill said that his organization frequently innovates when the CEO discovers that major competitors have introduced new initiatives. The rationale for change seems to be that if others are doing it, so should we.

Some senior managers are known for experimenting with virtually every new fad that has come along. One manager of an electronics plant commented to one of the authors recently:

Over the years we've tried quality circles, management by objectives, TQM, and JIT. We've re-engineered twice in the last decade, we've tried teamwork twice, and we've had more initiatives than I care to remember. Every time there's something new the CEO is calling meetings to tell us what to do. There is so much change going on that no wonder we're not efficient anymore. We just keep playing around with new ideas.

This comment is telling because it gives the reasons so many change programs fail. They fail because they are not thought through carefully, because they are imposed from the top down, and because most employees see them as faddish and impermanent. They also fail because they are given insufficient investment of both time and resources, and because they often disrupt the existing status and workplace norms. For example, a plant manager of a textile company commented that, following the introduction of teams, productivity increased but so did the operating costs of his plants. At the end of the year, the higher cost resulted in lower than average bonuses for him and other managers in the plant. As a consequence his enthusiasm for teamwork has waned and he is experimenting with ways to re-integrate it with old, more cost-effective operating systems.[1] As the plant manager's experience shows, change programs also fail because they do not fit in with existing production structures.

Change is also difficult for many managers because it presents them with situations which are unfamiliar or for which they are unprepared. Such problems often stem from difficulties in reconciling day-to-day operating procedures with broader strategic goals. The following are typical of the sorts of mistakes managers make in these areas:

- Many managers don't make a distinction between management work and the work they do every day. They think that what they are doing in the entrepreneurial and directives stages is the work of management—to give task assignments, to control costs and to get production out the door.

- Many managers don't recognize that a formal planning and review system is not the same thing as giving and monitoring task assignments. Often they don't know how to put in place a performance management system because they have never done it before. Further, they often abdicate to a training department the job of teaching managers the fundamentals of performance management then assume that if the training is done the job is complete. When they don't implement the procedures themselves, it just produces another "flavor-of-the-month" program gone sour.

- Many managers are so task-driven that all they can think of is short-term projects that get results, not long-term solutions to the more fundamental problems they face.

- Many managers don't have time to think about the future and how to put in place a system that holds people accountable for results and not task assignments. Most of their time, therefore, is spent fire-fighting problems that have been ignored too long.

Finally, solving technical problems and getting involved in day-to-day operating details can be more exciting than doing management work. There is a management principle that describes this phenomenon. It says that when called upon to perform management work and technical work during the same time period, a manager will tend to give first priority to technical work.

The reasons these obstacles exist are simple. Operating work is fun; management work is hard. Immediate results are easy to see when making technical decisions. It is the kind of work that made managers successful in the first place. Add to this list the fact that past promotions were based on their technical ability rather than their skill in managing people and it is easy to see why managers often resist the introduction of new performance systems.

All of these obstacles demonstrate the importance of instituting change through all the three legs of the stool—people, purpose and process. Yet they also suggest a pattern whereby change is systematically impeded in many organizations. Typically, the obstacles to change can be broken down into the following subcategories:

- Failure to recognize the need for change.
- A superficial recognition of the need for change.
- Failure to systematically implement change.
- Failure to sustain change.

We now consider each of these in more detail.

Failure to Recognize the Need for Change

In 1972, IBM and GM were listed number 1 and number 4 in the Fortune 500 rankings. Into the early 1980s, IBM was ranked as the most admired company in the survey. Yet by 1992, both of these companies were struggling and loosing huge quantities of money. Both had legions of very intelligent managers and both had at one time in their histories been remarkable innovators. What went wrong?

The answer to this question is quite simple. Both companies refused to acknowledge the need for change. Both assumed that their size and obvious success would insulate them from the sorts of problems others companies were facing in the 1980s as new technology, new production systems, and new customer demands took shape. The arrogance of size is not new, neither is it unique to industry. Large firms, like many political and economic leaders, cloak themselves in a mantle of indifference that prevents them from recognizing the need for change. Sometimes it's because they fail to listen to the experts that tell them change is necessary. At other times, it's because they have surrounded themselves with cronies who are unwilling and even fearful of informing them of needed reforms. The business literature is replete with examples of CEOs who managed by fear. This also includes many entrepreneurial firms and family-run businesses. When they succeed, their leaders are seen as heroes with a forceful but dynamic style. But when they fail, as many do, it's often too late to do anything about the company.

But in neither IBM's nor GM's case was the management style particularly autocratic. They had merely lost touch with the nature of competitive reality, which can happen in the coordinative phase of an organization's evolution as Part I explains. In GM's case, managers assumed the old standardized, mass production model that was producer driven would continue to flourish. Even when Toyota's cars were gobbled up eagerly by consumers, looking for cost/quality combinations that GM (and other U.S. car manufacturers) couldn't provide, GM's response was to petition Congress for tighter import controls and higher tariffs on Japanese cars coming into the United States. Like a lumbering giant they stumbled along, their size and non-auto operations eventually saving them from bankruptcy.

Companies such as these adhere to the old command-and-control model and have failed to realize that the operating environment has changed. Their whole operating philosophy and corporate culture is built around such a paradigm and is therefore resistant to change because they do not perceive the need for change. They are caught in the paradigm paralysis trap. When the environment in which they competed was stable, such a system worked well and was arguably the most efficient way for them to allocate their resources. The norm was predictability and consistency, and the administrative hierarchies that they created were perfectly suited for such operations. But when that environment changed, flexibility replaced consistency and quality became as important as cost. They were ill equipped to even recognize the warning signs of change, let alone make the actual changes needed. They had built structures that ensured stability and control, but these structures also made innovation difficult.

In other instances, firms do not perceive the need for change because they see change as disruptive. Edgar H. Schein[2] talks about the various anxieties that managers have in firms when they confront the possibility of change. Since organizations are, according to him, an accumulation of prior learning based upon prior success, senior executives' ability to see what is going on in the outside world is limited. They are unwilling to embrace change because it appears too difficult, disrupts established procedures, and can hurt their success record.

Other companies that fail to recognize the need for change often assume that the competitive environment is unchanging and that past practices will continue to provide success. Such companies, as Gareth Morgan argues, are trapped by the status quo and have become myopic.[3] They have convinced themselves that their current reality is the reality, and in doing so refuse to acknowledge that their strategies and/or operating systems are no longer appropriate for the environment in which they compete. In these instances, competitors sneak up from the fringes and steal market share before their presence is even acknowledged by senior management.

Superficial Recognition of the Need for Change

Any review of the popular business press will provide numerous examples of firms that have embraced change. In fact, most firms are willing to experiment with new ideas, new technologies, and even new techniques. The problem comes in the reasons for the change effort. In many instances firms have embraced change because others are doing it. If one's major competitors have introduced new production systems or new technologies then perhaps one also should. Many CEOs are particularly susceptible to this form of thinking. In some instances they are prompted by the Board of Directors to consider something new. In yet other cases they learn about a new management practice at an executive retreat or a management seminar, or they are cajoled into adopting a program by their downstream customer. In addition, they might read about new practices in the trade or business press. Whatever the scenario, they become convinced of the necessity of changes and immediately initiate moves with senior management to implement the changes.

The problem with such proposed changes is that they might not be appropriate to the maturity of the firm or the nature of the firm's production. CEO insight is not always correct, and if senior management is unable to resist the pressure for change by arguing to the contrary, then inappropriate changes might be introduced. Such imitative behavior is surprisingly widespread among senior managers. Chris Tilly and Charles Tilly have argued that managerial decision making is often irrational, partly because managers lack sufficient information to make informed decisions and partly because they often merely imitate the behavior of others.[4] CEOs are not immune from such behavior. Rarely does senior management understand the complexity of organizational change, especially the details that are crucial for its sustained implementation.

For example, in a recent study of the apparel industry[5] it was found that several firms had introduced new work practices because the CEOs had decided that they would be a good idea. There was no systematic rationale for their introduction. In one instance, the CEO had heard about new automatic cutting machines and how these could be used to save on labor costs of skilled fabric cutters. He instructed one of the plant managers to try these machines. When the plant manager pointed out that such machines were more suitable to long production runs of standardized items—precisely the sort of production the firm was trying to move away from—his protests were ignored. The CEO was convinced of the efficacy of such machines because several of his executive friends had found them to be useful and a way of trimming labor costs. They did in fact reduce labor costs since the firm was able to lay off three highly skilled cutters and replace them with the machine and one semiskilled worker. But the constant reprogramming that was necessary for numerous style changes dramatically reduced the flow of fabric for those working in garment assembly and overall production rates deteriorated.

The result of such misguided innovation is often chaos, inefficiency, and resistance among the workforce. Instead of improving the performance of the firm, change inhibits success. Furthermore, if it occurs frequently, it can erode overall efficiency or lead to an institutionalized resistance to change. Managers and workers alike might become so used to change initiatives that they ignore them or doctor them in such a way as to limit their impact on existing procedures. In other words, change doesn't really filter down to operating levels, or if it does, it is concealed so as to marginalize its impact.

Failure to Systematically Implement Change

This failure of senior management to comprehensively implement change gives the impression that change efforts are not that important. Accordingly, they are seen as just another "flavor the month." Since most people dislike change because it disrupts established routines and is unpredictable, it's not surprising that change is embraced halfheartedly. Many firms behave in a similar fashion. Whatever the impulse for change, its implementation is often unsystematic or short-lived. In other instances powerful structural or cultural forces impede its implementation. The result is that many in the organization might not take it seriously, or see it as sufficiently threatening to actively resist it. Consequently, it is doomed to failure, despite the good intentions surrounding its inception. We examine each of these possibilities in detail.

Unsystematic Implementation. When an apparel company introduced just-in-time production techniques to lower inventory costs and speed product throughput, the plant manager was amazed that the finished goods sat in a warehouse because distribution failed to make the necessary changes to expedite delivery. This made him wary of introducing new changes in the future unless he could be assured that company-wide measures were being implemented. Whatever gains his part of the production process might yield are cancelled unless they are part of a total systematic restructuring. Similarly, at a mining company, the introduction of cross-functional teams in processing collapsed because adequate levels of training for workers that would enable them to perform effectively was not provided. The expected gains from teamwork did not occur because the workers lacked the skill for effective implementation. Finally, a well-known U.S. airline spent millions of dollars retraining its flight attendants to improve their "customer friendliness," but failed to provide similar training for check-in agents—the first point of contact group that passengers encounter before boarding a flight.

In each of the above examples, firms had the insight to recognize that a problem existed but failed to understand the magnitude of the change necessary. As we've argued with our three-legged stool analogy, organizations are interconnected structures. Changing one aspect of the structure without considering the effect that such change has on other aspects is a naïve but all too often common practice. As a consequence, change in one area of the organization can actually be disruptive for other areas. At best, the organization may simply not realize the benefits of change; at worst, such change could result in diminished efficiency and added costs.

All too often a successful firm recognizes the need for change, and innovates, but at the same time it retains many of the old ways of working, tinkering with production systems rather than radically overhauling them. Firestone and Laura Ashley were both successful companies that failed to make the necessary drastic changes when their competitive advantage eroded. They were victims of what Donald N. Sull calls "strategic blinders."[6] The firms were caught in a particular strategic mind-set that impeded their opportunity to innovate. They were complacent about their customer markets, content to peddle the same old goods in the same way. They failed to recognize that such markets were changing. When they did recognize the need to change, the innovation was superficial and consequently ineffective.

In recent years, the benefits of cross-functional teams have become obvious to many managers, but many have sought implementation in a piecemeal approach. They have either invested insufficient resources to maintain the program or made changes in parts of the organization while ignoring the need to change elsewhere. In the spirit of the old command-and-control system, some CEOs have imposed teamwork upon the firm but retained the parallel hierarchy of managerial control. Workers have been encouraged to work together in semi-autonomous work groups, to make decisions about daily operating procedures, and to take "ownership" of the product or job that they are doing. But at the same time, they remain part of a hierarchy that is rigidly authoritarian. They are fearful of making mistakes, lack the resources and the confidence to make decisions, and are pulled off of team activities to help in the technical work of their functional departments. Not surprisingly, this has often led to dysfunctional organizations.

Most of the recent research literature on high-performance work practices gives further evidence that failure is often associated with the lack of a systematic approach. For example, a 1993 U.S. Department of Labor[7] study found that productivity gains and improved financial performance are most likely attained when a system that ties together the various constituent parts is introduced. Only when these parts are comprehensively brought together will a firm realize the full benefits of such innovations. Many companies, however, introduce new processes in some areas, but lack an integrating system that will organize the old and new activities in ways that yield benefits.

Short-Term Fix Approach. Many firms that introduce new practices do so in the belief that they will yield dramatic results in the immediate future. Since many innovate in response to a crisis, it is not surprising that they expect an instant solution to their problem. Even those firms that are financially sound have to operate in a business environment that is increasingly driven by fear of a drop in the company's value (associated with a falling stock price). In such circumstances, it is often difficult for senior managers to develop a long-term strategic perspective.

This short-termism is pervasive throughout U.S. industry, and arguably is an inevitable consequence of a system increasingly driven by the need to maximize shareholder value. Much has been written about how U.S. managers have never been given the luxury of making the long-term investments that their counterparts in Japan or Germany have. Wall Street's obsession with quarterly financial performance has placed immense pressure on senior managers to deliver short-term financial gains, often at the expense of sustained long-term performance. Consequently, many workplace innovations are evaluated solely by their ability to deliver immediate benefits. Even if short-term gains are not immediately expected, it seems many managers are reluctant to await the full benefits of such a system.

A pervasive problem with much innovation is that it is expensive. New work systems require training and preparation that inevitably disrupt existing procedures. They also involve large investments in time. Since many of the most innovative work practices involve a radical break with old operating norms, it takes time for workers and managers to adapt to the new systems. During this "learning" period, productivity can easily fall and costs rise. One plant manager complained to one of the authors of this book that the introduction of teamwork into his plant resulted in that division losing money for almost two years. It took that long for "the kinks to get worked out." Every quarter for two years he had to convince senior managers at company headquarters that soon they would see the benefits. He tried to convince them that such changes would lead to an improved competitive edge for the company, better positioning it for a dramatically changing market. Unfortunately, his pleas fell increasingly on deaf ears. In the third year, just when he thought the new systems were working smoothly and yielding improvements across a range of measures (quality, speed, productivity, etc.), the plant was closed and production moved overseas. Not only did he personally suffer financially (through lower than average bonuses), the company suffered by not having the patience to reap the rewards of its investment. Not surprisingly he was bitter at what he correctly identified as a shortsighted approach to problem solving, and remained pessimistic about such situations ever changing.

Stories such as these indicate the situational problems that confront many managers attempting to change. There are disincentives associated with long-term investments and an institutional climate that pressures managers to evaluate innovations in terms of their immediate (usually financial) benefits. To look for instant returns on investments is therefore rational for the manager, although not necessarily beneficial for the company. Furthermore, since many innovations involve a "paradigm shift," the level of uncertainty increases dramatically. As a consequence, it is not surprising that managers "tinker" with change. They attempt modifications rather than a complete overhaul; they innovate but endeavor to retain the old structures as a fallback. But this results in self-fulfilling behavior. Change does not yield the promised benefits because its implementation is unsystematic.

Structural Impediments to Change

There is a long history of social science research showing that innovation often does not occur because of system inertia. Firms cling to outmoded organizational forms long after such systems are appropriate because existing structures act as impediments to change. Michael T. Hannan and John Freeman,[8] for example, argue that structural inertia is more likely to occur in large, older organizations where established routines are firmly in place. In such instances, change efforts are up against not so much an active opposition to change, but simply the accumulated weight and legitimacy of past practices that prove to be immovable. GM is perhaps one of the best and most well-known examples of this type of problem.

In her study of the problems surrounding attempts to introduce new technology and new processes in firms, Maryellen Kelly[9] found managers' enthusiasm for change was frequently tempered by bureaucratic imperatives that ended up constraining their attempts to innovate. Such practices as the "cookie cutter" approach by corporate staff groups to further their own particular subgroup interests and the conflicting messages, demands, and ever-changing priorities sent down by corporate staff are all examples of bureaucratic imperatives that dampen efforts at the local level to innovate.

Similarly, Vicki Smith's[10] study of banks found rigid rules and structures were used by middle managers and supervisors to buttress their own positions against the instability associated with new flexibility imperatives. In this instance, managers used structures to reinforce their own positions when change threatened to disrupt their status. And in organizations where managers might take initiatives and encourage innovation they often run up against inner organizational walls along which resources and rewards are allocated and careers determined. The old hierarchies used such structures and their attendant layers of bureaucracy to maintain control. As firms grew in size, so the hierarchy proliferated as further bureaucratic divisional structures were born. But divisions do just that—divide—and the old divisional model of companies not only fragmented a company's resources, it acted as a further impediment to change. Yet because of its past resilience, it was hard for many managers to let go of this system.

Other examples of structural resistance are contained in Howard Risher and Charles Fay's book on why Taylorism retains its grip on American industry.[11] They point to industrial relations systems that have institutionalized distrust between management and workers, making collaboration difficult. These adversarial relations make employees suspicious of management overtures. They point to a track record of wage compression and benefit erosion as responses to past problems and are convinced that any managerial initiative will probably be detrimental to worker interests. Similarly, managers distrust workers, claiming that they are indifferent to the plight of the firm, are selfish, and resist any change that might promote overall efficiency. Such employment relations are a product of the business unionism that was discussed in Chapter 6, and they remain a powerful legacy that constrains many change efforts.

Cultural Impediments to Change

Because the hierarchical model proved so successful for such a long period of time and was clearly the most efficient way of organizing production in stable markets, its cultural legacy has endured long after its practical importance. Since most senior managers learned their skills under this model, they not surprisingly retain belief in its efficacy.

Organizations are socially constructed realities, and the norms and values that are implicit in a firm's culture are important determinants of behavior in that firm. In fact, many have argued that successful firms are ones that have a cohesive culture that is more important than the operational structure. If a firm has flourished under a hierarchical culture, then attempts to introduce new non-hierarchical systems will obviously be difficult because of the pervasiveness and resilience of the old culture. Even if innovation is led by a strong manager-leader, the cultural residue of the old system makes penetration of a new ideology difficult. It can often take a long time for change to occur.

Morgan argues in *Images of Organization* that many senior managers prefer the way the old system permits them to specify "detailed rules, protocol, and targets that in effect bind the organization into a specific mode of operation. The overcontrol negates any redundancy, variety, and innovative potential that the unit may possess because attention gets focused on the internal rules and controls instead of absorbing and dealing with the external challenges being faced."[12]

He also suggests that certain groups such as accountants can shape the reality of organizational life by emphasizing the primacy of financial considerations. By exerting a very strong influence on the organization's culture they can force decisions to be constantly viewed through the lens of financial performance. While this is not necessarily bad, it can nonetheless make innovation difficult by basing all decisions on strict accounting standards.

The centrality of competitive individualism in U.S. corporate culture can also act as an impediment to change, especially when promotion and incentive packages are often tied to individual achievement. Delegating decision making and authority in an organization is seen as tantamount to admitting that managers are no longer the individuals responsible for success. Because many of the innovative change programs embrace a cooperative aspect, it is difficult for many managers to accept what they often see as the loss of individual initiative.

For example, many of the workers at Levi-Strauss plants where teamwork was introduced in the late 1990s resented the new work systems because they felt they had to pick up the slack for other coworkers. A climate of suspicion and anger developed. Workers were made to feel guilty if they left the production line to take a bathroom break. Also, many of the managers responsible for the implementation of change tampered with the programs or were provided with insufficient training themselves. Consequently, these programs failed. Managers admitted afterwards that the new systems were so different from the old ways of doing things, with several going so far as saying that they were inconsistent with the culture of apparel manufacturing and its strong emphasis upon piecework. With this sort of entrenched culture it is not surprising that change is difficult and frequently subverted.

Failure to Sustain Change

While many senior executives recognize the need for change, their commitment to it often wanes after the initial implementation. Morgan has estimated that at least 70 percent of companies that adopt some new form of innovative work practices or undergo reengineering and/or restructuring to improve quality, productivity, or customer service have been unsuccessful in such endeavors only to abandon them.[13] The principal problem appears to be their inability to rid themselves of the old bureaucratic logic that structures much of the production process. They fail to change the old mind-set that remains pervasive. Changes are introduced but often in a programmatic fashion. People try them because they are forced to do so, but interest wanes as commitment from the top diminishes. They fail to counter the many political dynamics within the organization that mitigate against newness. Too many vested interests suffer with change, and often resistance to change only becomes apparent after a period of time when leadership interests might be focused elsewhere.

One of the forces at work here is the functional mind-set. It is a powerful inhibitor of change. Many companies fail to recognize this and assume that if they change various structures, people will start to think differently. Ann Majchrzak and Qianwei Wang have argued that many companies assume change will be sustained if functional units are replaced with process-complete departments. In doing this, firms believe "it will forge them instantly into a team intent on achieving common goals."[14] But as the authors point out, this rarely happens because the change is not systemic and firms underestimate what needs to be done.

It's important to recognize that most organizations have vested interests in the status quo. They adapt to the external environment, coping with change when it is absolutely necessary but avoiding it whenever possible. Even when change has been initiated, behavioral patterns tend gradually to return to the norms and values that are preeminent in the organization. For this reason, many change programs fizzle after a period of time. Ironically, organizations that claim to be dynamic and embrace change are often ones in which the status quo remains the most resilient. In such cases, employees are so familiar with new ideas that they adopt the attitude of "it too shall pass." They passively resist change because they know it will not be permanent.

As we have noted, in many cases change doesn't work because it has not been fully integrated into the fabric of all of the operating procedures, and the intended benefits therefore are not realized. In other cases, managers claim victory after too short of a period. Harvard's John P. Kotter argues that many times firms abandon their reengineering efforts after a couple of years assuming that the benefits have become permanent. However, as he states, "Within two more years, the useful changes that had been introduced slowly disappear. In two of the ten cases [studied], it's hard to find any trace of the reengineering work today."[15] It appears that the initiators become over confident about success, while those that resist change find increasing opportunities to point out weaknesses in it.

In other instances, change fails because it is the brainchild of one person who left the company. For instance Daimler-Chrysler faces such a problem today. Daimler-Chrysler is a very different company to that of the resurgent Chrysler of less than a decade ago. In rebuilding itself, Phoenix-like, out of the despair of bankruptcy, it created a dynamic fast-paced company culture built around the energy of senior executives. But now that Robert Eaton, the last person from that group, has left, Chrysler will (some say "has") become subsumed under Daimler. Not only will it effectively become a German company, but also arguably many of its competitive strengths might disappear under a different, more bureaucratic corporate culture.

SUMMARY

Firms are remarkably good at resisting change. They do so, as we have shown in this chapter, for a variety of reasons. In some instances, active resistance and deliberate sabotage of change programs point to the presence of powerful forces that mobilize to protect their interests against change. In other cases, the resistance is less intentional. Structures inhibit change and cultures make adherence to the status quo easier than embracing change. The legacy of the bureaucratic model is powerful, yet the need for a militaristic chain of command is less and less evident in today's dynamic marketplace. Firms continue to muddle through, playing with some new systems then abandoning them when the payback is not immediate.

Nobody likes change, mainly because it disrupts the status quo and is invariably unpredictable. And modern management, as a profession that was nurtured throughout the twentieth century, is loath to relinquish learned and established control techniques. But, as we have shown in previous chapters and as we shall further explain in the next chapter, a new dynamic requires change that is more than cosmetic. The tensions that have emerged in the last decades have created the need for a new alignment of operating systems to tap the creative talents of people. This requires a new culture and a new form of management-leadership. The foundation for the old paradigm is crumbling.

NOTES

1. See Ian M. Taplin, "Managerial Resistance to High Performance Workplace Practices" in *Research in the Sociology of Work* 10, 2001.

2. Edgar H. Schein, "How Can Organizations Learn Faster?" *Sloan Management Review* 10 (Winter, 1993): 33–40.

3. Gareth Morgan, *Images of Organization* (Thousand Oaks: Sage, 1997), 93.

4. Chris Tilly and Charles Tilly, *Work Under Capitalism* (Boulder, CO: Westview Press, 1998).

5. See Ian M. Taplin, op. cit., 11–13.

6. See Donald N. Sull, "Why Good Companies Go Bad," *Harvard Business Review* (July–August, 1999): 44.

7. See U.S. Department of Labor, Office of the American Workplace, *High Performance Work Practices and Firm Performance* (Washington, DC, August, 1993).

8. Michael T. Hannan and John Freeman, "Structural Inertia and Organizational Change," *American Sociological Review* (1984, 49/2): 149–164.

9. Maryellen Kelley, "New Process Technology, Job Design, and Work Organization," in *American Sociological Review* (1990, 35, 3): 299–333.

10. Vicki Smith, *Managing in the Corporate Interest: Control and Resistance in an American Bank* (Berkeley: University of California Press, 1990).

11. Howard Risher and Charles Fay (eds.), *The Performance Imperative: Strategies for Enhancing Workforce Effectiveness* (San Francisco: Jossey-Bass, 1995).

12. Morgan, op. cit., p. 114.

13. Morgan, op. cit., p. 142.

14. Ann Majchrzak and Qianwei Wang, "Breaking the Functional Mind-Set in Process Organizations," *Harvard Business Review* (September–October, 1996): 93.

15. John P. Kotter, "Leading Change: Why Transformation Efforts Fail," *Harvard Business Review* (March–April, 1995): 66.

14

Strategies and Structures for the Twenty-First Century

This final chapter briefly discusses the faces of change and then is divided into three sections. The first is a reflection on and summary of the external forces of change organizations face as they evolve. Next, we look at three strategies that help to ensure successful change. We conclude the chapter with a discussion of how organizational structures are changing given the profound shifts taking place in digital technology and the new emphasis on managing the human side of enterprise.

FACES OF CHANGE

In today's evolving network, organization leadership skills among managers are more vital than ever before. As we've seen in previous chapters, horizontal, team-driven organizations are becoming the norm. Such firms require not merely a manager but a leader, someone who can provide strategic direction, inspire trust, and have excellent communication skills. As we explained in Chapters 1 through 5, all organizations evolve through predictable stages. As they grow and mature, the methods required to control their size and complexity change. Recognizing this inevitability, senior executives have the responsibility to first understand where their business is in its evolution and then lead by articulating a strategic direction that anticipates the next evolutionary phase. They cease to be simply managers as they become management-leaders in this most important process. All organizational evolution—in structure, leadership, and maturity—is in response to and stimulated by change.

EXTERNAL DRIVERS OF CHANGE

Since a firm's size and complexity are largely the result of external drivers—changing customer requirements, public policy, and as we are seeing entering the twenty-first century, rapid improvements in communication technology—firms are constantly forced to deal with change. We now live in an age of unprecedented economic volatility, where change is omnipresent and much faster than in the past. Not only have business activities become increasingly globalized, thereby altering the face of change, but microprocessor technologies have unleashed a phenomenal growth in the velocity of change. The ability to recognize change *and* respond quickly and accurately to it determine the firm's ability to maintain flexibility, innovate, and adapt to a changing environment.

Even though today, more than in the last two decades, strategic leadership requires senior executives to look outside the firm at customer expectations, this perspective is often hard to achieve. The legacy of large hierarchical organizations is typically to focus inward. These firms see the outside world as an environment to compete against and one in which customers are manipulated by marketing to buy products. Such firms fail not only in their efforts to change but also in their profitability, as the previous chapter explained.

A powerful driver that can change this inevitability is the evolution of technology and its impact on the organization. An example is the PC industry. It has evolved from the early years of Steve Jobs and the Apple computer to one where innovation and creativity are needed again. Compaq's new president, Michael Capellas, describes the challenges facing his $39-billion-a-year behemoth when talks about "the third stage" of the PC era: "The first stage was design and innovate [*see our Chapter 1*]. The second was driving toward standardization and almost commoditizing the business [*see our Chapter 2*]. Now we are getting back to creativity."[1] Where outside consulting, reengineering, and other change initiatives failed, organizations are now forced to adopt the realities of a wired and networked economy.

Connectivity Is Changing Organizational Structures

Microprocessor technologies, particularly the advent of the Internet and its ability to connect people, are rapidly changing the structures and relationships both within and outside the firm, and with them change in corporate mind-sets. Hierarchy and bureaucracy minimize connections between people, making connections across departments, divisions, and within work groups infrequent and difficult. However, horizontal connectivity is beginning to shift power and control away from the top to those directly doing the work and interacting with customers. Speed and availability seven days a week and twenty-four hours a day are assuring connectivity on a scale only dreamed about a decade ago. Connectivity is stretching the linkage to the far corners of the economic world. In their book *Blur, the Speed of Change in the Connected Economy*, Stan Davis and Christopher Meyer make the point that "connectivity is putting everybody and everything online in one way or another and [this] has led to the death of distance, a shrinking of space."[2]

While the shrinking of space—and therefore also of time—has become much more prevalent today, it is not a new phenomenon. The U.S. apparel industry in the 1980s pioneered the "quick response" system—a system of tight coordination among fabric makers, clothing manufactures, transportation providers, and retailers.

For example, Benetton of Italy gained fame for cutting months out of the traditional supply chain by tying production to retail activity. Benetton built its own web of relationships long before there was a World Wide Web. To make their system work, the company had to give up a measure of control and rely instead on influencing others over whom they had little direct control. This is the nature of the emerging web of connectivity spanning the globe. Managers must still manage but interactive leadership builds alliances that hold a web of inclusion together. Benetton's system allowed stores to keep the hottest items in stock and left them little to unload in end-of-season sales. Speed drives such a "quick response" system; connectivity between continents enables the system to deliver today better than ever before. Their system of "quick response" is mirrored in all organizations today, only at a faster pace.

The Global Neural Network

The emerging system of communication being formed by accelerating connectivity is a brain-like structure made up of neural nodes and web-like synapses. The world is being laced with a network of nodes flashing and blinking at one another as they send their packets of data hurtling around the globe from computer to computer. The world is sprouting a massive growth of web sites, supply-chain networks, B2B connections, buying intermediaries, and auction sites. These are accelerating the connectivity between people at the same time as they dramatically increase the velocity and volume of business activity. Organizations facing these dynamic conditions can ill afford to ignore such changes or merely tinker with their organizations and structures. They need a vision of the future, solid management procedures to execute flawlessly, and an organizational structure that maximizes flexibility.

As the Pendulum Swings

The problem many in senior management face is the difficulty in both grasping the necessity for change and developing the appropriate vision to accomplish it. Couple this limitation with a rapidly changing external environment and the result is "paradigm paralysis." This paralysis isn't limited just to companies. Managers find themselves in the middle of an age of discontinuity where many of the old rules do not apply and the new rules of innovation, creativity, and customer focus have not yet been established. However, there are positive signs that the corporate pendulum is swinging away from excessive top-down management controls and toward leadership that is people-centered. We forecast that this emphasis on leadership will continue to dominate corporate strategy during the next decade.

Maintaining control while encouraging people-centered creativity is a tension paradox for many in senior management. Recognizing this, management-leaders need to know where their company is on the control/ creativity continuum as the pendulum swings between tight control and chaos, and they need to monitor performance in order to take action when things are moving too far in one direction or the other. This is a proactive approach, similar to what the Federal Reserve Board does when it raises or lowers interest rates, and is paramount to ensure a firm's continued growth and profitability.

Strategic Inflexion Points

Oscillations in the life cycle of society and organizations are a natural phenomenon. When they veer too far in one direction—as may have been the case with the industrial revolution—they create a "strategic inflection point." This concept describes a point in time when the underlying assumptions upon which past practices are based need re-evaluation. It is a time when the old ways and assumptions are challenged by the new. It is both a dangerous and yet opportunistic time. In such circumstances the challenge for senior management is to be proactive, creative, and jump the curve, preserving the old while funding the new.

Robert A. Burgelman and Andrew S. Groves of Intel coined the term *strategic inflection point* in a 1996 *California Management Review* paper entitled "Strategic Dissonance."[3] Dissonance, they argue, can be felt and predicted because everything has a life cycle. Products, organizations, and even empires usually follow the S-curve pattern depicted in Figure 14.1. They start off strong, plateau after a while, and then start going downhill. At point A on the first curve the firm is doing well, but senior management needs to be wary, anticipating the eventful decline of the first curve and looking for a second curve to climb. If management looks at the future

Figure 14.1
Life Cycle Decline

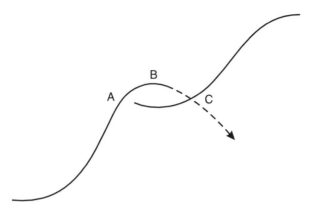

from point B, the firm is already in trouble and does not know it. Most firms don't start feeling the pain until they are at point C, when their backs are against the wall and they have few options. Before this happens, firms need to jump the curve to protect what they have, build on the past, and fund the new.

Unfortunately, mature products make the most money at a time when they are about to expire. As a consequence senior executives tend to be blinded by profit. The more successful the company, the harder it is to contemplate a downturn. However, like some light bulbs, they are brightest just before they burn out.

The Internet Creates an Industrial Strategic Inflection Point

Figure 2.3, in Chapter 2, suggests that new industrial life cycles emerge about every 55 years. If this is true, then the Internet is the new emerging technology. Building on the *analog* telecommunications life cycle started in the early 1950s, the *digital* revolution of the Internet is creating strategic dissonance for many firms today. E-commerce and Web retailing pose a sticky marketing dilemma for products sold through traditional retail outlets. For them the strategic question, and the dilemma, is to stay with "bricks," shift to "clicks," or try to do both. These are the choices. Trying to do both will probably result in neither being done well. For example, if consumer products manufacturers don't protect the volumes they currently have—through the likes of mass marketers like Wal-Mart—as they explore Internet possibilities, these firms face the prospect of being shut out as suppliers. If this were to happen they would loose cash flow vital to the support of existing plants and equipment and would possibly underfund the new Web medium. Balancing these two colliding strategic initiatives *within one organization* may also be too much for the managerial mind. The solution and the only way to survive according to Harvard's Clay Christenson is for firms "to set up a separate company to cannibalize the parent."[4] Without a separate entity that has its own cost structure and set of customers the parent will kill off the new project. This scenario is not a new dilemma for companies.

Change Is a Given

Today, new technology is changing the rules for many traditional companies forcing senior executives to rethink not only their customer relationships but the assumptions about how to manage and structure their firms for the future. They need to be careful not to fall into the trap of managerial rationality. If they do, they may end up shunning important new technologies and markets precisely because they are being good managers according to the old rules. That is, listening to shareholders and customers and focusing investments and research on the most profitable products that are currently in high demand by the best customers. This rational instinct works well when it's a matter of incrementally improving existing offerings. Yet when it comes to disruptive innovations like the Internet, rational management will fail.

This disruptive period in history may one day be labeled the "the age of discontinuity." If history teaches us anything about change, it is that incremental and piecemeal approaches that end up protecting old systems must be avoided and that quick fixes do not work. When changing organizational components the same potential liabilities exist. In Chapter 13, "Why Change Programs Fail," we suggest that the root cause behind most change program failures is not seeing the organization as a total system—changing one aspect, one condition, one process, one department—and not considering what had to be changed in other parts of the system to support the new initiative. Strategies and structures for the twenty-first century require a holistic approach to change. Without such an approach, the organization will reject the new and revert to its old ways of doing things.

THREE STRATEGIES TO ENSURE CHANGE SUCCEEDS

When faced with a strategic inflection point, three strategies to ensure change initiatives succeed are like the legs of a three-legged stool we described on Part I—the legs of purpose, process, and people, as Figure 14.2 shows. When considering a change or designing a new organization all three legs of the stool must be given equal consideration or the organization will be unbalanced; it will be unstable. As with the stool, organizations must be aligned around three key elements.

The first and most important corporate strategic leg is to clearly define

Figure 14.2
Three Elements of Strategy

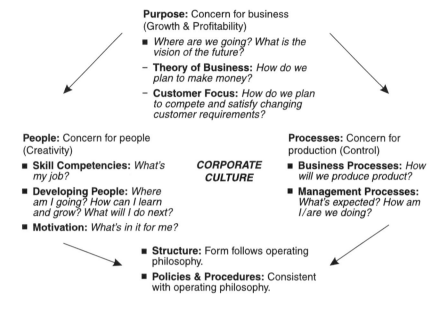

Purpose: Concern for business
(Growth & Profitability)

- *Where are we going? What is the vision of the future?*
- **Theory of Business:** *How do we plan to make money?*
- **Customer Focus:** *How do we plan to compete and satisfy changing customer requirements?*

People: Concern for people
(Creativity)

- **Skill Competencies:** *What's my job?*
- **Developing People:** *Where am I going? How can I learn and grow? What will I do next?*
- **Motivation:** *What's in it for me?*

***CORPORATE
CULTURE***

Processes: Concern for
production (Control)

- **Business Processes:** *How will we produce product?*
- **Management Processes:** *What's expected? How am I/are we doing?*

- **Structure:** Form follows operating philosophy.
- **Policies & Procedures:** Consistent with operating philosophy.

company *purpose*. It spells out the rationale for organizational existence. The purpose defines how the firm will be profitable and how it will satisfy customer needs. A concern for production describes a company's *process* leg. Production processes cover "how" the product is produced. Finally, employee skills, motivation, and commitment are the crucial third leg of any change effort. As much thought and effort must go into a strategy for *people* issues as goes into the other two legs of corporate strategy.

Figure 14.2 depicts the relationship between concerns for purpose, process, and people. A more detailed version is in Appendix D. As we argue in the previous chapter, many firms that embraced reengineering failed miserably in their attempts because their efforts were one-dimensional. They changed a procedure, cut a few unnecessary steps, or combined steps without paying attention to the deeper requirements of a change effort.

Typically, change efforts start with "a concern for improved production"—how to increase efficiencies, reduce costs, or shorten production cycle times. Take for example the change efforts that deal with redesigning how warehouse workers fill routine orders directly from the company's intranet, thus freeing up customer service representatives for more complex *and* different kinds of work. Both warehouse workers *and* customer service representatives will need training and new performance goals. This change requires both to do more, possibly resulting in a modification in the incentive compensation system.

Achieving such change is difficult—witness the fact, mentioned before, that 70 to 80 percent of the reengineering efforts of the early 1990s failed. Because management's unstated purpose was often the elimination of people, the impact of these reengineering efforts was resistance by the very people who had to make the reengineered processes work.

If there is a lesson to be learned from these many failed change efforts, it is the frequent absence of a clear rationale for change. To avoid such failures in the future, three questions need to be answered and then articulated with a clear strategy. They are: Why are we doing this? What are the implications for existing production processes? What will be the impact upon employees? Not coincidentally, each of these questions addresses the stability of the corporate legs—purpose, process, and people. We discuss these below in detail, showing how crucial they are in building competitive viability for firms in an age of discontinuity.

Purpose: A Concern for Profitability and Growth

For profit making corporations there are two categories that define a firm's purpose. One deals with how the firm plans to make money and the other with how the firm plans to grow.

Profitability of the Firm. Peter F. Drucker links making money to what he calls the company's *theory of the business.*[5] Drucker argues that what underlies the decline of so many large and successful organizations worldwide is that their theory of business no longer works. The story is a familiar one: a company that was a superstar only yesterday finds itself stagnating. The root cause of nearly every one of these crises is not that things are being done poorly. It is not even that the wrong things are being done. Indeed, in most cases, the right things are being done—but fruitlessly. What counts for this apparent paradox? Drucker argues that the assumptions about how to make money may no longer fit the firm's emerging reality. These assumptions are what Drucker refers to as a company's theory of the business.

Nike, for example, makes great gross margins, not from manufacturing product, since it has no factories, but instead from brand awareness. Getting teams and sports legends to wear its colors and footwear is its theory of business. As another example, Wal-Mart brought low prices and selection to rural America with superstores, but its theory of business is based on volume buying, superior logistics, and low inventories.

Profitability, earnings per share, discounted future cash flows, shareholder value, or other fiscal measures track the economic viability of a firm's business model. But what drives all business models is the customer. Knowing exactly what customers want and being able to deliver it to them is what ensures continued profitability. Today's customers are more discerning and expect value and a degree of customization hitherto unknown. Making profits therefore means knowing customers better than ever before.

How to Grow the Business. Meeting or exceeding customer expectations is what ensures not only corporate life but also corporate growth. To achieve this in today's technologically savvy marketplace, closer ties with customers are necessary. Micro marketing and the Internet are showing the way. In place of shotgun approaches to marketing are interactive customized approaches between customer and supplier. The result is a stronger relationship with customers that today enables firms to monitor micro data about their customers, and thus provides unprecedented levels of customer satisfaction. Customers, as Cisco's CEO John Chambers recently stated, must be made "the center of your culture."[6] Similarly, Hewlett-Packard has undergone a dramatic refocusing of their core activities following a new direction from its leadership team. Finally, Southwest Airlines has built a sustained pattern of success in an intensely competitive industry by developing a wide range of activities that tightly fit and reinforce each other. Their activities are united around a common purpose but complement each other, as Michael Porter[7] argues, in ways that create significant economic value. Furthermore, everyone in the company understands the importance of this strategic fit and how it delivers value to customers.

From a commitment to more individualized marketing flows an articulation of the firm's operating philosophy. Within this operating philosophy are the other two legs of a firm's strategic tripod.

Process: A Concern for Production

Many of the productivity improvements in today's organization are the effects of a digital economy. Not only has computer software automated many business processes that were hitherto manual, the falling cost of computer automation suggests this trend will continue. To ensure competitiveness, strategic initiative must continue to focus on ways of maximizing the benefits of such automation. But at the same time micro marketing and adding value for customers can nonetheless be costly and firms must continually define and control cross-functional processes to ensure that added costs do not outweigh benefits.

The Production Process—Controlling Operations. Part III dealt with management techniques for controlling operations and using leadership to influence people. Some major concepts covered in Chapters 10 through 13 are:

- In order to move to a teamwork-driven environment, an organization must first put in place a *vertical* system of accountability right down to the shopfloor or where the actual work takes place. This requires the art of delegation.

- Once performance measures and decision-making authority are in place, then an organization can begin to think about creating a *horizontal* organization through teamwork as well as encouraging cross-functional communication. Horizontal structures function through the operating review meeting (ORM), a management technique to ensure operating results at all levels. The ORM is a short-term planning and review process that defines what managers and team members are expected to do to ensure financial results.

With a vertical system of accountability and a horizontal performance management system in place, decision making is pushed further and further toward the workers actually doing the work. Through this process not only does hierarchy become flatter by eliminating layers of bureaucracy that hindered change in the past, it becomes more fluid. With data and information harnessed at the point of production (where it is needed most) and disseminated throughout the firm (where it can be best acted upon), the use of information becomes a core competence for a firm. If teams and networks are to function effectively, they must be legitimized and made part of an open culture, where trust permits information to be shared, and communication drives all work done.

When leaders communicate a strategy and make delegated decision making a reality, the old manager-subordinate structure becomes one of partnership. With more discretion invested in employees who possess the necessary skills and training to act responsibly, firms can harness the full informational potential of all of their employees, not just the ones at the top of the old hierarchy. This is what is meant by open communication and a workplace notable for trust.

The Management Process—Controlling Results through People. In the same way that an autopilot can guide a craft with minimal supervision, so too can firms begin to streamline managerial intervention. Management processes are just like production processes; once they are defined and systematized they can be passed to those closer to the work being done. With today's emphasis on cross-functional teams, natural work groups, and continuous improvement task forces, senior executives must delegate some of their planning and review activities to those actually doing the work. The traditional command-and-control structures had teams, but they were vertical. Employees belonged to the sales team or the internal audit team, and the boss was responsible for managing the group. With the growing evolution of networking across traditional boundaries, team and project management skills—planning and reviewing results—are vital to the success of an evolving horizontal organization. If business processes are to achieve the levels of flexibility and quality that many argue are fundamental for success today, then the people that are part of these processes must have their own set of processes to do the job at hand.

An example of a company that excels in both business and management processes is Toyota. In a *Harvard Business Review* article about how Toyota integrates product development, authors Durward K. Sobek III, Jeffery K. Liker, and Al C. Ward explain how Toyota created a *formalized* tight-loose set of management processes to share knowledge, speed up product development, and achieve integration across projects over time, as well as within projects. Well known for its social processes, Toyota balances these with highly formalized rules for team member interaction, communication, and problem solving. Because they can become unproductive if not designed and conducted effectively, Toyota even goes so far as to place limits on the use of cross-functional teams. Such rigid policies appear on the surface to limit project development efficiencies, but the tight constraints actually improve team effectiveness. To ensure each project team has the flexibility it needs to be productive Toyota adds freedom within the constraints. The point is that upper management takes the time to specify the management processes and behaviors by which team members are to interact. "The result is a deftly managed process that rivals the company's famous production system, lean manufacturing, in effectiveness."[8]

People: A Concern for Workers

If the production processes require management skill to maximize production efficiencies, by providing a structure of control, leadership skill is required to unleash creativity in people. Tomas V. Morris, former professor of philosophy at Notre Dame, in his book *If Aristotle Ran General Motors*, stresses that an important requirement for day-to-day worker satisfaction "is the performance and active experience of meaningful creation. And that's one reason why empowering people, pushing a creative scope for decision making as far down the corporate hierarchy as possible into the front lines, is so important."[9]

Thanks to receptive capital markets and the venture capital community, there is a tremendous opportunity to tap the creative potential of the population. The free flow of capital, most visible in Silicon Valley, is hatching ingenious new companies by the score that rely strongly on creativity. Admittedly many fail, and large numbers are overvalued as investors continue to hype their potential rather than what they have actually achieved. Nonetheless, they have unleashed a degree of dynamism and a flurry of entrepreneurial activity that has not been seen in decades. As established firms scramble to ride the bandwagon of this digital success they have come to realize the necessity of growing their own "human" assets. With fewer but higher-skilled employees in many firms, the critical factor becomes one of labor retention. How does one retain workers in whom large investments (training, etc.) have been made? While casual dress days are appealing to some, and stock options attract others, the most important component remains the work itself. Creativity remains uppermost in the minds of many

employees as they search for employment that rewards them both financially and emotionally.

To understand what is unleashing this wave of creativity is to understand
what people want most out of their jobs. Besides meaningful and creative
work, Morris digs even deeper and suggests that business should be about
people in a partnership for a shared purpose.[10] This is the same conclusion
that others have come to, but which remained ignored by many firms in
the old command-and-control system. While not all employees want to be
decision makers, many want to be more involved in day-to-day activities.
Not only that, they believe they can help improve the profitability of the
firm if their practical knowledge is regularly solicited. It is such a partnership for a shared purpose that can become the cornerstone of harnessing
the creativity of all employees.

One of the misconceptions about creativity is that it thrives best in an
unstructured environment. Nothing could be further from the truth. Vinton
Cerf, the father of the Internet revolution, devised TCP/IP as a set of standard protocols that serves as the common "language" of the Internet. His
comment is that, "People often take the view that standardization [control,
limits, boundaries, etc.] is the enemy of creativity. But I think that standards
help make creativity possible—by allowing for the establishment of an infrastructure, which then leads to enormous entrepreneurial creativity and
competitiveness."[11] Like organization or DNA, diversity blossoms when
there is a tightly defined infrastructure with unlimited possibilities for creativity.

Skill Competency. "People power" is predicted to be the next productivity lever in developed countries. High tech can only engender so much
in the way of increased productivity. If productivity increases are to continue, worker input must be more effectively utilized. This involves workers
having the appropriate skill sets to match the jobs that they do and it
requires putting forth adequate effort to maximize the use of such skills.
We have already noted the importance of increasing worker discretion to
raise effective effort. Too often, however, increasing effort is nothing more
than intensification of effort or work speedups. This was part of the old
manufacturing ideologies in which productivity gains were achieved by
finding ways to make workers work harder. But workers in more participatory work settings have a wider range of opportunities to realize productivity gains. They work smarter rather than working harder.

Smarter workers need ongoing training and skill acquisition. Companies
must invest in workers and workers must continually add to their own
human capital. The marketplace for skilled workers, especially those in
high-technology fields, is very tight. Firms in such fields must compete for
new employees and find ways to retain them. Investing in people demonstrates a commitment by the firm to employees. Making the job challenging

and the rewards appropriately exciting helps the firm keep its strongest asset.

Developing People. The old human resource model that underlay earlier (1980s) attempts to rethink the management of employees all too often resulted in the marginalization of employee issues. As a consequence of power struggles over resources within firms, most of which were won by finance or marketing departments, human resource issues were relegated to secondary status. As people issues have been reinstated as one of the principal concerns for firms, firms are realizing just how important attracting and developing human resources are for their survival.

In the high-technology sector, a firm such as fast-moving Cisco has been able to improve retention of workers and raise productivity by ensuring that its workers remain committed. It has done this through ongoing skill development programs and delegating decision-making authority to employees. Many firms make the mistake either of not following extensive training with appropriate delegation or of granting considerable autonomy to teams, but not providing adequate training or infrastructural support for such teams. In either case, the result is employee frustration.

To fully capture the efficiency benefits of a restructured workplace, firms must commit themselves to organizational learning and knowledge creation. In what some authors[12] have termed high-performance work systems (HPWS), the accumulation of shopfloor production experiences leads to organizational learning which in turn translates into productivity increases. These HPWS can also foster improved adaptability that permits the firm to respond quickly to subsequent market or technological changes.

However, a commitment to such a system without due consideration of the purpose and process aspects of the tripod can be disastrous. For example, Levi-Strauss has a long history of success as a company in which people matter. But recently their failure to pay sufficient attention to their business processes became particularly problematic when their market share dropped and they were forced to lay off many of their employees and close plants. People are important but only when their function is part of an interdependent business strategic whole in which purpose and process are clearly addressed. In this case, inadequate attention to one crucial aspect (process) undermined their legacy of success in another (people).

It may seem trite to reiterate the following point, but communication remains fundamental to organizational success. Whereas information was guarded and territorial in the past, if firms are to succeed in a fast-moving marketplace, they must disseminate information widely among the workforce. Part of this dissemination can be built into the organizational culture, usually by the senior executive becoming a "listener" as much as a speaker. If he/she is a management-leader, open, two-way communication is more likely to occur. The more communication occurs the more it becomes an integral part of the organization, and with it workers' trust becomes solidified. With more open communication, the interests of the firm are more easily aligned with those of its employees because assumptions about the firm (its theory of business) are shared among all the parties. Employees will be easier to motivate when what they want from work is the same as what the firm wants.

STRUCTURE: THE NEXT EVOLUTION OF ORGANIZATIONAL FORM

The next few decades promise to be extremely interesting. The pace of change today and the currently evolving organizational forms point to an uncertain but somewhat predictable future. One of the few things we can confidently predict about the organizational forms of the near future is that they will be even more shaped by their external environment. For example, in recent years there has been an increased awareness of the need to better manage relations with external suppliers and buyers. Supply-chain management has become an integral part of daily activities in many firms, and even automobile industry giants such as Ford and GM are reducing their number of suppliers and establishing partnerships with them rather than seeing them as low-cost contractors. In its new plant in Brazil, for example, Volkswagen has divided its sprawling factory into sub-areas in which component suppliers bring prefinished products to assemble in the vehicles. Instead of a large contingent of workers on VW's payroll, their suppliers provide not only components but also the workers to install them. VW merely coordinates the activities of these various suppliers within its own factory.

Jessica Lipnack and Jeffrey Stamps argue, in *The Age of Networks*, that organizations can realize many new opportunities by forging networks both from within and externally. While the thrust of their book lies in its advocacy of interlocking teams and the breakdown of hierarchies within firms, by also pointing to interfirm collaborative advantages, it highlights the true benefits of networking outside the firm.[13]

Ironically, in arguing as others have for the need to build networks in firms, Lipnack and Stamps reinvent an organizing principle that preceded the growth of factories almost 200 years ago. At the dawn of the industrial revolution, owners of capital searched for ways of assembling simple products that they could subsequently market. In the cottage industry that emerged, local artisans labored on product assembly at home, using parts supplied by an industrialist. This was known as the "putting out system," and the finished product was collected and subsequently marketed by the industrialist, while the artisans were paid on a piece rate basis. The inefficiencies of this system were identified by Adam Smith, who argued for greater specialization in what would subsequently become the factories of the nineteenth century.

However, in many places such as northern Italy, where a network system of continued artisanal production persists to this day, the benefits of a more collaborative set of interfirm relationships are still apparent.[14] In Italy, the state provides much of the necessary infrastructure that permits small firms to externalize some of their costs, enabling them to further work a system that is both very old and very new. In the United States some of the infrastructural costs to encourage new business enterprise are born by local government. This support is evident in Silicon Valley, and on the East Coast around Massachusetts' Route 128, and within North Carolina's Research Triangle. The high concentration of research universities in these areas helps cross-fertilize new ideas, which, together with local fiscal initiatives (tax breaks, indirect subsidies, etc.), encourage high-technology entrepreneurial activity.

What is apparent in these and other cases is that organizations can flourish by specializing in one or more things, developing functional complementarities through collaboration. These networks are less hierarchical than their counterparts of 200 years ago. They also rely upon information sharing and strategic goals that are designed to be mutually beneficial to all partners. They are founded on trust between members and the assumption that growth will often be qualitative rather than quantitative. In this new guise, firms abandon hierarchy within and seek collaboration/cooperation in many of their external relations. The former provides increased adaptability and the latter a means to rationalize activities across a wide range of key value-added linkages. Such organizing principles are bound together by leaders whose strategic vision rests on their ability to garner input from everyone within the firm and from strategic alliance partners.

In the past when mass production was the norm, size typically was the means whereby firms developed their core competencies. Such an approach was geared to maximizing efficiency. In the new organization, where the aim is effectiveness, size matters less than the bundle of interdependencies than heighten the flow of information. The core competencies are now shaped by the firm's ability to develop appropriate frameworks where trust, collaboration, and exchange of information occur. A more cooperative venture is necessary, with leaders establishing the parameters for information flow as well as the broad strategic goals. Rather than doing one thing well, core competency is now about doing many different things that collectively promote effectiveness. For example, it is hard to point to one thing that Southwest Airlines does well since its success comes from a combination of crucial interdependent activities. Such bundling of activities is its core competence and together they permit the airline to have the lowest passenger per mile costs in the industry.

SUMMARY

When contemplating change, the last thing senior executives need to concern themselves with is an organization chart. The organizational *form* should follow the vision of how the firm in the future should *function*. All too often when there is a corporate problem senior executives start discussing the organization chart, concentrating on a person or business unit that is producing poor results. Instead, when a firm realizes change is necessary, it needs to start by analyzing the effectiveness of its three most fundamental components—*purpose, process, and, people.* "A company is a system—you have to have the courage and capability to tackle everything at once," says Carly Fiorina the HP CEO, who in just over a year on the job has attempted to reinvent the company. "To change the company, you have to operate on the whole system—the strategy [purpose], structure [processes], the rewards [people], the culture."[15]

Starting with a macro view of the firm's evolution and the assumptions underlying each of the three strategic legs of the firm will help avoid a piecemeal approach to change. There are six steps to a well thought out change effort:

1. Determine where the firm is in its corporate life cycle. In Part I Figure I.1 provided an overview of corporate evolution, and Chapters 1 through 5 discussed this evolution in detail.

2. Revisit the *purpose* of the enterprise and determine if the desired operating philosophy is in alignment with its theory of business and the strategic direction of the firm.

3. Before considering teams or a network organization, determine if accountability for results resides at the bottom of the organization. Chapter 10 laid the foundation for a *vertical* performance management system that ensures accountability.

4. Once performance measures exist for the operating work, workers know what they are accountable for and how they are doing. Then it's appropriate to consider teams, teamwork, and cross-functional processes to stimulate creativity and innovation and the management-leadership of alliances and partnerships.

5. In the emerging *horizontal* organization, as Chapter 12 pointed out, interactive *leadership* is key to senior management's ability to foster collaboration towards the common goal. A pioneering article on establishing a horizontal organization appeared in *Business Week* and chronicles a logical way to approach this task.[16] See appendix E for a summary of these steps.

6. Finally, tactical plans need to be created to move the organization forward to integrate both its *people* and *process* considerations so that they are consistent with the strategic direction of the firm, or its *purpose.*

NOTES

1. David Kirkpatrick, "Please Don't Call Us PC," *Fortune*, 16 October 2000, 114.

2. Stan Davis and Christopher Meyer, *Blur, The Speed of Change in the Connected Economy* (New York: Warner Books, 1999), 6.

3. Robert A. Burgelman and Andrew S. Groves, "Strategic Dissonance," *California Management Review* 38, no. 2 (Winter 1996): 8.

4. Jerry Useem, "Cannibalize Yourself," *Fortune*, 6 September 1999, 134.

5. Peter F. Drucker, "Theory of the Business," *Harvard Business Review* (September–October, 1994): 96.

6. Scott Therm, "How to Drive an Express Train." Interview with John Chambers, *Wall Street Journal*, May 30, 2000.

7. Michael Porter, "What Is Strategy?" *Harvard Business Review* (November–December, 1996): 70.

8. Durward K. Sobek II, Jeffery K. Liker, and Al C. Ward, "Another Look at How Toyota Integrates Product Development," *Harvard Business Review* (July–August 1998): 38.

9. Tomas V. Morris, *If Aristotle Ran General Motors: The New Soul of Business* (New York: Henry Holt, 1997), 110.

10. Ibid, xiv.

11. "How Do You Invite Your Brain to Encounter Thoughts That You Might Not Otherwise Encounter?" *Fast Company* (April 2000): 106.

12. See E. Appelbaum, T. Bailey, P. Berg, and A. Kalleberg, *Manufacturing Advantage: Why High Performance Work Systems Pay Off* (Ithaca, NY: ILR/Cornell University Press, 2000), 230–231.

13. Jessica Lipnack and Jeffrey Stamps, *The Age of Networks* (New York: John Wiley, 1994).

14. See Michael Best, *The New Competition* (Cambridge: Harvard University Press, 1990), and Bruce Kogut, ed., *Country Competitiveness* (Oxford: Oxford University Press, 1993).

15. Patricia Sellers, "The 50 Most Powerful Women in Business," *Fortune*, 16 October 2000, 132.

16. John A. Byrne, "The Horizontal Corporation," *Business Week*, 20 December 1993, 76–81.

Appendix A: Calibrating Your Organization

A simple survey of employees will determine the extent to which *performance management* exists in your organization. The seven questions employees need to be able to confidently answer are:

	Yes	No
1. Do you know where we are going?	___	___
2. Do you know what your job is?	___	___
3. Do you know how your job contributes to the rest of the organization?	___	___
4. Do you know what level of performance is expected of you in your job?	___	___
5. Do you know how we are doing as a business?	___	___
6. Do you know how you are doing: A. Against the expectations of your supervising manager?	___	___
B. Of your peers?	___	___
7. Do you know what is in it for you?	___	___
TOTAL	___	
	___ percent	

Note: The percent of "Noes" to "Yeses" will give you a quick operating measure of performance management within your organization by level and function.

Appendix B: Planning Terms: Desired Results and Activities

Most organizations have a confusing array of planning terms. For example, employees when discussing commitments often use the word *result* (a business goal) and *objective* (activity) interchangeably. When they do, they can focus on activities—because they are easier—and get caught in the "activity trap." Activities produce organizational results only if workers see how they are connected to a firm's results.

To help clear up the confusion, Figure B.1 simplifies planning terms and puts them into two categories: those that define desired business *goals*, and those that deal with *activities*. Another reason for making the distinction is that activities that are undertaken without knowing why they are being done often produce compliance rather than commitment. Therefore, when managers, individuals, and teams plan, they should predetermine a level of performance they want and then determine what needs to be done to get there. Articulating a desired goal statement makes the work (activity) meaningful because it explains "why" the work needs to be done.

Study the left-hand column of Figure B.1; it defines goal areas. At the top of this column is the word *vision*. Vision is a fuzzy planning word, one that is hard to define, yet it expresses the way the organization "could be." It is an envisioned result, something the organization might attain if articulated and communicated clearly. An *operating philosophy*, on the other hand, communicates how the organization plans to produce its goods and services, how it will treat employees, or the way it wants to interface with the end user. While these statements are rare, they can even be used to communicate how the organization wants to manage— for example delegated decision making, team structures, and exception reporting of results.

Next are planning term pairs. *Strategy* communicates the desired direction of a firm and what it strives to be; *tactics* are the activities used to achieve a strategy.

Figure B.1
Planning Terms: Desired Results and Activities

Concreteness	**Business Results** *Answers Why*	**Activities** *Answers How*

FUZZY

Vision & Values

Operating Philosophy

Mission Statement

Strategic Goals.......................................Tactics

Performance Measure.............................Projects

Operating Goals.................................Action Plans

Policy...Procedures

Decision................................Task Assignments

Commitment....................Compliance

HARD

To improve business operations, *projects* are undertaken. A return on investment is typically the measure. Another pair of planning terms is the *action plan*, which is implemented to achieve an *operating goal*. Looking at this pairing from the other direction, goal commitments need an action plan to make them a reality. The next example deals with *policy*. Consider this policy: "Employees must not accept a gift from a vendor." This is a predetermined level of ethical behavior—a desired result. It is not subject to interpretation, and applies to the whole organization. *Procedure* on the other hand, prescribes how the work is done. Concreteness and clarity in both are essential. Lastly, a *task assignment* specifies what is to be done, where it's to done, by whom, and in what time frame. Tasks are often given without an explanation of "why" the task needs to be done. The "why" is unexpressed and resides in the head of the person assigning the task—usually because they want it done a certain way.

When an organization focuses its attention on activities, accountability for results is weak, and workers often do the work not knowing why they are doing it. This leads to *compliance* behavior. On the other hand, when organizations focus on outcomes and people understand "why" the work needs to be done, *commitment* is improved because understanding and acceptance are negotiated.

Appendix C: Performance Measures

In a traditional corporate measurement system each department or function has its own set of measures that are used to inform top management about results. Production tracks *on time delivery*, sales looks at *bookings*, accounting monitors *bad debt*, and so on. But this is a segmented view of the firm; it does not measure the subtle drivers of performance like customer satisfaction and employee morale.

Having a handle on such "soft" performance measures, many believe, can pinpoint problems before they hit the bottom line, and can assist in better company results. According to the report "Measures That Matter" from Ernst & Young's Center for Business Innovation, institutional investors give a one-third weight to such nonfinancial measures.[1] At the top of their list were quality and execution of corporate strategy, management credibility, innovativeness, and the ability to attract talented people. Rather than "Are we making any money?" these soft measures help to answer the broader question, "How are we playing the game?"

This larger picture requires a balanced scorecard that considers both the hard and soft measures of corporate effectiveness. Since Robert S. Kaplan and David P. Norton[2] wrote about the balanced scorecard, the concept has become a popular management tool. Numerous companies have designed scorecards, and major investments have been made in the technology and tools to support their delivery to management.

Companies that use a balanced scorecard track not only financial indicators like gross profit margins on new products, revenue growth, and return on investment, but also business process measures in softer areas. Great companies don't talk about profits; they talk about drivers. It is their belief that tracking manufacturing yield rates and process cycle times gives bottom-line results. Managing strictly by the financials won't necessarily get better financial results, because the financials only indicate where the firm was—they are history.[3]

ALIGNING WITH BUSINESS STRATEGY

Unfortunately, some of the early adopters of scorecards struggled in getting full value from their investments. As they gained experience in using scorecards and performance measures, they sought to further refine the concept and develop a better understanding of the critical success factors for deployment such as:

• Linking the scorecard to the overall business strategy.
• Integrating the scorecard into the overall management process.

While finding the scorecard useful, many executives need a more explicit linkage to their overall business strategies. These strategies generally focus on points of competitive differentiation in a company's product or service offering. Therefore, forward-thinking companies "bias" their scorecards to the dimensions that most closely support their strategic direction.[4] For example, a company that seeks leadership through customer service would link, or bias, its scorecard measures directly to customer service goals. It should be possible to review a company's scorecard and discern all the key elements of its strategy. If a strategy addresses innovation, customer retention, or employee empowerment, there should be relevant performance measures for each. Astute CEOs go so far as to use the scorecard as a guide for conducting calls with Wall Street analysts, since it provides them with a frame of reference to explain performance and plans.

INTEGRATING SCORECARDS WITH LEGACY MEASURES

Many companies are finding that it is difficult to integrate their scorecards into their planning, budgeting, and resource allocation processes. Too often, managers are focused on making budgets, which results in the scorecard becoming "a nice to have" rather than an essential management tool. Similarly, the linkage between changes in scorecard metrics and subsequent changes in priorities and resource allocations is often blurred.

The solution is to ensure that a scorecard meets three basic criteria:

• The measures on the scorecard must be the same measures around which planning goals are set, budgets are developed, and projects are prioritized; in fact, the scorecard becomes the agenda for the management planning process.
• Incentive compensation needs to be tied directly to scorecard performance.
• Scorecard logic must be cascaded down the organization to ensure consistent linkage between individual goals and measures of overall business strategy.

NOTES

1. David A. Light, "Performance Measurement: Investors' Balanced Scorecard," *Harvard Business Review* (November–December 1998): 17.
2. Robert S. Kaplan and David P. Norton, "Using the Balanced Scorecard as a

Strategic Management System," *Harvard Business Review* (January–February 1996).

3. Joel Kurtzman, "Is Your Company Off Course? Now You Can Find Out Why," *Fortune*, 17 February 1997, 129.

4. Kaplan and Norton, op. cit., 76.

Appendix D: An Integrated Strategic Model

Figure D.1
An Integrated Strategic Model

Purpose: Concern for business (Growth & Profitability)

- **Where are we going?** *What is the vision of the future?*
- Theory of Business: *How do we plan to make money? What is our operating philosophy?*
- Customer Focus: *How do we plan to compete and satisfy changing customer requirements?*

Processes: Concern for production (Control)

- **Business Processes:** The end-to-end value added chain
  - Horizontal cutting across functions
  - Supplier, internal, and customer
  - A balanced scorecard of metrics aligned with strategy to measure organization effectiveness

- **Management Processes:**
  - The planning and review of operating results. *What's expected?*
  - Performance metrics for work-group and individuals. *How am I/we doing?*

CORPORATE CULTURE

People: Concern for people (Creativity)

- **Skill Competencies:** *What's my job?*
  - Technical skills
  - Leadership: Establishing an emotional connection & communicating effectively.
  - Management skills: Planning, coaching, and reviewing results
  - Interpersonal skills: Teamwork

- **Developing People:** Career planning, training & personal development plans. *Where am I going? How can I learn and grow? What will I do next?*

- **Motivation:** Job satisfaction, recognition, making a contribution, stock options. *What is in it for me?*

- **Structure:** Form follows operating philosophy.
- **Policies & Procedures:** Consistent with operating philosophy.

Appendix E: Creating a Horizontal Organization

When contemplating the creation of a horizontal organization consider these seven steps from a classic *Business Week* article:[1]

1. **Organize core business processes, not tasks**: Instead of creating a structure around functions or departments, build the company around core business processes. Ask, what is the firm's core competency? Why do we excel? What makes us unique? Focus on this and outsource the rest. Assign an "owner" to each macro process and begin defining accountability and performance measures.

2. **Flatten hierarchy**: To reduce supervision, combine fragmented tasks, eliminate work that fails to add value, and cut the activities within each process to a minimum. Use as few teams as possible to perform an entire process. Consider starting with three process teams, one for suppliers linked to manufacturing, another for internal production, and finally one for attracting and retaining customers.

3. **Use teams to manage everything**: Make teams the main building block of the organization. Create subteams within the three core business processes. Limit supervision by making the team manage itself. Clarify the team purpose. Hold it accountable for measurable process goals.

4. **Let customers drive performance**: Make customer satisfaction—not stockholder value or profitability—the primary driver and measure of performance. Mass customization and one-on-one marketing are the cornerstones of the emerging markets. Profits will materialize if customers are satisfied.

5. **Reward team performance**: Change the appraisal and pay systems to reward team results, not just individual performance. Radical as it may seem, base top management bonuses on the results of team performance. Encourage employees to develop multiple skills and pay them for their knowledge and skill sets.

6. **Maximize supplier and customer contact**: In addition to electronic communications, bring employees into direct, regular contact with suppliers and customers.

Remember in a high-tech world you need "high touch." Add supplier or customer representatives as full working members of in-house teams and solve problems together.

7. **Inform and train all employees:** Don't just spoon-feed sanitized information on a "need to know" basis. Trust workers with raw data, but train them on how to turn it into information. Make them accountable to perform their own analyses and make team decisions.

NOTE

1. John A. Byrne, "The Horizontal Corporation," *Business Week*, 20 December 1993, 76.

Index

About the Authors

DOUGLAS SCOTT FLETCHER is Principle and Senior Consultant at Performex in Newport Beach, California. He has done extensive consulting in the areas of performance management, cross-functional teams, and personal performance improvement.

IAN M. TAPLIN is Professor of Sociology, Management, and International Studies at Wake Forest University. He has done extensive research on work re-organization and restructuring in the American and British garment industries.